VOICES FROM

Dickens' LONDON

VOICES FROM

Dickens'

LONDON

MICHAEL PATERSON
FOREWORD BY PETER ACKROYD

David and Charles

This book is dedicated to my mother Evangeline (1928–2000)
who had read the entire works of Dickens by the age of ten,
an achievement I still find deeply impressive.

A DAVID & CHARLES BOOK
Copyright © David & Charles Limited 2006, 2007

David & Charles is an F+W Publications Inc. company
4700 East Galbraith Road
Cincinnati, OH 45236

First published in 2006
First paperback edition 2007

Text copyright © Michael Paterson 2006, 2007

A catalogue record for this book is available from the British Library.

ISBN-13: 978-0-7153-2281-9 hardback
ISBN-10: 0-7153-2281-8 hardback

ISBN-13: 978-0-7153-2723-4 paperback
ISBN-10: 0-7153-2723-2 paperback

Printed and bound by Creative Print & Design Group,
Ebbw Vale, Wales, UK
for David & Charles
Brunel House   Newton Abbot   Devon

Head of Publishing   Alison Myer
Commissioning Editor   Ruth Binney
Editor   Ame Verso
Art Editor   Mike Moule
Design Assistant   Emma Sandquest
Production Controller   Kelly Smith

Visit our website at www.davidandcharles.co.uk

David & Charles books are available from all good bookshops; alternatively
you can contact our Orderline on 0870 9908222 or write to us at FREEPOST
EX2 110, D&C Direct, Newton Abbot, TQ12 4ZZ (no stamp required UK only);
US customers call 800-289-0963 and Canadian customers call 800-840-5220.

CONTENTS

Foreword by Peter Ackroyd   6

Introduction   9

1 THE PLACE   14

2 THE PEOPLE   34

3 SHOPS AND SHOPPING   60

4 CITY AND CLERK   86

5 TRANSPORT AND TRAVEL   108

6 ENTERTAINMENT   132

7 THE POOR   192

8 CRIME AND PUNISHMENT   234

9 THE RESPECTABLE   264

Gazetteer   298

Chronology   302

Bibliography   304

Sources   306

Index   308

Picture Credits   320

FOREWORD

The air of 19th-century London is full of voices – voices pleading and voices celebrating, voices remonstrating and voices lamenting, voices melancholy and voices triumphant. In his introduction to this vivid and memorable volume, Michael Paterson suggests that the inhabitants of Dickens' London 'did not look, speak, smell or behave like us'. But by the miracle of continuity we do still speak approximately the same language; through that language, in the passages that Michael Paterson has extracted from the voluminous materials of the age, we can re-enter the society and culture of the period in an immediate and unmediated manner.

London was then a vast echo-chamber of voices. And those voices were much more strident and diverse than any to be heard in the present century. Modern dialects have almost completely disappeared, at least in the streets of London; certainly it is no longer possible to hear the regional accents of the city itself. Modern communications, and the diffuseness of vocal fashions, have rendered differences obsolete.

But there were, in the 19th century, a hundred different groups (we might almost call them tribes) holding fast to their own identities in the face of perilous circumstances. This was the period when London itself was becoming the first megalopolis in Europe, but in these early years the different groups within the city instinctively clung to their idiosyncratic speech and habits. There were the Irish, the Italians, the Jews, the immigrants from Africa and the Caribbean, the Germans, the French. Each area of London, too, had its own accent; the voices of Southwark would have been different from the voices of Islington, and a trained

Londoner would be able to identify the area from which a speaker came with some precision. And there were of course differences of class, with the labouring poor speaking a very different language from the middle-class cleric or the upper-class parliamentarian.

This leads to the phenomenon of the Cockney accent itself, of course much illustrated in the fiction of Dickens. We hear it in the colloquies of Samuel Weller and his father. In one letter between them (which, given the prevailing level of literacy, it is almost impossible for the elder Weller to have written) we read that 'The doctor says that if she'd svallo'd varm brandy and vater artervards she mightn't have been no vus her veels wos immediately greased and everythink done to set her agoin as could be inwented'. We notice particularly the substitutions of 'v' and 'w' as well as the employment of 'wos' for was and 'vus' for worse. All these are characteristic of London speech of the era, but they are only particular tokens of a general looseness or liquidity of language. Cockneys were lazy speakers, who did not care to articulate the full sound of any word they used. In the 19th century you would have heard 'reckleck' for recollect, 'Eye open' for High Holborn, 'nuffink' for nothing and 'ax' for ask. Some of these variants are still in use, at least in certain parts of London, and their persistence is an indication of the fact that Cockney speech of the 19th century had not changed in its essentials from that of the 15th century. It was an oral rather than a written dialect and was thus not susceptible to the ordinary processes of historical change.

The voices of Londoners would also have been more colourful and more strident than those of the 21st century because the city itself was noisier, more theatrical and more sonorous. Foreign observers noticed that the local dialect was 'harsh', but that was, of course, the effect of London as a harsh city. The noises of the streets alone, as recorded by Michael Paterson, are enough to suggest the background against which the voices of London are to be heard. He anatomizes all the notes of the cacophony that was the city's perpetually unfinished symphony – there were the Italian organ grinders, the street balladeers, the raucous cries of the various street sellers, the Hindoo beggar with his drums, the acrobats with their clarionets, the bagpipes of wandering groups of musicians known then as 'pfifferari', the whistling and singing of the tradesmen and the apprentices. It was said, with some justice, that it was impossible to hold a conversation on any busy London street. So the voices were raised, clamant and strident against the general roar of the city.

The voices were not subdued out of politeness or fear. There were no standards of decency in the street, and there was certainly no police force to curtail the behaviour of the more obstreperous or energetic Londoners. Swearing was so common that laws were passed to inhibit it; the laws, of course, had no effect. Vulgarity and indecency were an intrinsic part of the repertoire of the crowd. Everything was brusque, and rough, and direct. The reasons are not hard to find. Life was shorter and more dangerous; the privations of ordinary existence were overwhelming, the horrors of disease and death immediate. Is it no wonder, then, that the speech and conversation of the people were often violent and improvident? It would be odd if they were not. The emotions of the age were in that sense much closer to the surface of life. There was no need for equivocation or hesitation.

There is another factor of some importance in the voices of Dickens' London. The life of the city was innately theatrical. Everyone wore his or her appropriate costume, from the old clothes seller to the city clerk, and of course the popular theatre was then the dominant means of cultural expression to which everyone consciously or unconsciously aspired. So there was a rhetoric, and a colour, to the voices of the 19th-century city – a circumlocution, sometimes, that Dickens himself captures very well in characters as different as Mr Micawber or Mrs Gamp. Out of this babble of voices, Michael Paterson has been able to extract the essence of London itself. Read this book and re-enter the labyrinth of the now ancient city.

PETER ACKROYD

INTRODUCTION

Fog everywhere. Fog up the river, where it flows among green meadows; fog down the river, where it rolls defiled among the tiers of shipping, and the waterside pollutions of a great (and dirty) city. Fog on the Essex marshes, fog on the Kentish heights. Fog creeping into the cabooses of collier-brigs; fog lying out on the yards, and hovering in the rigging of great ships; fog drooping on the gunwales of barges and small boats. Fog in the eyes and throats of ancient Greenwich pensioners, wheezing by the firesides of their wards; fog in the stem and bowl of the afternoon pipe of the wrathful skipper, down in his close cabin; fog cruelly pinching the toes and fingers of his shivering little 'prentice boy on deck. Chance people on the bridges peeping over the parapets into a nether sky of fog, with fog all round them, as if they were up in a balloon, and hanging in the misty clouds.

No author has ever known, or described, London as well as Charles Dickens. He could bring to life the fog-bound Thames, the gas-lit parlours, the noisy taprooms and the solemnly quiet offices of merchants and lawyers. His eye for detail and his gift for characterization peopled these with a varied cast of often implausible Londoners, but ever since they have moved and entertained readers throughout the world who might never have been to the city. Many of the clichés that crowd our imaginations when we think of London, or of the Victorians, can be traced back to his writings. For many readers, Dickens is London – his novels were famously popular in the Soviet Union, where his audience was persuaded that the conditions he described in the 19th century still existed. The city was not his only subject – he dealt, after all, with America, Continental Europe and Revolutionary Paris – and many of his scenes were set in other parts of England – Kent, East Anglia, Yorkshire – nevertheless it is with the capital that he was overwhelmingly occupied, and it is therefore with London that he is chiefly identified.

During the years that Dickens knew it – from 1822 to 1870 – London was the largest city in the world. This period saw three different monarchs on the throne: George IV, William IV and Victoria. It witnessed one major war (against Russia in the Crimea) and several political upheavals: the Great Reform Bill, Chartism, and agitation over the Corn Laws. There was considerable technical innovation, most obvious in the development of railways. There were widespread outbreaks of disease, most notably cholera, that visited terror and suffering on the city's poorer inhabitants. Crime was out of control, and an expanding population – for the city doubled in size between 1800 and the 1850s – brought overcrowding and increased misery.

Dickens described his lifetime with such power and vividness that his name has been lent to it: the phrase 'Dickensian' immediately evokes for us images of stovepipe hats, cheeky urchins, wisecracking ostlers and benevolent elderly businessmen, crowded into a fog-shrouded, cobbled, steepled and domed city of narrow alleys and comfortable, old-fashioned chop-houses. To anyone who has seen a Christmas card or a chocolate box, this seems an era of almost ludicrous quaintness, all stagecoaches and crinolines. There is a perception that these were quiet years. Europe had several revolutions; Britain had the Great Exhibition. In reality, there was nothing either quaint or quiet about this era.

The city of Dickens is a place lost to us beyond recall. It is difficult to imagine its dirtiness and danger and its extremes of wealth and poverty. Its people did not look, speak, smell or behave like us. The ways they dressed, the times at which they ate, the slang they used and the accents in which they talked, the ways in which they worked or celebrated or took their amusements, often bear no resemblance to our experience. Even the currency they used has gone, though it survived until a generation ago.

If a single word could sum up for us their environment, it would be 'brutal.' This would describe not only the manners of Londoners in public before the modern era, but also the sort of life that most people would live in the absence of the checks and balances we take for granted: compulsory free education, sick-leave, affordable medical care, paid holidays, unemployment benefit, old-age pensions and legislation to prevent domestic violence, or cruelty to animals, or persecution of minorities. Without any of these safeguards, brutality and desperation were everywhere.

Those who dislike the Victorians are fond of viewing them in terms of 'hypocrisy' and 'exploitation'. Despite an apparent fixation with respectability and a widespread habit of churchgoing, they are seen as guilty of immorality and of ignoring the hardships of those around them, whether these were prostitutes or child-labourers or slum tenants. While there were of course people who were guilty of these things, by and large the Victorians were no more moral or immoral in their private behaviour than any era before or since. Churchgoing was less universal, and sexual licence more common, than the purveyors of stereotypes would have us believe.

But we have no business to generalize about the callousness of the Victorians. In Dickens' London there were bare-knuckle boxing, bull-baiting and public hangings, yet these things were constantly condemned. There was deep and genuine concern for the plight of the unfortunate. The scale of London – and therefore of urban problems – had no precedent in history, and to those who sought to do good the task seemed overwhelming. Nevertheless hundreds of organizations came into being to address specific evils. Dickens' lifetime, and the decades after it, saw a vast effort to house, feed and educate the poor, whether through the Ragged Schools, the Salvation Army or Dr Barnardo's Homes. This mass movement of philanthropy and social concern – entirely the result of private endeavour – represented the greatest outpouring of kindness in British history, the precursor to the famine-relief campaigns of our own time. It is worth emphasizing that this work was begun and followed through almost entirely by the Christian Church or by people professing its beliefs.

For all its almost impenetrable distance, we are not without links to the London of Dickens, for a number of things that are familiar to us had their beginnings at that time: buses, photography, stamps and post-boxes, package tourism, the London Underground, organized football, and public lavatories.

Though Dickens' novels give an illuminating picture of his time, there is a great deal that they do not explain about everyday life. There is no reason why they should, for his original audience needed no such information. They understood his terminology and references without difficulty. We, of course, need some assistance. Fortunately there is no lack of people to take us through the labyrinth of language, behaviour and topography, for numerous other authors described the city and its inhabitants at this time. Of these, I have chosen to make repeated use of several, in the hope that their comments, writing style and personalities, quickly recognized by readers of this book, would make them seem like old friends – or flesh-and-blood guides – to their world.

One cannot, for instance, look at the London of this era without the help of Henry Mayhew. His genuine concern for the city's unfortunates led him to undertake exhaustive research into the lives of those he encountered in the streets. These interviews, published in 1851 under the title *London Labour and the London Poor*, give us an unprecedented insight into the circumstances, livelihood, past histories and aspirations of what was London's most populous class. Read today, they make the same impact as when they first appeared over a century and a half ago.

The journalist George Augustus Sala is another of my chosen guides. In 1858, his collected writings about the capital were issued in book form under the title *Twice Round the Clock*. His wit and cynicism are often endearing, and he has a gift for lampooning the pomposity of the 'respectable'. He is also the best source of detail about the social habits and rituals of the era – apart from Dickens himself. Dickens, though like Sala a journalist, clearly exaggerated much of what he described; Sala, whose desire was not to change society but simply to mirror it, often provides a less subjective view .

Outsiders' impressions have been very useful in examining the life of London, and two that I have chosen were both Germans. Max Schlesinger was a tourist who came to the city at almost exactly the century's mid-point. He saw with unjaded eyes the things that the British took for granted. His observations, long since forgotten but recorded in a book entitled *Saunterings in and About London*, are amusing and thought-provoking, and deserved, I felt, to be offered to a new generation of readers. His compatriot, Prince Hermann Pückler-Muskau, also offered incisive and entertaining views. For a below-stairs perspective I have used the journal of William Tayler, a footman at the time of Queen Victoria's accession, whose endearingly idiosyncratic spelling marks him out from the other authors. His writings, discovered in Oxfordshire by his descendants and published by Westminster City Archives, are delightful, and they too deserve a wider audience.

Dickens himself, naturally enough, has been a source of much information. In particular, I wished to highlight his earliest published work – *Sketches by Boz* – which provides a charming and very entertaining series of glimpses of life in the 1830s. This has not been adapted for television as have his later and more famous novels, and is therefore much less known, but it repays study, and has much insight to offer. Finally Francis Grose, whose *Classical Dictionary of the Vulgar Tongue* was a bestseller in the 1820s, has been my tutor in the language of the time.

A brief note on the currency of Dickens' London, which may confuse modern readers: there were 12 pence to a shilling and 20 shillings to a pound. A shilling was equivalent to 5p in today's money. Half a crown was two shillings and sixpence, or 12½p. A sovereign was a gold coin worth £1, and a half-sovereign therefore 50p. A guinea was worth £1.05. A farthing was a quarter of a penny. In the text shillings are denoted as s and pennies as d. (At the time of writing GB £1 = US $1.91.)

I would, of course, like to thank several people for their kindness in assisting with this book. As always, my principal debt is to my wife Sarah. This book, more than any other I have written, has been a joint effort, and could not have been produced without her. I would also like to thank my dear friend Eduardo Rego, a native of Rio de Janeiro, whose passion for Dickens galvanized my own interest, Sandy Malcolm for technical help, Carolyn Rowland-Jones for valuable information about Charles Lamb and Bryn Hyacinth at the Cuming Museum in Southwark for valuable suggestions. I would also like to thank Mr Nick Humphrey of the Victoria and Albert Museum for his helpful advice. At David & Charles I thank Ruth Binney, Ame Verso and Alison Myer. Val Porter and Beverley Jollands also deserve considerable gratitude for their skill and dedication in editing and proofreading the text, as does Tony Hirst for indexing. I also thank Mrs Thelma Grove of the Dickens Fellowship for kind and useful advice.

MICHAEL PATERSON

The PLACE

The journey from our town to the metropolis was a journey of about five hours. It was a little past mid-day when the four-horse stage-coach by which I was a passenger got into the ravel of traffic frayed out about the Cross Keys, Wood Street, Cheapside, London.

We Britons had at that time particularly settled that it was treasonable to doubt our having and our being the best of everything: otherwise, while I was scared by the immensity of London, I think I might have had some faint doubts whether it was not rather ugly, crooked, narrow and dirty.

Thus Pip, the hero of *Great Expectations*, headed for London as a boy by coach from the north Kent coast. Charles Dickens had made the same journey, at the age of ten, in 1822, and we can assume that his experience was similar. To retrace this route provides an insight into the city as he first encountered it. If you had seen London from afar, as he did, your first impression would have been of a distant, dirty smudge of smoke. Coming nearer, you would have made out the steeples of churches and (often just as tall) the masts of shipping in the Thames. St Paul's Cathedral would have been unmistakable, set on the top of Ludgate Hill and rising head and shoulders above its surroundings.

At this point, if not before, the imaginations of those seeing the great metropolis for the first time would almost certainly have begun to stir. Another impressionable small boy, David Copperfield, described the combination of excitement and fear that the sight evoked in him:

What an amazing place London was to me when I saw it in the distance, and I believed all the adventures of my favourite heroes to be constantly enacting and re-enacting there, and I vaguely

**made it out to be fuller of wonders and wickedness than all the
cities of the earth.**

By the time the city's landmarks were clearly visible, the coach would
perhaps be crossing the great expanse of Blackheath and descending the
steep hill into the village of Deptford (the passengers might be asked
to get out and walk down, to ease the burden on the horses). There
would be more traffic: carriages filled with people; carts, many pulled
by donkeys, laden with produce; enormous broad-wheeled wagons
lumbering behind teams of slow-moving horses, their cargoes covered
with tarpaulins. There would also be scores of men, women and children
on foot, many of them carrying heavy loads. Before the invention of the
bicycle or the arrival of cheap public transport, it was usual for people to
walk, even though it might take all day to reach their destination.

Market gardens were another sign that the city was near. Slow
transportation meant that freshness could only be assumed if the produce
travelled the shortest possible distance from grower to consumer, and
in all directions around London thousands of acres were given over to
feeding the city. Whatever was in season was packed in baskets, loaded
on to backs or into carts, and carried to the markets. As these began their
business early in the morning, the farmers and gardeners – or more likely
their wives and children – might well have to travel for half the night. In
addition, flocks and herds of livestock, driven perhaps for days from the
farms of Kent, blocked the traffic and strayed to nibble the roadside grass,
their bellowing and bleating accompanied by the crack of drovers' whips,
the shrill whistles of small boys or the yaps of darting sheepdogs.

Cheek by jowl with these rural elements was a distinctly urban feature,
and one that also suggested the city was close at hand: the vast rubbish
tips, or 'dust heaps' of London's refuse. These often swarmed with people,
sorting through them in search of usable items. Henry Mayhew, the
author of studies of the London poor, described them in 1851:

**The dust-yards ... are generally situated in the suburbs, and they
may be found all round London ... Frequently they cover a large
extent of ground in the fields, and there the dust is piled up to a
great height in a conical heap, and having much of the appearance
of a volcanic mountain.**

Located on the road to London from Kent there were numerous inns and stables, outside which swarms of grooms and stable-boys washed down vehicles, curry-combed horses or swept the yards. However quaint this seems, it would have been no more remarkable to contemporaries than a petrol station would be to us. Much else was so functional that it barely merited a glance: milkmaids labouring under wooden yokes; crowds of red-sailed Thames barges on the river; and the creaking sails of the windmills found all over the city's outskirts.

There was no clear distinction between town and country. Along the Old Kent Road was a good deal of what would now be called 'ribbon development'. Behind Georgian terraces or pretty rows of Regency cottages (many of which are still there) a traveller could glimpse fields with haystacks or sheep and cattle grazing. At the Bricklayer's Arms the built-up area began in earnest. By now the coach would be rattling over cobblestones and the passengers would notice an increase in both noise and discomfort as the coach turned right toward London Bridge.

However noisy today's traffic may be, it is insignificant by comparison with the din that filled the city in Dickens' time. Countless iron-shod wheels rattled all day over cobbled streets behind clopping horses. Shouting was constant as, without any form of traffic control, drivers relied on aggression to push their way through the crush of vehicles. The sound, thrown back by the walls of narrow streets, was so loud that it would not be possible to hold a conversation on the pavement, nor to leave street-facing windows open in summer.

London Bridge was one of the city's sights. Though it would soon (in 1831) be replaced by a modern structure, the bridge that Pip and Copperfield crossed was over 600 years old. It had been built as a series of narrow arches, buttressed with solid piers or 'starlings', which slowed the flow of the river and gave the upstream side the stillness of a lake. The bridge had once been cluttered with shops and houses, but these had been cleared away 60 years earlier. David Copperfield saw it in the company of a young teacher while on his way to Salem House School:

We went on through a great noise and uproar that confused my weary head beyond description, and over a bridge which, no doubt, was London Bridge (indeed I think he told me so, but I was half asleep).

To look north across London Bridge toward the towers and steeples
of the ancient city must have seemed the most awe-inspiring sight
ever, though what would probably strike us would be the untidiness
of everything. The embankments that now stretch along both shores,
with their solid granite walls and elegant iron lamp-posts, would not be
built for another 40 years. Without them the river was much wider, and
its banks were a jumble of warehouses, cranes, docks, jetties and slime-
covered flights of stone or wooden steps.

The river itself was a vital, bustling workplace. London had the
largest port and shipyards in Britain, as well as being the world's biggest
industrial centre, and much of its life revolved around the import, export
and processing of goods. Below the bridge was the Pool of London,
where ships from all over the globe could be seen lying at anchor, their
decks and holds alive with activity as sailors and stevedores went about
their work. Hosts of small craft – skiffs, lighters, cutters – plied to and
fro or bobbed in the wake of larger vessels. Among the sailing ships with
their masts and spars there might be a paddle-steamer, its massive side-
wheels thrashing the water as it came about, its whistle shrieking and its
funnel belching clouds of noxious black smoke that hung and drifted.
Crossing London Bridge, visitors of Dickens' time could see the source of
London's wealth and power set out before them.

By the time they reached the Thames, our visitors would long since
have noticed another abiding aspect of London life: the smell, which
must have been overwhelming. First, there was the smell of coal fires.
The vast forest of reeking chimneys filled the air with smoke, which
covered buildings with unsightly layers of soot and left dirty black smuts
on clothing and faces. There were the multifarious stenches of industry:
breweries, foundries and forges, chemical works and, worse than all of
them, tanneries, with which the coach passengers would already have
become acquainted while travelling through Bermondsey. There was
also the aroma of horses, on which so much of London's transport and
commerce depended – the smell of a stable multiplied a millionfold.
There was the scent of hundreds of thousands of people, whose tightly
packed lives did not allow them opportunities to keep themselves,
their clothes or their homes clean. At dusk, when the 'parish lamps',
or streetlights, were lit, the air filled with the cloying stench of burning
whale-oil, for gas would not be introduced until 1828. George Augustus

Sala, journalist, friend of Dickens and fellow-observer of the life of
London, analysed this aspect of the city in great detail:

**The fumes of the vilest tobacco, of decaying vegetables, of
escaping (and frequently surreptitiously tapped) gas, of deceased
cats, of ancient fish, of dubious mutton pies, and of unwashed,
unkempt, reckless humanity; all these make the night hideous and
the heart sick.**

Worst of all was the stink that assailed the nostrils at London Bridge.
The murky, greenish-brown waters below were filled with the sewage of a
million people, and the river was not only the destination of much of the
city's bodily waste but also the source of a good deal of its drinking water.
Crossing the bridge in a coach would cause the inside passengers to
slam the windows shut, no matter how warm the day, while those sitting
outside would hold handkerchiefs over their faces. Only people who
spent their lives on or near the river ever got used to it. Small wonder
that town-dwellers looked so unhealthy, or that those visiting from the
country could expect quickly to become ill.

Across the river, travelling up Bishopsgate and left into Lombard
Street, the coach would pass through what was then, and remains,
London's banking district. Progress would be slow through the narrow
and congested streets, but a large vehicle and a robust coachman, using
language that would probably shock some passengers, could usually force
a way without difficulty. On the right was the Bank of England – its
impressive new building, designed by the great architect Sir John Soane,
still taking shape (it would not be completed until 1833) – while on the
left was the Mansion House, the home of London's Lord Mayor. Going
westward along Cheapside, a much broader thoroughfare, Pip would
have seen the towering steeple of St Mary le Bow, to be born within the
sound of whose bells is the traditional definition of a Cockney. As the
coach turned right into Wood Street, the great bulk of St Paul's would
have been glimpsed a short distance to the west, and he might have
heard the tolling of its huge 17-ton bell, 'Great Paul'.

No visitors to the city could have remained unaffected by what they
had seen, especially country people accustomed to knowing everyone in
their town or village by sight, and to seeing them in the street perhaps

dozens of times a day. In London there were more people than they would ever have encountered before. The sheer size and volume of everything must have been profoundly disconcerting. In foul weather London's dirtiness, overcrowding and rudeness would have been even more in evidence. Dickens wrote of it in *Bleak House*:

> **Smoke lowering down from chimney-pots, making a soft black drizzle, with flakes of soot in it as big as full-grown snowflakes. Dogs, indistinguishable in mire. Horses, scarcely better; splashed to their very blinkers. Foot-passengers, jostling one another's umbrellas, in a general infection of ill-temper, and losing their foothold at street corners, where tens of thousands of other foot-passengers have been slipping and sliding since the day broke.**

Everywhere there was dirt and a visible lack of hygiene. From street-corner pumps, people would be drawing drinking water that was an unpleasant brown colour and smelt disgusting. Scuttling out of sight behind barrels or under warehouse doors, rats would be ubiquitous in broad daylight, as would mangy feral cats and dogs, which might make a grab at meat hanging outside a butcher's shop until chased away by an apprentice with a broomstick (dead dogs and cats, unless they had been someone's pet, would not merit a glance as they lay in the street or floated in the Thames). This same meat, hung outdoors, would be covered with flies and spattered by passing traffic. And there was worse. Half-concealed under rags down a back alley, one might glimpse the bluish corpse of an abandoned baby or, early in the morning and especially in winter, the stiffened body of someone who had frozen to death overnight while sleeping.

The traffic in Dickens' London was terrifying. Vehicles did not keep to the left, but drove as near the middle of the road as they were able. Unless a constable happened to be nearby, there would be no prospect of crossing a busy road except by taking the plunge and risking the wheels and hooves. Drivers, perched high above the pedestrians and armed with whips, could be formidable obstacles to safe passage. Small boys often hopped on the backs of carriages and wagons to ride, causing passers-by to call to the driver, 'Whip behind!' At least the pavements were safe from traffic. There were iron bollards on the corners to prevent the wheels of wagons mounting the kerb. Though the rumble and rattle of vehicles was deafening, there were occasions on which the noise might be reduced: on residential streets in which someone was ill, their family could pay to have straw strewn, a practice that continued into the 1930s.

Only on Sundays did the city seem less intimidating. Then it was free of commercial traffic and a dreary emptiness settled over the streets. Other than the churches, almost everything was shut – shops, libraries and places of entertainment. Even the 'improving' spectacles so beloved of the 19th century – picture-galleries and museums – were unavailable. In winter, especially, the gloom could be utterly dispiriting. Arthur Clennam experienced it in the opening pages of *Little Dorrit*:

> It was a Sunday evening in London, gloomy, close and stale. Maddening church bells of all degrees of dissonance made the brick-and-mortar echoes hideous. Melancholy streets, in a penitential garb of soot, steeped the souls of the people who were condemned to look at them out of windows in dire despondency ... Everything was bolted and barred that could by possibility furnish relief to an overworked people. No pictures, no unfamiliar animals, no rare plants or flowers, no natural or artificial wonders of the ancient world – all taboo with that enlightened strictness, that the ugly South-Sea gods in the British Museum might have supposed themselves at home again ... Nothing for the spent toiler to do but compare the monotony of his seventh day with the monotony of his six days, think what a weary life he led, and make the best of it.

Though London was overwhelmingly impressive to Dickens' contemporaries, it would seem to us small and parochial. There were large structures that attracted admiration, most of which are still standing – St Paul's and Westminster Abbey, the Tower, Mansion House, Somerset House, Carlton House – but almost all of the great public buildings and spaces that we associate with the 19th century, such as the Houses of Parliament, the Royal Courts of Justice, the National Gallery and Trafalgar Square, belong to a later period. These, like the enormous steel-and-glass office buildings of recent decades, have given us a sense of scale that was entirely lacking in the reign of George IV. Virtually no secular building was higher than five storeys. The skyline was low (as it still is in central Paris) and punctuated by graceful spires and steeples, with only an occasional eyesore in the form of a factory chimney.

This modesty of scale was perhaps most noticeable in Whitehall, where the great white-stone departments of state now stand. Here there were a few impressive structures – the Banqueting House, the Admiralty, Melbourne House – but otherwise the country was administered from a warren of unpretentious buildings. Many of the departments in which the everyday business of government went on were housed in dank, shabby and rat-infested premises, as unimposing to look at as they were uncomfortable to inhabit. The Palace of Westminster itself, home to the Houses of Parliament, was a similarly random assemblage of rooftops, chimneys, buttresses and passageways, having grown organically from its medieval core. The whole ensemble would be swept away by fire in 1834 but for the moment, despite a veneer of dignity, it certainly did not look like the seat of government of the world's richest nation. London's most famous sound, the tolling of Big Ben, was not to be heard until 1860. The famous chime, which has been copied all over the world, was itself borrowed from Great St Mary's, the university church in Cambridge.

As in our own time, the East End of London, which stretched along the Commercial Road and Mile End Road to the new docks at the Isle of Dogs, was the poorer side of the city. The West End, based on St James's and Mayfair, lay astride Piccadilly, which ran as far as the turnpike at Hyde Park Corner before petering out in the village of Brompton. South of the river were the workaday districts of Bermondsey and the Borough, beyond which, across fields or marsh, lay the more salubrious suburbs of Newington, Camberwell, Kennington and Lambeth. To the north a new and dignified quarter, composed of huge white-stuccoed Palladian terraces and villas, was being laid out by George IV's favourite architect, John Nash, around the Regent's Park. On the slopes beyond – Primrose Hill, Hampstead and Highgate – fashionable houses looked down on London, but in this direction there were also meaner districts. One of these was Camden Town, then on the edge of the built-up area, where the young Dickens and his family lived when they arrived in London.

This neighbourhood was associated with respectable lower middle-class families and the genteel poor. It was to be the fictitious home of the Micawbers and of Bob Cratchit. Those who lived in the suburbs would normally have gone everywhere on foot, for few places in central London would have been more than an hour's walk away, and there would be short cuts across farmers' fields or waste ground. Mr Wemmick, a legal clerk in *Great Expectations*, walked every day from his home in Walworth to his office near Smithfield, a journey of between 50 and 60 minutes.

Even the city centre still had a somewhat rural atmosphere. From the upper-storey windows of many town houses it was possible to see fields. (The sales particulars for a house in Piccadilly announced: 'The views from it over the THREE PARKS, and the Country to the SURREY HILLS, are uninterrupted.') Livestock was herded through the streets to market; flocks of sooty-fleeced sheep grazed in Hyde Park and milk could be bought, straight from the cow, in St James's Park. In Haymarket, farmers sold hay a stone's throw from the shops and clubs of St James's.

London was the largest city in Europe, and growing. All cities seem perpetually incomplete because they are constantly expanding, demolishing and rebuilding, and in the London of that era construction was everywhere in evidence. Its central thoroughfares echoed with the sounds of demolition – the clinking of chisels and pickaxes, the shouts of workmen, the crash of falling masonry. A modern eye would notice that scaffolding was wooden (as is often still the case in eastern Europe) and that no attention was paid to the mens' safety or protection.

On the edges of the city, the virtually endless noise of hammering and banging carried across the fields. At roadsides along the approaches to London, or amid open ground, terraces of houses or detached villas were built by speculators. Often they would stand in awkward and unsightly isolation for years, or even decades, before continuing development closed the gaps between them and brought an overall harmony to a district. All around these building sites would be the activity, and the litter, of the trades involved: carpenters' and glaziers' workshops, tile-works and brickworks. Lime kilns for making mortar were often constructed in the suburbs, and one of these can still be seen at Walworth. Dwellings were built in a hurry, but the fact that so many are standing today is a tribute to their solidity. Many were simple and functional in design – like the ubiquitous late-Georgian 'brick box' houses, many thousands of which are still inhabited by Londoners; others could be more pretentious, exhibiting small flourishes such as elaborate fanlights, pilasters, urns and statuary, to appeal to the 'upwardly mobile' in what was a highly status-conscious age.

A Perambulation

London's historic heart was the mile-square district known as 'the City', which dated from Roman times and had become the centre of the capital's international trade and finance. Amid its narrow streets and sunless courts could be found the offices of a multitude of brokers, traders, private banks and joint-stock companies – as well as the Bank of England, the Royal Exchange and numerous commodities exchanges – representing an immense concentration of wealth. They included Britain's largest commercial organization: the East India Company, whose headquarters, East India House in Leadenhall Street, was one of London's sights.

While the City is still devoted to wealth and commerce, a striking difference between Dickens' youth and our own time is that very few people now live there. In the early 1820s it was home to wealthy merchants, middle-class clerks and poor labourers, and there were numerous shops. The sight of delivery boys with baskets of goods, or of servants running errands or hanging out washing, gave the City a lived-in atmosphere that has all but vanished. Dickens recalled his childhood impressions of the area in 'Gone Astray', an article he wrote some 30 years later for his magazine *Household Words*:

> Up courts and down courts – in and out of little squares – peeping into counting-house passages and running away – ever staring at the British merchants, and never tiring of the shops – I rambled on, all through the day. I particularly remember that when I found myself on 'Change, and saw the shabby people sitting under the placards about ships, I settled that they were misers, who had embarked all their wealth to go and buy gold-dust or something of that sort ... I came to the India House. I had no doubt of its being the most wonderful, the most magnanimous, the most in all respects astonishing, establishment on the face of the earth. Thinking much about boys who went to India [East India Company cadets], I got among the outfitting shops. There, I read the list of things that were necessary for an India-going boy, and when I came to 'one brace of pistols', thought what happiness must be reserved for such a fate!

Also in the City was the medieval Guildhall, the heavily restored and venerable building that served as the focus of ceremony and administration for the City of London. Within its immense hall were two wooden statues, each 4.5m/14ft 6in high, of the giants Gog and Magog, mythical figures connected with the legend of London's beginnings. Carved in 1708 to replace earlier statues, they were to be destroyed by an air-raid in 1940. They were a symbol of London and one of its best-known 'tourist attractions'. In 'Gone Astray', Dickens finds himself lost in London and decides to use the occasion to explore. His objective is to see the Guildhall giants and, after a lengthy and tiring walk, he finds them:

> I began to ask my way to Guildhall. I was too knowing to ask my way to the Giants, for I felt it would make people laugh. I remember how immensely broad the streets seemed now I was alone, how high the houses, how grand and mysterious everything ... I came into their presence at last, and gazed upon them with dread and veneration. They looked better-tempered, and were altogether more shiny-faced, than I had expected; but they were very big, and, as I judged their pedestals to be about forty feet high, I considered that they would be very big indeed if they were walking on the stone pavement. I was in a state of mind as to these and all such figures, which I suppose holds equally with most children. While I knew them to be images made of something other than flesh and blood, I still invested them with attributes of life – with consciousness of my being there, for example, and the power of keeping an eye on me. Being very tired, I got into the corner under Magog, to be out of the way of his eye, and fell asleep. When I started up after a long nap, I thought the giants were roaring, but it was only the City ...

Ten minutes' walk west of the Guildhall is St Paul's and its churchyard. There has been a church on this hilltop site since the 7th century, but the present one, built after the Great Fire, was completed in 1708. In the 19th century its surroundings had none of the tranquillity associated with cathedrals, for in the narrow streets abutting its north side were the evil-smelling and highly inflammable premises of tallow chandlers.

Beyond these was Newgate Market, where animals were sold and slaughtered, as they were in neighbouring Smithfield. From the cathedral could thus be heard squealing pigs and lowing cattle. The great church itself, which has now been restored to its original whiteness, was then as filthy as the rest of London's buildings. Unless attending a service, visitors paid twopence for admission. For this sum they could climb the steps to the dome, try out the 'Whispering Gallery' and visit the tomb of Lord Nelson in the crypt. The building was as dirty inside as outside; the soot-covered statues of numerous worthies, often depicted expiring amid attendant cherubs and allegorical figures, appeared to a canon of the Cathedral some years later as if 'black angels are conveying Ethiopian heroes to their long rest'. St Paul's was not heated adequately, and to sit through a service even in mild weather could be a feat of endurance. Another canon, Sydney Smith, remarked:

> The thermometer is several degrees below zero. My sentences are frozen as they come out of my mouth, and are thawed in the course of the summer, making strange noises in various parts of the church.

Gas lighting was introduced in 1822 but illuminated only the choir. Once the setting sun no longer reached the windows, the rest of the huge building must have seemed an ocean of darkness.

Below St Paul's were the Sessions House (a major courthouse) and Newgate Prison, as well as Smithfield with its noisy animals. In *Great Expectations*, Pip explored the region and noticed its twin functions as abattoir and seat of justice:

> I came to Smithfield; and the shameful place, being all asmear with filth and fat and blood and foam, seemed to stick to me. So I rubbed it off with all possible speed by turning into a street where I saw the great black dome of St Paul's bulging at me from behind a grim stone building which a bystander said was Newgate Prison. Following the wall of the jail, I found the roadway covered with straw to deaden the noise of passing vehicles; and from this, and from the quantity of people standing about, smelling strongly of spirits and beer, I inferred that the trials were on. While I looked

about me here, an exceedingly dirty and partially drunk minister
of justice asked me if I would like to step in and hear a trial or so:
informing me that he could give me a front place for half-a-crown,
whence I could command a full view of the Lord Chief Justice in
his wig and robes.

Westward lay Fleet Street, which connected the City with Westminster
and the shops and squares of aristocratic London. Here were other
famous sights. One was the clock on the church of St Dunstan-in-the-
West. The clock itself thrust outward over the street, but set above it
were the mechanical figures of a pair of giants, who at each hour struck
two bells with their clubs. The young Dickens described these 'obliging
monsters' in 'Gone Astray', and David Copperfield and his aunt made a
point of seeing the clock when she came to London to settle his career:

We made a pause at the toy-shop in Fleet Street, to see the giants
of St Dunstan's strike upon the bells – we had timed our going, so
as to catch them at it, at twelve o'clock.

The clock of St Dunstan's remained in place until 1830. Another
small boy who had marvelled at it grew up to become the Marquess of
Hertford, a wealthy art collector. When the church was demolished, he
bought the clock and removed it to his home in Regent's Park. In 1936
it was returned to its original setting, but, set well back from the street
on the rebuilt church and with its chimes drowned by traffic noise, it
is unnoticed by many passers-by. The toy-shop was chiefly famous for
the fact that 'Mrs Salmon', a maker of waxworks and the predecessor
of Madame Tussaud, had her exhibition above it. Inside were effigies of
statesmen and celebrities. Outside was a model of the soothsayer Mother
Shipton, which, at the touch of a lever, would aim a kick at passers-by.
    A little further on was Temple Bar, the City's western limit. This was
guarded by a baroque arch, designed by Christopher Wren and constructed
in 1672. Upon it, in less peaceful times, had been displayed the heads of
executed traitors. Here too the young Dickens found fascination:

When I came to Temple Bar, it took me half an hour to stare at
it, and I left it unfinished even then. I had read about heads being

exposed on the top of Temple Bar, and it seemed a wicked old place, albeit a noble monument of architecture and a paragon of utility.

The narrow arch was a serious obstruction, and was dismantled in 1878. It was re-erected, in St Paul's Churchyard, only in 2004.

Beyond Temple Bar, Fleet Street became the Strand. Now part of London's theatre district, in Dickens' time this was one of the city's principal shopping thoroughfares. Despite this, it was only 9m/30ft wide where it passed St Clement Dane's church, and was thus as congested and traffic-choked as any side street. Most of its shops would seem to us very small. Many had goods hanging outside, or had bow windows to gain more display space. Surprisingly often they advertised themselves as 'warehouses', 'depots' or 'manufactories', since, in many cases, goods were not only sold but made, finished and stored on the premises. We are not accustomed to thinking of central London as a manufacturing centre, but in the 19th century it boasted thousands of small workshops producing everything from gloves to glassware.

Further along was Exeter 'Change, built in 1676 and, effectively, London's first shopping centre (it was guarded by a doorman dressed as a Beefeater). On the ground floor were stalls – an indoor bazaar. Upstairs was, of all things, a menagerie. The roaring of lions and tigers could be heard in the street, especially at feeding times. Its most famous inhabitant was Chunee the elephant, who once appeared on stage at Covent Garden. In 1826 he had to be shot after going berserk in his cage, an event commemorated by a popular print.

Today at the west end of the Strand are Charing Cross Station and Trafalgar Square. Neither was there in Dickens' youth. Until 1874 the area was dominated by Northumberland House, the town residence of the Dukes of Northumberland. Its wide street frontage was crowned with a lion (the emblem of the ducal family), standing on a plinth nearly 12m/40ft above the street, and this was for generations a London landmark. It was, in fact, the very reason that the young Dickens 'went astray'. He told how he came to get lost:

When I was a very small boy indeed, both in years and stature, I was taken out by Somebody (shade of Somebody forgive me for remembering no more of thy identity!), as an immense treat, to be

shown the outside of Saint Giles' Church. We were conversational
together, and saw the outside of Saint Giles' Church with
sentiments of satisfaction, much enhanced by a flag flying from the
steeple. I infer that we then went down to Northumberland House
in the Strand to view the celebrated lion over the gateway. At all
events, I know that in the act of looking up with mingled awe and
admiration at that famous animal I lost Somebody.

Work began on the laying out of Trafalgar Square in 1829. This involved
the clearing away of a number of shops, courts and alleyways, but the
most significant casualty was the Royal Mews, which housed the stables
and carriage-houses of the King, and is now situated behind Buckingham
Palace. At that time it occupied an elegant 18th-century building with
a yard in front. Between the Mews and Charing Cross was the Golden
Cross Inn, with its faux-Gothic entrance, castellated and pinnacled,
facing down Whitehall from behind the statue of King Charles I. It
was one of London's best-known coaching inns, and like many of these
establishments comprised a warren of taprooms, coach offices, waiting-
rooms and bedrooms. Five minutes' walk from the blacking factory in
which Dickens worked as a boy, it was the setting for a scene in *David
Copperfield* in which David met Daniel Peggotty in St Martin's Lane:

In those days there was a side-entrance to the stable-yard of the
'Golden Cross', nearly opposite to where we stood. I pointed out
the gateway, put my arm through his, and we went across. Two or
three public rooms opened out of the stable-yard; and looking into
one of them, and finding it empty, and a good fire burning, I took
him in there.

The inn was also the starting point for the first outing of the Pickwick
Club. To get out of the stable yard the coach had to pass under an arch,
and outside passengers had to duck their heads. The story told to Mr
Pickwick by the talkative Alfred Jingle as they departed was based, at
least partially, on a real occurrence:

'Heads, heads – take care of your heads!' cried the loquacious
stranger, as they came out under the low archway, which in

those days formed the entrance to the coach-yard. 'Terrible place
– dangerous work – other day – five children – mother – tall lady,
eating sandwiches – forgot the arch – crash – knock – children
look round – mother's head off – sandwich in her hand – no
mouth to put it in – head of a family off – shocking, shocking!'

West of this area, fashionable London began. Nearby was Haymarket,
with the Theatre Royal and Royal Italian Opera House, and Carlton
House, the residence of George IV. Designed by Henry Holland and set
back from the street behind a screen of Ionic columns, it was naturally
the centre of London Society. Its neighbours were the elegant clubs –
more raffish, and devoted to gambling, than in the reign of Victoria
– along Pall Mall and St James's Street.

Regent Circus, now Piccadilly Circus, was a short walk from
Haymarket. Here Nash's new Regent Street, which would be completed
by 1823, was meeting Piccadilly in a graceful curve, or 'quadrant'. On
both sides long arcades of Doric columns, behind which were shops,
made this street one of the wonders of Europe and gave London its only
thoroughfare that could bear comparison with Paris. It ran northward
through Portland Place to terminate at Regent's Park.

Piccadilly, on the other hand, was two centuries old and its eastern
end was crowded with shops and dwellings. Among them was Burlington
House, one of the great aristocratic town houses that were a feature of
London until the 20th century, with its huge gate and high front wall.
West of it, past the fashionable shops in Burlington Arcade, the street
became almost entirely residential. The mansions of the rich lined
the north side, their windows looking across Green Park to where the
King's new home, Buckingham House (now Palace) was being rebuilt.
The last of these great establishments was Apsley House, the Duke of
Wellington's residence, which stood by the turnpike gate at Hyde Park
Corner. The gate marked the western extremity of the metropolis; and
Apsley House had the splendid address 'Number One, London'.

These streets were by no means the whole of Dickens' London, but in
his youth a single afternoon would have been sufficient to see everything
that mattered. It was through innumerable walking excursions, driven by
his ceaseless, restless curiosity, that he built up the knowledge of London
which provided his novels with such vividness and power.

The Changing City

This was the city Dickens found on his arrival in 1822. For a few more years it would retain its Georgian intimacy, but great convulsions were on the way. The first and most significant change was the arrival of the railway. In 1836 a station was built at Spa Road (later renamed London Bridge) as the London end of the line to Greenwich, and 12 years later this line was pushed westward through the crowded and historic district of Southwark to a new terminus at Waterloo Road. In 1838 the first of the large-scale London stations was built at Euston Square. It was followed by others, of varying sizes, at Fenchurch Street (1841), King's Cross (1852), Paddington (1854), Victoria (1860), Charing Cross (1864), Cannon Street (1866) and St Pancras (1868). They were like secular cathedrals. When it opened, King's Cross was the largest station in Britain, but it was soon dwarfed by its neighbour, St Pancras, which had an arched glass roof 73m/240ft wide. The railway termini began the change in the scale of buildings that would gradually transform London.

As well as the stations, the railway lines themselves involved widespread demolition as they sliced through whole neighbourhoods, truncating streets, sweeping away buildings (an early casualty was Wellington House, Dickens' old school in Camden) and even removing natural features such as hills. Armies of labourers, mostly from Ireland, spent years gouging the steep cuttings and building the lengths of brick tunnel, filling the air with noise and dust and causing intense, seemingly endless congestion. Dickens remembered the disturbances of these years in a famous passage in *Dombey and Son*:

> The first shock of a great earthquake had, just at that period, rent the whole neighbourhood to its centre. Traces of its course were visible on every side. Houses were knocked down; streets broken through and stopped; deep pits and trenches dug in the ground; enormous heaps of earth and clay thrown up; buildings that were undermined and shaking, propped up by great beams of wood … Everywhere were bridges that led nowhere; thoroughfares that were wholly impassable; Babel towers of chimneys, wanting half their height; temporary wooden houses and enclosures, in the most unlikely situations; carcases of ragged tenements, and

fragments of unfinished walls and arches, and piles of scaffolding, and wildernesses of bricks, and giant forms of cranes, and tripods straddling above nothing ... In short, the yet unfinished and unopened Railroad was in progress; and, from the very core of all this dire disorder, trailed smoothly away, upon its mighty course of civilization and improvement.

By the end of the 1850s most of the lines from London to other regions were in operation, but work then began on the Metropolitan Railway, the world's first underground transit system. The digging of the tunnels caused immense inconvenience along one of the city's major thoroughfares for almost ten years.

Simultaneous with this was another great excavation project: the creation of a sewerage system. The problem of the city's waste had continued to grow. Hot summers were dreaded by Londoners because of the stench and sickness they drew from the river. June 1858 brought the 'Great Stink', when the Thames was choked with effluvium and infested the Palace of Westminster with such pestilential vapours that Parliament could scarcely function. A report by a government medical officer expressed the shock felt at this state of affairs:

Never, perhaps, in the annals of mankind, has such a thing been known before, as that the whole stream of a large river for a distance of seven miles should be in a state of putrid fermentation. The cause is the hot weather acting upon the ninety millions of gallons of sewage which discharge themselves daily into the Thames. It is quite impossible to calculate the consequences of such a moving mass of decomposition as the river at present offers to our senses.

The solution was already to hand, however. London had a Metropolitan Commission of Sewers and its Chief Engineer, Joseph Bazalgette, produced a scheme for diverting all of London's sewage from the Thames and channelling it eastward, through new systems of pipes to the north and south of the river, to treatment plants far outside the city in Essex and Kent. Work began in 1860 and lasted throughout the decade. This involved massive disturbance as dozens of major streets were dug up, but the years of inconvenience were worthwhile.

Another significant step had been taken when Parliament passed the Metropolitan Interment Act in 1850. Perhaps the most unpleasant aspect of London's stench had come from overcrowded, city-centre churchyards, used for centuries and ill-adapted to cope with a steadily rising population, so that corpses had had to be buried too near the surface. The Act allowed the creation of vast new suburban cemeteries, such as those at Highgate and Kensal Green, which made a significant contribution to the cleanliness of the capital.

Not only railways and sewers cut through London's crowded districts. Trafalgar Square provided London with an ornamental centrepiece when it was completed in 1867. New streets, on a scale appropriate to the city's increasing might and wealth, were built to rationalize the flow of traffic and to cope with its increased volume. These included King William Street (1830), Moorgate (1846), New Oxford Street (1847), Victoria Street (1852) and Queen Victoria Street (1867). Most impressive of all was Holborn Viaduct (1869), which bridged the valley of the Fleet River and eliminated the steep hill up which westbound traffic had had to struggle. Like the other large avenues, this involved the demolition of an entire district and the wholesale eviction of its inhabitants. Many moved to outlying communities, as the coincidental development of a suburban rail network enabled them to live at a distance and work in the centre.

Public buildings began to rival the railway stations in size and magnificence. The National Gallery (1838), the Royal Exchange (1843) and the new British Museum (1847) were overshadowed by the Crystal Palace (1851), a temporary structure that was considerably enlarged three years later when it was established permanently on another site. The Houses of Parliament were completed in 1860, to be followed a few years later by the Foreign Office.

These developments represented the greatest changes in layout, appearance and character in London's history – a level of disruption not to be seen again until the Blitz in 1940. The place that Dickens saw in 1822 had more in common with the London of the Middle Ages than with that of today. By the time of his death, 48 years later, it was a city that we would recognize ourselves.

The PEOPLE

To a modern visitor, the 'human landscape', the crush of people in the streets, of Dickens' London would seem disturbingly unfamiliar. Almost everything about the Londoners of the time – their clothes, hairstyles, language and even their smell – would bear little resemblance to the population of today. The first thing an observer would notice about them would be their unhealthy appearance. Contemporary foreign visitors often mentioned the strapping build of Englishmen, the soft complexions of the women and the attractiveness of the children, and they may indeed have looked more robust than the peasantry of poorer European countries, but to us the great majority of people would seem smaller, thinner and more malnourished: the overworked adjective 'pinched' would apply to many faces. Although there were both brawny and overweight individuals, the appearance of many of their contemporaries reflected a lifetime of unhealthy and inadequate diet.

The lined, shrivelled and toothless faces of the elderly (and some who seemed to be in their 70s would only have been about 40 years old) was witness to the fact that men and women could begin their working lives as small children and have no prospect of retirement. 'Good Mrs Brown', the hag who accosted Florence in a scene from *Dombey and Son*, might have been no older than middle-aged:

> She was a very ugly old woman, with red rims round her eyes, and a mouth that mumbled and chattered of itself when she was not speaking. She was miserably dressed, and carried some skins over her arm. She seemed to have followed Florence some little way at all events, for she had lost her breath; and this made her uglier still, as she stood trying to regain it; working her shrivelled yellow face and throat into all sorts of contortions.

Everywhere there were the visible signs of disease: the pitted faces of smallpox victims, the bow-legged gait of sufferers from rickets, the ravaged noses of untreated syphilis, the distorted limbs of those crippled in war, or in accidents at a time when little thought was given to 'health and safety'. Disability was more common, more obvious and more harrowing than we are used to. Even men and women in their 20s might have no teeth left.

General behaviour would also seem strange to us and more like that of the poor in some developing country than in the capital of England. One would be aware of people spitting in the street, and blowing their noses with their fingers. Men would walk arm in arm. Members of either sex would urinate, or even squat to defecate, in corners, unregarded by passers-by. Women would carry baskets, jugs and other loads on their heads, a practice now associated with rural Africa or India, and swarms of begging children would follow prosperous-looking people as they do in the streets of Morocco or Mexico City. Children, even infants, would be openly swigging alcohol. People of both sexes used tobacco, either taking snuff or smoking pipes made of white clay. Cheap and brittle, these were constantly breaking, and wherever a group had gathered for any length of time the ground might be littered with discarded bowls and stems.

In Dickens' London there were huge numbers of working children. The tasks these youngsters carried out were not a playful aping of adult occupations but a grim and relentless matter of survival. Piping little voices called out the virtues of matches, thread, or toys that they themselves could not play with. Mere tots would sell flowers or newspapers, sing ballads, carry parcels, black the shoes of pedestrians or lead blind men. In Dickens' boyhood, it was still common to see a chimney-sweep accompanied by a black-faced 'climbing boy'.

Much in evidence also was that stock 19th-century figure, the crossing-sweeper. Usually young boys or old men, crossing-sweepers looked after personal pitches that had to be jealously guarded. A glance at the road surface would show why they were necessary. Horse dung, spread by the rolling wheels of traffic and turned by rain to a brown slush, was sprayed by passing vehicles over the skirts and trouser-legs of those on the pavements, and a woman would have found it difficult to cross an unswept street without fouling the hem of her dress. Henry Mayhew discovered a female crossing-sweeper, who described her occupation:

I have been on the crossing fourteen years; but just now it is very poor work indeed. I have no regular customers at all. I like the winter-time, for the families is in. Though the weather is more severe, yet you do get a few more ha'pence. I take more from the staid elderly people than from the young. At Christmas, I think I took about eleven shillings, but certainly not more. The most I ever made at that season was fourteen shillings. The worst about Christmas is, that those who give much then generally hold their hand for a week or two.

A shilling a day would be as much as I want, sir. I have stood in the square all day for a ha'penny, and I have stood here for nothing. One week with another, I make two shillings in the seven days, after paying for my broom. I have taken threepence ha'penny today. Yesterday it was threepence ha'penny too. Years ago I made a great deal more – nearly three times as much. I come about eight o'clock in the morning, and go away about six or seven. I should not think crossings worth purchasing, unless people made a better living on them than I do.

Arguably the most striking feature of the time was people's abominable rudeness. On crowded pavements, pedestrians would barge and shove without any apology. A German traveller, Max Schlesinger, observed:

A Londoner jostles you in the street, without ever dreaming of asking your pardon; he will run against you, and make you revolve on your own axis, without so much as looking round to see how you feel after the shock; he will put his foot upon a lady's foot or dress, exactly as if such foot or dress were integral parts of the pavement, which ought to be trodden upon; but if he runs you down, if he breaks your ribs, or knocks out your front teeth, he will show some slight compunction, and as he hurries off, the Londoner has actually been known to turn back and beg your pardon.

Of course all this is very unpleasant to the stranger, and the more delicate among the English do not like it. None but men of business care to walk through the City at business hours; but if, either from choice or necessity, you find your way into those crowded quarters, you had better walk with your eyes wide open.

> Don't stop on the pavement, move on as fast as you can, and do
> as others do, that is to say, struggle on as best you may, and push
> forward without any false modesty. The passengers in London
> streets are hardened; they give and receive kicks and punches
> with equal equanimity.

Even indoors, if one sought refuge in some public building, there would
be no escape from this barbarism:

> Much less excusable is the kicking and pushing of the English
> public at their theatres, museums, railway stations, and other
> places of public resort. Nothing but an introduction to every
> individual man and woman in the three kingdoms will save you
> from being, on such occasions, pushed back by them. You have
> not been introduced to them; you are a stranger to them, and
> there is no reason why they should consult your convenience.
> The fact is, the English are bears in all places, except in their own
> houses; and only those who make their acquaintance in their dens
> know how amiable, kind and mannerly they really are.

Londoners' language was as offensive as their behaviour, and neither the
underclass nor the aristocracy had a monopoly on colourful invective.
One author, Captain D. Shaw, lamenting from a distance during the
Edwardian era that the city's modern-day inhabitants were not as full-
blooded as his own contemporaries, invoked the example of the great
Duke of Wellington:

> Persistent swearing may sound curious to the student of today, but
> in those halcyon days everybody swore. The Iron Duke, as is well
> known, never opened his mouth without a superfluous adjective.

Everywhere there would be boys, men and sometimes women carrying
the articles and equipment necessary for peripatetic trades. An old-
clothes man, probably a bearded Jew, would be holding half a dozen coats
and waistcoats and wearing several hats stacked on his head. Sellers of
hot pies, gingerbread, chestnuts and potatoes would have to be able to
carry not only the food itself but a charcoal stove in which to prepare it,

while those who dealt in apples, oranges or strawberries needed only to manage a two-handed basket and might carry this on their heads. Sellers of brushes, footstools, clothes-horses and picture-frames might be almost invisible under the burden of a day's supply of these things, draped over both shoulders, balanced on their heads or strapped on their backs. A seller of pots and pans and kitchen-utensils – nothing less than a walking ironmonger's shop – would make slow and clanking progress and might well have difficulty in turning round. A print-seller (perhaps the most fortunate of this fraternity in terms of baggage) would display his wares inside a downward-pointing open umbrella. Chair-menders had to carry with them great sheaves of cane in addition to their tools and were a common sight in residential streets, sitting at work on the kerbside. A knife-grinder worked from a barrow on the pavement, pumping a treadle with his foot to keep the grindstone turning. There were delivery boys with barrows and lidded baskets, aproned butchers' boys carrying meat in wooden trays, and milkmaids (there were very few milkmen) who had to balance two bulky and heavy metal cans, weighing well over 45kg/100lb when full, on a wooden yoke.

Another and older trade associated with women was also highly visible, indeed impossible to ignore: prostitutes were everywhere – at the gates of dockyards and barracks, in the streets of Mayfair and in the lobbies of theatres. Today it is possible to live for years in London without seeing prostitutes; in Dickens' time one could not spend even an hour without being aware of them. Their major hunting ground was in the Haymarket, where after dark large numbers would stand in clusters or patrol the pavements, importuning and grabbing at the sleeves of passing men. There were places even in the centre of London's fashion and culture that in the evenings were 'no-go areas' for families or for the respectable. In the 1850s Mayhew examined this aspect of the West End and wrote:

A considerable number [of the women] have come from the provinces to London [and] some are young milliners and dressmakers, at one time in business in town but, being unfortunate, are now walking the Haymarket. There are also a considerable number of French girls, and a number of Belgian and German prostitutes, who promenade this locality ... In the course of the evening, we see many of the girls proceeding with young and middle-aged and sometimes silverheaded frail old men, to Oxenden Street, Panton Street and James Street, near the Haymarket, where they enter houses of accommodation. Numbers of French girls may be seen in the Haymarket, and the neighbourhood of Tichbourne Street and Great Windmill Street, many of them in dark silk patelots and white or dark silk bonnets, trimmed with gay ribbons and flowers.

Besides these exotic and elegant courtesans there were crowds of poorer, shabbier and more desperate women. Mayhew described them too:

They consist of domestic servants of a plainer order, the daughters of labouring people, and some of a still lower class. Some of these girls are of a very tender age – from thirteen years and upwards ... Many of these young girls cohabit with young pickpockets about Drury Lane, St Giles's, Gray's Inn Lane, Holborn, and other localities – young lads from fourteen to eighteen, groups of whom may be seen loitering about the Haymarket, and often speaking to them. Numbers of these girls are artful and adroit thieves. They occasionally take watches, purses, pins and handkerchiefs from their silly dupes who go with them into those disreputable places.

Below even these were the lowest class of prostitutes:

These faded and miserable wretches skulk about the Haymarket, Regent Street, Coventry Street, Panton Street and Piccadilly, cadging from the fashionable people in the street and from the prostitutes passing along, and sometimes retire for prostitution into dirty low courts with shop boys, errand lads, petty thieves and labouring men, for a few paltry coppers. Most of them steal when they get an opportunity.

Another conspicuous aspect of street life was the number of men with advertising boards. Dickens himself was to coin the term 'sandwich board' when the phenomenon of street advertising developed in the 1830s. The city's streets were filled with advertisements. Virtually every available stretch of fence or wall was covered with printed notices, pasted up to the furthest height that a man with a long-handled brush could reach. In the belief that a sign could attract more attention if it moved, and was accompanied by noise (whether a drum, a trumpet or a shouting voice), large numbers of men were set to walking the streets with placards, usually on poles, touting everything from medicines to circuses; at election time they would also display the results in this manner. Sometimes they would be dressed in unusual costumes, or might be accompanied by unusual objects. For example, among the advertising men sketched by the artist George Scharf were two whose job was to demonstrate the merits of a type of waterproof boots. They did this by carrying a trough of water with a pair of the boots actually suspended in it. A foreign visitor, Prince Hermann Pückler-Muskau, commented:

> Every day sees some new invention. Among them may be reckoned the countless advertisements, and the manner of putting them 'en evidence'. Formerly people were content to paste them up; now they are ambulant. One has a pasteboard hat, three times as high as other hats, on which is written in great letters, 'Boots at twelve shillings a pair – warranted.' Another carries a sort of banner, 'Only three-pence a shirt.' Chests, like Noah's Ark, entirely pasted over with bills, and of the dimensions of a small house, drawn by men and horses, slowly parade the streets, carrying more lies than Munchausen ever invented.

Even more noticeable would have been the street performers – jugglers, acrobats, card-sharps, organ-grinders, singers and players – who provided diversion, or created a nuisance, depending on the nature or the mood of their listeners. George Sala, who lived in a street of houses near Charing Cross, was not numbered among their admirers. He imagined the anguish of having them all pass beneath his windows at the same time:

> So sure as the clock of St Martin's strikes eleven, so sure does my quiet street become a pandemonium of discordant sounds ... First Italian organ-grinder, hirsute, sunburnt, and saucy, who grinds airs from the 'Travatore' six times over, follows with a selection from the 'Traviata', repeated half a dozen times, finishes up with

the 'Old Hundredth' and the 'Postman's Knock', and then begins
again. Next, shivering Hindoo, his skin apparently just washed
in walnut juice, with a voluminous turban, dirty white muslin
caftan, worsted stockings and hob-nailed shoes, who, followed
by two diminutive brown imps in similar costume, sings a dismal
ditty in the Hindoostani language, and beats the tom-tom with
fiendish monotony. Next comes a brazen woman in a Scotch cap,
to which is fastened a bunch of rusty black feathers, apparently
culled from a mourning coach past service. She wears a faded
tartan kilt, fleshings, short calico trews, a velveteen jacket,
tin buckles in her shoes, and two patches of red brick-dust on
her haggard cheeks, and is supposed to represent a Scottish
highlander. She dances an absurd fling, interpolated occasionally
with a shrill howl to the music of some etoliated bagpipes screeded
by a shabby rogue of the male sex, her companion, arrayed in
similar habiliments. Next come the acrobats – drum, clarionet
and all ... Close on their heels follows the eloquent beggar,
with his numerous destitute but scrupulously clean family, who
has, of course, that morning parted with his last shirt. Then a
lamentable woman with a baby begins to whimper 'Old Dog Tray'.
Then swoop into the street an abominable band of ruffians, six
in number. They are swarthy villains, dressed in the semblance
of Italian goatherds, and are called, I believe, pifferari. They play
upon a kind of bagpipes – a hideous pig-skin-and-walking-stick-
looking affair, and accompany their droning by a succession of
short yelps and a spasmodic pedal movement that would be a near
approach toa sailor's hornpipe, if it did not bear a much closer
resemblance to the war-dance of a wild Indian ...

I can do nothing with these people. I shout, I threaten, I shake
my fist, I objurgate them from my window in indifferent Italian,
but to no avail. They defy, scorn, and make light of me. They
are encouraged in their abominable devices, not merely by the
idlers in the street, the servant-maids gossiping at the doors,
the boys with the baskets, and the nurse children [those in the
care of 'baby-farmers' or childminders], but by the people at the
windows, who seem to have nothing to do but to look from their
casements all day long.

Naturally clothes would have formed a major part of one's impressions. People's appearance was much fussier, with many layers of clothing. All men wore waistcoats, even in summer, buttoned almost up to the chin. Labouring men often dressed in short monkey-jackets, as did boys. Others wore knee-length coats (a short, double-breasted one was called a spencer), often with a swallow-tail and brass buttons. Only in the middle of the century did the frock coat become the standard dress of Victorian gentlemen. Gloves were worn by men at all times of year. They were often of beautiful leather and in striking colours, such as green or sky-blue and, like the canes carried by many, were an emblem of gentility.

Trousers were of all sorts. Knee-breeches ('small clothes') had been replaced only at the beginning of the century by full-length 'pantaloons' (sometimes called 'American trousers') but thousands of men continued to wear them until well into Victoria's reign. Many workmen wore them with thick wool or cotton stockings and lace-up boots or shoes, and they might be worn with buttoned, calf-length gaiters against the mire in the streets. Some pantaloons were narrow in the leg and stopped a little above the foot. 'Tights', a variation on this theme, were skin-tight and buttoned just above the ankle, but there was also a fashion for loose, baggy trousers. The understrap (a strap and buckle under the instep that kept trouser-legs taut) was borrowed from military uniform and continued in fashion until the arrival of peg-top trousers in mid-century.

Jerseys (sweaters) were not worn by anyone except fishermen and seafarers, though woollen scarves or 'comforters' were used in winter. In summer men might wear white trousers and substitute straw hats for felt, but otherwise their costume made little concession to the climate. Without dry-cleaning (the only way to take dirt out of wool clothes was by rubbing them with fuller's earth, an absorbent clay), garments would have been crumpled and uncomfortable, and any outer clothing would soon have been stained with soot.

Until after the middle of the century, men's shirts were baggy-sleeved and had an elaborate, crimped frill on the front. This and the large, sticking-up collar were an important part of a man's appearance. Whenever possible they had to be snow-white. In descriptions of his characters, Dickens often made a point of mentioning 'clean linen' in a manner that suggests this was not especially common. Above the collar, a neck-cloth or stock would be worn; it would be wrapped several times around the throat and tied in a bow at the front. Many men were too poor to wear a shirt at all: the high necks of waistcoats left little of the throat visible and this could be covered by a stock.

While in later generations male dress was characterized by dark colours and sober cut, the men of Dickens' time had greater opportunity for individualism and exuberance. The formal dress worn by members of the respectable professions might include coats of blue, red or buff, and trousers with a loud check (there was a fashion in the 1840s and 1850s for a black-and-white tartan called shepherd's plaid) or a wide stripe down the leg.

Men's shoes in the earlier part of the century were low heeled, low in the instep and tied with a ribbon like women's shoes; they were called 'pumps'. There were also boots of many types, from the lace-up version worn by workmen to the pull-on 'Wellington boots'. Another style, which became universal after the middle decades, was the elastic-sided boot. Many shoes for both men and women were still 'straights', made exactly alike rather than designed for the left or right foot, and intended to be gradually 'accustomized' by the wearer (some surviving pairs have had 'L' and 'R' written inside them by their owners). Boots and shoes fitted to feet had been available since about 1810, but they did not become universal until much later, and agricultural labourers continued to wear straight hobnail boots until well into the 20th century.

There would have been thousands of people, mostly children, without shoes. Many of the poor never wore them, and therefore did not have what were called 'shoe feet', which could adapt to being encased in leather. In inclement weather they might wrap their feet in rags, which quickly became sodden. Another extraordinary sight would have been that of women click-clacking along the pavements in pattens – wooden soles strapped on the shoes and raised off the ground by iron struts. Prince Hermann Pückler-Muskau remarked that, in wet weather:

... people must go on stilts. Englishwomen of the lower classes do indeed wear an iron machine of the kind on their large feet.

Everyone, of either sex, wore a hat; to appear in public without one would draw curious glances, and probably derisive remarks. It was an irritating trick of urchins on crowded pavements to tip people's hats over their eyes from behind. A crowd of men would present a sea of top hats, a form of headgear that had arrived almost as the 19th century began and was to dominate male wardrobe until long after it ended. The top hat was first worn on the streets of London in 1797 by a man called John Hetherington, who was arrested as a result. It looked so unusual that he was booed by passers-by, and four different women fainted on seeing it. He was charged with breach of the peace for wearing 'a tall structure having a shiny lustre calculated to alarm timid people' and ordered not to repeat the offence.

Within 20 years top hats were everywhere. Even workmen wore them when digging up the roads. The sleek, expensive ones seen on gentlemen were of beaver pelt; those worn by poorer men were of rabbit and soon came to look shaggy when they had been in the rain. They became part of the uniforms of policemen and postmen and, since both these types of public servant spent a great deal of their time outdoors, their hats were topped with black oilcloth that gleamed like patent leather. The top hat was therefore common to all classes in Dickens' time and only gradually did it become the emblem of the office clerk. Before that, in the 1840s, it grew in both height and width of brim to become the 'stovepipe', which was to flourish for 30 years.

There were multitudes of caps. The peaked version was a Regency innovation, its visor and high crown inspired by the headdress of Britain's Russian and Prussian allies in the war against Napoleon (Dickens wore such a cap when working as a 'writing-clerk' in a legal firm). A decidedly civilian version of this, soft-crowned and sporting a tassel, was worn largely, though not exclusively, by boys rather than men. It has come to be associated indelibly with Dickens' characters, particularly David Copperfield, but, an ancestor of the modern school cap, it is still worn on festive occasions by students in some Scandinavian countries. From this evolved the 'cheese-cutter' of the mid-Victorians – a soft, pork-pie hat with a vertical leather peak descending over the brow. Labourers wore woollen stocking-caps, or a curious round peakless hat not unlike those still seen in Afghanistan. Some skilled artisans also wore a square hat of folded newspaper, which was something of a professional trademark. One of these can be seen on the carpenter in Tenniel's illustrations for *Through the Looking Glass* and they can also be found in Italy, where workmen still make them.

For most of Dickens' lifetime, men had a habit of parting their hair at the back of the head and combing it forward across the temples, and it was often grown, or styled, in large forward-thrusting spikes. Though beards and moustaches were relatively unfashionable in the first half of the century – Dickens did not grow his own goatee until the 1850s – men often wore hefty side-whiskers. In the 1860s these developed into the extravagant 'dundrearies' that became a male hallmark of the decade: very long whiskers that hung from the jowls and were linked by a moustache, leaving the chin bare.

Women's hair was pinned in a bun, like the young Queen Victoria's, or piled on top of the head. From the 1820s to the 1860s there was a fashion for side-curls (elaborate festoons of ringlets that hung down from the temples), often hung with ribbons. Though this made them look very feminine, many young women, even those who were clearly considered attractive, would seem plain and unremarkable to the 21st-century eye. The modern essentials of mass-produced cosmetics were of course unavailable, as were suntans (they went to great lengths to avoid exposure to the sun. Anyone, man or woman, with sunburned skin would be taken for a manual labourer or a market stall-holder). The development of photography, the cinema and the 'beauty industry' have since created notions of beauty that were unknown to that era.

Women wore at least a lace cap when outdoors, and working women, whether milking cows in a dairy or washing sheets in a laundry, wore a shapeless cotton 'mob cap', tied at the forehead, that kept the hair under control. Those more careful of their complexions wore a 'poke bonnet', in fashion from the Regency until the late 1850s, with a projecting brim that hid much of their faces except from the front (Dickens refers to young men 'looking under the bonnets of milliners' apprentices').

Women's shoes were simple. Ladies wore flat-heeled pumps, made of silk or satin if they were rich, leather if they were not. By the 1820s these were frequently square-toed and had straps that crossed over the instep and tied around the ankle. Boots gradually became popular. These were ankle-length and were also flat-heeled. The uppers were of silk or satin and the tips of the toes – the only part that was expected to be visible – were of patent or kid leather. With all of these, stockings would be worn. They were usually made of white cotton and would be tied with garters, or held in place with buckled leather straps, above the knee.

Dresses, in Dickens' early years, were still of the simple high-waisted design, inspired by Ancient Greece, that had been worn by Jane Austen's heroines. By the 1830s skirts had widened, the desire for hourglass waists had brought back the corset, necklines had risen and long sleeves had evolved into the puffed shape seen in Cruikshank's illustrations. Regency dresses had often been only ankle-length, but by the 1830s hems dragged along the ground, as they would do for the rest of the century. (When Joseph Paxton designed the Crystal Palace, he had wooden floors laid with narrow gaps between the planks, on the principle that dust and litter would be swept into these spaces by the skirts of female visitors, thus saving expensive cleaning!) By 1850 the crinoline or 'hoop skirt', a ludicrous and impractically wide skirt kept in shape by a cage-like frame, had begun its 20-year domination of fashion.

Every woman wore a shawl. Usually of thick wool, cotton or tweed, it kept the upper body warm and in foul weather would be worn over the head. It was also ideal for carrying small children, or other burdens such as firewood or groceries. An immensely practical garment, it was a blanket, rug, overcoat, hat and shopping-bag combined.

Class Distinction

It would have been relatively easy to categorize people at a glance as belonging to a particular class, profession or trade. Dickens' contemporaries would not have understood the present-day desire of people at the top, or in the middle, of society to be mistaken for those in lower strata. The clothing of the rich was expensive and elegant. The bourgeoisie could also afford to be well dressed by the city's legions of expert tailors and dressmakers, and looked as much as possible like their betters. The aspirational poor, though their clothes no doubt showed a good deal of patching and mending, would also try to dress neatly. Policemen, shop assistants and parish officials would all behave with considerably more respect toward anyone who looked comfortably off.

In Dickens' fiction, the character most representative of respectable poverty is Mr Micawber in *David Copperfield*. Though his clothes were drab and probably secondhand, he managed by the judicious use of small touches and accessories to present an image of elegance:

I went in, and found there a stoutish, middle-aged person, in a
brown surtout [greatcoat] and black tights and shoes, with no
more hair upon his head than there is upon an egg, and with a
very extensive face, which he turned full upon me. His clothes
were shabby, but he had an imposing shirt-collar on. He carried a
jaunty sort of a stick, with a large pair of rusty tassels to it; and a
quizzing-glass hung outside his coat – for ornament, I afterwards
found, as he very seldom looked through it, and couldn't see
anything when he did.

Of those below this level, a description of both clothing and
physiognomy that probably fitted hundreds of thousands of Londoners
of the time is this picture of Bill Sikes in *Oliver Twist*:

A fellow in a black velveteen coat, very soiled drab breeches, lace-
up half-boots, and grey cotton stockings. He had a brown hat on
his head, and a dirty belcher handkerchief round his neck.

Sometimes the line between the classes was deceptively thin, as noted
by the German visitor Max Schlesinger:

The women of England do not betray their social position by their
dress. Coloured silks, black velvets, silk or straw bonnets with
botanical ornaments, are worn by a lady's maid, as well as by the
lady. Possibly, the maid's dress may be less costly; the lady, too,
may sweep her flounces with a distinguished air: there may be
some difference or other, but who can see all and know all by just
looking at people?

Everywhere there were brilliant official costumes and extraordinary items
of dress that identified people's professions or status and added greatly
to the theatre of the streets, whether it were the hats of market porters
(shaped so that they could carry goods on their heads) or the cocked
hats and capes of parish beadles. There were Yeoman Warders in their
Tudor bonnets at the Tower of London, and veteran sailors in tricorn
hats and blue-and-gold coats at the Naval Hospital in Greenwich. There
were the 'blue-coat boys', pupils of the charity school Christ's Hospital,

whose uniform of blue gown and yellow stockings (a colour supposedly chosen because it repelled rats) had been unchanged since Tudor times and is still worn today. There were postmen in bright red coats and police constables in dark blue ones, and there were hosts of coachmen, grooms and footmen in gorgeous liveries with powdered hair or cockades in their hats, who accompanied their employers about town or waited for them, standing about in conspicuous groups, outside shops and clubs.

Soldiers were part of this pageant of the streets. The scarlet-and-blue uniforms of the Guards regiments that protected the monarch were a conspicuous feature of London, and the men themselves were more visible than they are now. Today, members of the Armed Forces do not appear in uniform in public unless they are on duty. In those days they had no other clothes, and wore their scarlet coats in taverns, theatres, shops and in the streets. They were quartered in several places in the city: at the Tower, at Kensington, at Charing Cross Barracks (immediately behind the National Gallery) and at St James's (later Wellington) Barracks near Buckingham Palace. Today the British are convinced that the drill and bearing of these regiments are unmatched by any army in the world, but they have not always made such a favourable impression. An anonymous author who was himself an army officer observed the Guards outside the King's residence at Carlton House one day in the 1820s:

I have seen individuals of the Foot Guards, on duty at Carlton House, so ill-made, so slouching in their gait, and their fine appointments in such dull order, and so ill put on, that I have really cast my eye about in fear, lest some foreign officers should pass by. I saw three Russian officers, remarkably fine soldierly-looking young men, coming down Pall Mall, and the sentinels were relieving: out of the whole relief, except the corporal, there was not one fine, smart-looking soldier. I saw these officers attentively observing them, and talking with each other in that quiet way, in which, as modest gentlemen, they alone could express their disappointment. For cleanliness, handling of the firelocks, carriage, and marching, when actually under arms, our English soldiers are equal to any in the world; but the moment they are dismissed, or the moment they march at ease, under a

careless non-commissioned officer, or are left to stand sentry by
themselves, with no reproving eye on them, they cease to look
like what they really are, and can appear.

The British public did not like soldiers. The army at that time was
associated with the control of civil disorder, and thus with repression
(the infamous 'Peterloo Massacre' in Manchester, in which cavalry had
dispersed an outdoor meeting of radicals and killed a number of people,
had taken place as recently as 1819). In addition, their badly made
and ill-fitting uniforms caused any attempt at swagger to be met with
derision, as the same anonymous author explained:

> They dare not walk as they know they could and should. There
> is nothing the common people in England, even to the children,
> so much delight in as the lowering and laughing at all display of
> pride in a common soldier; they have many a saying, and many
> a trick to provoke him with. I have often, from a window, seen
> and smiled at this kind of thing. 'Heads up, soldier!' uttered by a
> little ragged urchin of a chimney-sweeper, will disconcert many a
> soldier for the length of a street. 'Lord, what a fine fellow I am!'
> and many such phrases, will do the like; whereas by a simple
> lounging gait they escape it all. There is not a British soldier, from
> the Duke of York to the young drum-boy, who is not aware of the
> thing, and the mass of the common people know it also.

Ironically, in the midst of London's splendid human cavalcade, anyone
whose appearance was different would be noticed at once. This was
especially true of foreigners or visitors from the country, whose rural
clothes – corduroy and gaiters, perhaps even a smock – announced their
presence even before their accent could betray them. London's swindlers
and pickpockets were naturally on the lookout for precisely this sort
of person. Dickens, in his article 'Gone Astray', described a country
friend of his father's who, although his appearance impressed the young
narrator, must have stood out amid the urban throng:

> I have an impression that he was got up in a striking manner – in
> cord breeches of fine texture and milky hue, in long jean [denim]

gaiters, in a green coat with bright buttons, in a blue neckerchief, and a monstrous shirt-collar. I think he must have come (as I had myself) out of the hop-grounds of Kent. I considered him the glass of fashion and the mould of form; a very Hamlet without the burden of his difficult family affairs.

Londoners' Language

While the clothing of strangers might arouse comment, characteristics that they could not help were also held up to ridicule. 'British reserve' was an invention of a later era. Georgians and early Victorians were a good deal more brusque, discourteous, argumentative and outspoken than their descendants. Foreigners, the handicapped, the overweight or those who otherwise stood out could expect little privacy or mercy, particularly from street urchins, at a time when it would never have occurred to anyone to care about the sensitivities of minorities. Mary Seacole, a black Jamaican-born woman who was to become a celebrity in Britain through her welfare work in the Crimean War, recalled her first encounter with this attitude as she and a friend walked through the streets:

I shall never forget my first impressions of London. They are as vivid now as though the year 18-- (I had very nearly let my age slip then) had not been long ago numbered with the past. Strangely enough, some of the most vivid of my recollections are of the London street-boys who began to poke fun at my and my companion's complexion. I am only a little brown – a few shades duskier than the brunettes whom you all admire so much; but my companion was very dark, and a fair (if I can apply the term to her) subject for their rude wit. She was hot-tempered, poor thing! And as there were no policemen to awe the boys and turn our servants' heads in those days, our progress through the London streets was sometimes a rather chequered one.

Small boys would call out 'Hip!', the equivalent of 'Oi!' in today's parlance, as preamble to whatever 'gum' (abusive language) would follow. Country visitors to London might be addressed derisively as

'Hobnail', 'Rodger', 'Johnny Raw', 'Tom Coney' or 'Chaw Bacon'. A fat man would be 'Mister Double-Tripe' or 'Guts and Garbage'. Boys would shout 'Glass Eyes!' at a wearer of spectacles, and a man with red hair might be pursued by cries of 'Hip! Michael! Your head's on fire!' Those with dark skin would be addressed as 'Blueskin', 'Snowball', 'Lilly-white' or 'Chimney-chops'. A short person would be called 'Whipper-Snapper', 'Jack Spratt' or 'Minikin'. An ugly man might be 'Jackanapes' and could be subject to the much-heard quip: 'You have killed a baboon, and stolen his face.' A man with peeling skin (often the result of syphilis) would be 'Peel Garlick'. Any man who looked effeminate would be 'Miss Molly' or 'Twiddle-Poop'. A Scotsman would be 'Sandy' (or 'Sawny', imitating Scots pronunciation) and north-country seamen, such as those who sailed the colliers from Tynemouth, would be 'Jock' or 'Crowdy-Headed Jock' – a reference to the food (oatmeal and cream laced with whisky) on which these men were supposed to subsist.

Jews were a community small in numbers (there were only 20–30,000 in the whole of Britain in the early decades of the century) but of long standing. Many of them had been assimilated into English society (a convert to Christianity, Benjamin Disraeli, became Prime Minister in 1868) but those who kept to their own religion were viewed as outsiders. Jews were active in finance as well as trade in jewellery and all manner of secondhand goods. At the lower end of commerce, they had a near-monopoly on used clothing, and their cry of 'Old Clo'!' was one of the familiar sounds of London. When Disraeli stood for election to Parliament in 1837, he was heckled with shouts of 'Shylock' and 'Old Clothes'.

Dickens' novels therefore reflect an attitude that was commonplace. Fagin became the most well-known Jew in literature since Shylock, and his appearance became symbolic of evil:

A very old shrivelled Jew, whose villainous-looking and repulsive face was obscured by a quantity of matted red hair. He was dressed in a greasy flannel gown, with his throat bare.

Oliver Twist was completed in 1839. Twenty-four years later, Dickens was reprimanded for his negative portrayal of Fagin by Eliza Davis, the wife of a Jewish banker. She suggested that he had done her people a great wrong and that he should make amends. He did so, to her complete satisfaction, by creating the character Riah in *Our Mutual Friend*. This man, also a Jew of advanced years, was patient and altruistic (he helped the young girl Lizzie to escape from her rival suitors, Headstone and Wrayburn). His nature was contrasted with that of his cantankerous employer, Fascination Fledgeby, who was given all the same character traits of miserliness, suspicion and indifference to the plight of others that Fagin had displayed:

> 'Now, old 'un,' cried Fascination in his light raillery, 'what dodgery are you up to next, sitting there with your eyes shut? You ain't asleep. Catch a weasel at it, and catch a Jew!'
>
> 'Truly, sir, I fear I nodded,' said the old man.
>
> 'Not you!' returned Fledgeby with a cunning look. 'A telling move with a good many, I dare say, but it won't put me off my guard.'
>
> The old man shook his head, gently repudiating the imputation, and suppressed a sigh. It was an edifying spectacle, the young man in his easy chair taking his coffee, and the old man, with his grey head bent, standing awaiting his pleasure.
>
> 'Now!' said Fledgeby, 'fork out your balance in hand, and prove by figures how you make out that it ain't more.'
>
> Riah obeyed, and then taking a bag from his breast, and referring to the sum in the accounts for which they made him responsible, told it out upon the table. Fledgeby told it again with great care, and rang every sovereign.
>
> 'I suppose,' he said, taking one up to eye it closely, you haven't been lightening any of these, but it's a trade of your people's, you know.'

Despite this effort at positive portrayal, it would be some time before Jews ceased to be accosted with cries of 'Old Clothes!'

The biggest foreign community was the Irish, known as 'Teagues' or 'Patlanders'. By 1801 they had made up 6 per cent of the city's population, but the building of canals, roads and railways was to bring in many thousands more. They were far too numerous to constitute a 'minority group' in the sense that they needed to assimilate or lost their identity. Many came from the same parts of Ireland, and kept a feeling of community and corporate identity, though they also absorbed enough native culture to become that hybrid species, the 'Irish cockney'. Filling the streets with their exotic brogue, they came to form a whole substratum. They were generally considered the bottom of the pile, for the poverty of many in Ireland was even worse than that in London. Mayhew interviewed two street boys who gave their impressions of the place from which these immigrants came. One told him that he:

> Had heer'd of Ireland. Didn't know where it was, but it couldn't be far, or such lots wouldn't come from there to London. Should say they walked it, aye, every bit of the way, for he'd seen them come in, all covered with dust.

Once arrived, the Irish packed into what were then known as the 'rookeries', or slum districts of the city, and lived the same life of overcrowding, disease and drunkenness as the poorest of the natives. When Oliver Twist followed the Artful Dodger through an extremely squalid district to Fagin's headquarters, he discovered that:

> There were a good many small shops, but the only stock in trade appeared to be heaps of children, who, even at that time of night, were crawling in and out at the doors, or screaming from the inside. The sole places that seemed to prosper, amid the general blight of the place, were the public houses; and in them the lowest orders of Irish were wrangling with might and main.

Blacks formed another, albeit tiny, ethnic group. They had lived in London since Tudor times and there were more of them in the early part of the 19th century than there would be later, but they were sufficiently few that their presence in the streets would be noticed and commented upon. They might belong to any trade, or might be sailors ashore between voyages. A number were beggars, and Mayhew described how:

> The Negro mendicant, who is usually an American Negro, relies on the abject misery and down trodden despair of his appearance, and generally represents himself as a fugitive slave. At the time that the suppression of the slave trade [abolished in the British

Empire in 1833] created so much excitement, this was so excellent a 'dodge' that many white beggars, fortunate enough to possess a flattish or turned-up nose, dyed themselves black and [pretended to be] real Africans.

There are but few Negro beggars to be seen now. It is only common fairness to say that Negroes seldom, if ever, shirk work. Their only trouble is to obtain it. Those who have seen the many Negroes employed in Liverpool, will know that they are hard-working, patient, and, too often, underpaid. A Negro will sweep a crossing, run errands, black boots, clean knives and forks, or dig, for a crust and a few pence. The few imposters among them are to be found among those who go about giving lectures on the horrors of slavery, and singing variations on the 'escapes' in that famous book 'Uncle Tom's Cabin'. Negro servants are seldom met with in police reports, and are generally found to give satisfaction to their employers. In the east End of London Negro beggars are to be met with, but they are seldom beggars by profession. Whenever they are out of work they have no scruples, but go into the streets, take off their hats, and beg directly.

Black beggars were known as 'St Giles' blackbirds' and one interviewed by Mayhew gave a picture of life that was probably all too typical:

I do porter's work mostly, but I do anything I can get. I beg more than half the year. I have no regular lodging. I sleep where I can. At some places they don't care to take a man of colour in. I sometimes get work in Newgate Market, carrying meat, but not often. Ladies give me halfpence oftener than men. The butchers call me 'Othello', and ask me why I killed my wife. I have tried to get aboard a ship, but they won't have me. I can lift almost any weight when I have had a bit of something to eat. I don't care for beer. I like rum best. I have often got drunk but never when I paid for it myself.

Not all black Londoners lived, as this man did, on the edge of destitution. His brother had become a servant in a wealthy household, though this had not improved his own lot:

> He never takes any notice of me now. He is doing very well. He
> lives with a great gentleman in Harewood Square, and has a coat
> with silver buttons, and a gold-laced hat. He is very proud, and
> would not speak to me if he saw me.

There were numerous migrants from other parts of Europe, such as
Italians, Germans and Frenchmen (who, apart from a general reputation
for effeminacy, had recently been Britain's enemy and were therefore
subject to especial ridicule), many of whom worked as manservants,
cooks, waiters, barbers or teachers, as well as merchants. England had a
reputation as a haven for 'asylum seekers' – political troublemakers who
had left their own countries either voluntarily or through compulsion
(Karl Marx was in London during Dickens' lifetime, Lenin a few
decades after his death). They were, often to the fury of their countries'
governments, at liberty to associate, attend meetings, speak and write
without interference from the police. It was also easier for such people to
find anonymity in the world's largest city.

Italians were the largest group of European origin, and had been in
London since the arrival of Lombard bankers in the Middle Ages. More
recently (in the 18th century), there had been a wave of Italian fencing
instructors, as well as manservants brought back from the Grand Tour
by wealthy Englishmen, who had settled in the city. By the 19th century
there was a steady trickle of poor Italian immigrants, many of whom
made their livings as street entertainers. One observer, Charles Knight,
was charmed by this new type of London street-character:

> An Italian was now and then imported with his guitar; and his
> knowledge of harmony compensated for his somewhat cracked
> voice. We have some fears that the immigration of Italian boys is
> declining. We do not see the monkey and the white mice so often
> as we could wish to do. And then these Italian boys themselves,
> with their olive cheeks and white teeth – they are something
> different from your true London boy, with his mingled look of
> cunning and insolence. They will show you their treasures [many
> of them 'exhibited' animals or mechanical toys] with a thorough
> conviction that they are giving you pleasure, and if you deny the
> halfpenny, they will still have a smile.

Though these groups were large and disparate, London was big enough to swallow them all and its character was overwhelmingly English. Society in that era had a homogeneity that is now unimaginable.

We would have a good deal of difficulty in understanding the accents of Dickens' Londoners, for their pronunciation of English was somewhat different from ours. It was characterized by the transposing of v's and w's. Cockney dialect was recorded by numerous 19th-century writers and commentators and is frequently used by Dickens' characters. Imitating it must have added to his original readers' fun in declaiming his novels aloud, and he himself, with an actor's ear for voices, will have been able to imitate it superbly when giving his own public readings. The hungry convict Magwitch, for instance, asked Pip: 'Do you know what wittles [victuals] is?' The cockney songs of the era abound in this patois, with titles such as 'The Poor Vorkhouse Boy' and 'Villikins and his Dinah', and one of the catchphrases of the time was Thomas Hudson's exclamation, 'Dash my Vig!' A popular song – 'The Ratcatcher's Daughter of Islington', about the tragic obsession of a peddler of white sand – demonstrates how widespread was this gutteral pronunciation:

> The Ratcatcher's daughter run in his head,
> And he didn't know vot he was arter,
> Instead of crying 'Vant any lily-vite sand?'
> He cried, 'D'ye vant any Ratcatcher's daughter?'
> The donkey pricked up his ears and laughed!
> And vondered vot he vos arter,
> To hear his lily-vite sandman cry,
> 'Vill you buy any Ratcatcher's daughter?'

It is never more obvious than in the exchanges between Sam Weller and his father Tony in *Pickwick Papers*. Weller Senior even wrote in this way, his solemn news interspersed with the imagery of the coaching world:

> My Dear Sammle,
> I am werry sorry to have the pleasure of being a Bear of ill news
> your Mother in law cort cold consekens of imprudently settin
> too long on the damp grass. The doctor says that if she'd svallo'd
> varm brandy and vater artervards she mightn't have been no vus

**her veels wos immediately greased and everythink done to set her
agoin as could be inwented ...
N B he vill have it spelt that vay vich I say ant right ... and am
Samivel infernally yours,
Tony Veller**

English slang, especially the 'flash' terminology of criminal Londoners,
would be almost incomprehensible to us. 'Blunt' meant money. A coach
was called a 'rattler', a wagon was a 'vardo' and a cart was a 'drag'.
Horses were called 'prads'. A 'slap-bang' was an eating-house – a café
– so-called because the proprietor refused credit, insisting that payment
was slapped on the counter. A 'flat' was a gullible or stupid person
and a 'flash cove' one with knowledge of the world. Many words had
meanings entirely different to those they have today: 'foxed' meant
drunk, not confused; 'crank' meant pert; 'dowdy' meant coarse or vulgar.
'Randy' meant obstreperous or unruly; 'smug' meant neat or spruce;
a 'slum' meant a room; 'bingo' was a nickname for brandy. A 'rap' or
'rapper' meant a lie or a false oath. To 'yam' was to stuff oneself but to
'snack' meant to share ('to go snacks' was to be partners). 'A 'kiddy' was
not a child but a young man.

Other phrases were simpler to interpret. For example, 'high-living'
meant living on the top storey of a building. There were delightful
expressions for everyday things or situations: 'dew-beaters' was a
slang term for feet; 'pockets to let' meant that one was broke; and a
parson whose sermons went on so long that the Sunday dinners of his
congregation were ruined was known as a 'spoil-pudding'.

Popular phrases that are encountered in Dickens' novels can
sometimes be deciphered by their context. 'Walker!' meant the
equivalent of 'Come off it!', an expression of mocking disbelief, as can
be seen from this passage at the end of A Christmas Carol, in which the
reformed Scrooge calls to a small boy from his window:

'Do you know the Poulterer's in the next street but one, at the
corner?'
  'I should hope I did.'
  'Do you know if they've sold the prize Turkey that was hanging
up there?'

'It's hanging there now.'
'Is it? Go and buy it.'
'Walk-ER!'
'No, no, I am in earnest.'

Some phrases have long since been lost to the English language. 'Cag-mag' was the term for cat's meat – inferior meat unsuitable for human consumption, and thus by extension for anything substandard. This explains the otherwise unintelligible outburst of a lisping Jewish supplicant of the lawyer, Mr Jaggers, in *Great Expectations*:

> I remarked this Jew, who was of a highly excitable temperament, performing a jig of anxiety under a lamp-post, and accompanying himself, in a kind of frenzy, with the words, 'Oh, Jaggerth, Jaggerth, Jaggerth! All otherth ith Cag-Maggerth, give me Jaggerth!'

Some words meant more or less the same as they do now, and sound surprisingly modern: To 'diddle' meant to cheat. The 'gob' was the mouth (a bridle was known as a 'gob-string'); 'spread' was a slang term for butter and 'cow-juice' for milk. The 'bog house' was the lavatory. Extraordinarily, a 'pig' was the term for a policeman and, using another phrase that sounds as if it would be more at home in the 1960s, Schlesinger reported that:

> ... in the broadest part of Holborn, there are on either side certain suspicious-looking lanes, in which pawnbrokers and cobblers 'hang out'.

Of all the things – dress, behaviour, outlook – that illustrate the gulf between ourselves and the Londoners of Dickens' time, it is perhaps their everyday language – this foreign-sounding pronunciation and unintelligible vocabulary – that most separates us from them. We have become accustomed, through numerous film and television adaptations of his novels, to seeing Dickens' contemporaries as more or less the same as us, but through their speech we can appreciate that they belonged to a different world.

SHOPS and Shopping

For Regent Street to be seen to the best advantage, it should be
visited on a summer's day in the afternoon, when the splendid
carriages, and elegantly attired pedestrians, evince the opulence
and taste of our magnificent metropolis.

The brilliant ever-shifting scene presented daily in Regent
Street is dizzying in its confusion. The fire-flies of fashion
glance rapidly hither and thither, and the West End streets are
thronged with a promiscuous jungle of carriages, horsemen and
horsewomen, cabs, omnibuses and wagons; the pavements being
crowded with fashionable loungers. With what dignified ease and
gorgeously bedizened footmen attend their mistresses or lounge
about in attitudes of studied grace.

This was how in 1866 the *Illustrated London News*, one of the
foremost magazines of the day, described Regent Street. Throughout
Dickens' lifetime it was London's most exclusive shopping thoroughfare.
It owed its success to the elegance of its architecture and to the fact that
its breadth and grandeur made it suitable for promenading by carriages
and pedestrians. Coincidental with its building had been the invention
of plate glass. This meant that far more goods could be put on show
in large shop windows, and could be displayed more attractively, even
artistically, as a source of temptation to passers-by. This in turn meant
that window-shopping became a pleasure and that walking or driving up
and down a shopping street came to have social importance.

The street had taken years to plan and build, involving the demolition
of scores of often small and mean houses and shops. Its purpose was
not simply to provide the capital with an ambitiously large avenue of
shops; it was also intended to establish a frontier between the noisome

alleys of Soho to the east (there were few side-streets leading off Regent Street in that direction) and the district of Mayfair to the west. It was visited in the afternoons by a largely female crowd of the wealthy and the celebrated (though of course it emptied in August when the Season ended); it was also a street in which members of Society might live, for above the shops were sets of apartments (in *Nicholas Nickleby*, Lord Frederick Verisopht occupied one of these).

Regent Street's greatest glory was the 'quadrant', with its curving colonnades that gave shelter to shoppers in bad weather. Their rows of Grecian pillars gave to this corner of London the Georgian dignity of Bath or Edinburgh, but they were to be demolished in 1848, exactly 25 years after they were built, because one of the shop-owners complained that they made his premises too dark.

The street was not an immediate success when it opened in 1823, but it soon attained ascendancy, it was a cornocupia whose name became synonymous with luxury and exclusiveness. Behind its windows could be seen all the beautiful and expensive goods that the world's leading industrial and trading nation could assemble. It cast such a shadow over other shopping areas that the Strand and Holborn, as well as Ludgate Hill and St Paul's Churchyard, began an inexorable decline as centres for the buying of drapery and luxury goods. Its neighbour, Piccadilly, was still at that time largely a street of hotels, private mansions and public exhibition halls (the Egyptian Hall and St James's Hall were both within a few steps of Regent's Circus) and was therefore no rival.

To the north, Oxford Street was on the way to becoming another major shopping street, though on a more modest scale. Its history had given it a somewhat raffish reputation, for its western end had been the site of public hangings until the 1780s and it had only gradually transformed from a not-quite-respectable residential area, haunted by jockeys, prize-fighters, gamblers and prostitutes, into a commercial quarter. One important business that had traded there was Dickins & Smith (later Dickins & Jones), established in 1790, but this followed the fashionable to Regent Street. Oxford Street's first significant retail venture appeared in 1834 with the opening of the Pantheon Bazaar, a converted theatre that became an important shopping centre.

To the west, some competition was offered by Savile Row, which was already famous for its tailors (the first had opened for business there in

1806), and by Bond Street, which like Piccadilly had been a district of
hotels, lodgings and private houses, but which had since the 1790s been
associated with tailoring, hairdressing, wigmaking and jewellers' shops.
Another area that was coming into prominence was Tottenham Court
Road. Some distance north of the centre, and bordering Bloomsbury,
Tottenham Court Road shared the revival of the district when new
stuccoed terraces and squares were grafted on to the 18th-century
suburb. The first to arrive, the draper James Shoolbred, opened for
business in 1817, but it was to be more than three decades before other
major drapery firms followed: Maple's and Heal's stores opened there, the
former in 1841 and the latter two years later. Both met with immediate
success (and are still there) and this encouraged the influx of other, often
similar, businesses.

As for Knightsbridge and Chelsea, these were beyond the pale of
fashion. The Brompton Road was memorably described, at around the
time that H.C. Harrod took over a Mr Burden's modest grocery and
wholesale tea business there, as 'a district of second-rate gentry and
second-rate shops'. A history of Harrod's store, written for its centenary
in 1949, imagined a cab journey along the Brompton Road that captured
the nature of this scruffy outlying community as Dickens, who explored
every quarter of London on foot, would have known it:

> Curiosity drives us on a little further – through a Knightsbridge
> that is unexpectedly slummy; past a Sloane Street without a
> single shop in it; and into the beginning of the new Brompton
> Road, which not long before had lain through fields but was now
> gradually becoming the shopping centre of a modest residential
> area. We cannot go on into the rural wilds of Kensington, it is
> time to turn back.
>
> There are shops of a sort at the beginning of the Brompton
> Road. Our cab has stopped in front of a block of dwelling-houses
> called Middle Queen's Buildings: all of them used to have front
> and back gardens, but many of the front gardens are now built
> over to make flat-roofed, single-storeyed shops. There are two
> cobblers, a surgeon, a solicitor, an apothecary, a clergyman, a
> schoolmaster and a draper, among the tenants of Middle Queen's
> Buildings; and our cab has happened to stop in front of number

eight, a little grocer's shop belonging to Philip Henry Burden, with wire blinds across its windows.

The horse's hooves clatter while the driver turns the cab, and, as we prepare to return, a flash of understanding comes to one or other of us – 'Harrod's ought to be somewhere here.'

Opening Up

The shops in Regent Street, like those in humbler thoroughfares, opened at eight o'clock every weekday (including Saturday). The apprentices and assistants, many of whom lived on the premises, emerged just before that hour to manhandle the heavy wooden shutters off the windows. Boys and young men also appeared with watering-cans to sprinkle the pavement in front of the shop. The floors inside and the street outside were swept with stiff twig brooms for the convenience of customers. Dickens captured this scene in an essay entitled 'The Streets – morning':

Half an hour more, and the sun darts his bright rays cheerfully down the still half-empty streets, and shines with sufficient force to rouse the dismal laziness of the apprentice, who pauses every other minute from his task of sweeping out the shop and watering the pavement in front of it, to tell another apprentice similarly employed, how hot it will be today, or to stand with his right hand resting on the broom, gazing at the 'Wonder', or the 'Tally Ho', or the 'Nimrod', or some other fast mail coach, until it is out of sight, when he re-enters the shop, envying the passengers on the outside of the fast coach, and thinking of the old red brick house 'down in the country' where he went to school.

George Sala described the ritual of shop opening as seen among the large emporia and the smaller establishments in the streets behind them:

There is a ceremony performed with much clattering solemnity of wooden panels, and iron bars, and stanchions, which occurs at eight o'clock in the morning. 'Tis then that the shop-shutters are taken down. The great 'stores' and 'magazines' of the principal

thoroughfares gradually open their eyes; apprentices, light
porters, and where the staff of assistants is not very numerous,
the shopmen, release the imprisoned wares, and bid the sun
shine on good family 'souchong', 'fresh Epping sausages',
'Beaufort collars', 'guinea capes', 'Eureka shirts', and 'Alexandre
harmoniums'. In the smaller thoroughfares, the proprietor often
dispenses with the aid of apprentice, light porter and shopman
– for the simple reason that he never possessed the services of any
assistants at all – and unostentatiously takes down the shutters
of his own chandler's, green-grocer's, tripe or small stationery
shop. In the magnificent linen-drapery establishments of Oxford
Street and Regent Streets, the vast shop-fronts, museums of
fashion in plate-glass cases, offer a series of animated tableaux
of poses plastiques in the shape of young ladies in morning
costume, and young gentlemen in whiskers and white neckcloths,
faultlessly complete as to costume, with the exception that they
are yet in their shirt-sleeves, who are accomplishing the difficult
and mysterious feat known as 'dressing' the shop window. By
their nimble and practical hands the rich piled velvet mantles
are displayed, the moiré and glace silks arranged in artful folds,
the laces and gauzes, the innumerable whim-whams and fribble-
frabble of fashion, elaborately shown, and to their best advantage.

The dressing of shop windows, then and now, required a degree of skill
and practice. Assistants worked gingerly and in stockinged feet amid
the cluttered displays: adjusting, buttoning and pinning clothes on the
sometimes surprisingly realistic wax or plaster dummies, placing price-
labels and arranging goods in piles or rows or baskets until one of their
superiors, watching from outside, was satisfied. The result was often
highly impressive. Dickens had in mind the splendours of Regent or
Oxford Street, and the contrast with the poverty of many who gazed at
them, when he wrote this passage in *Nicholas Nickleby*:

Emporiums of splendid dresses, the materials brought from every
quarter of the world; tempting stores of everything to stimulate
and pamper the sated appetite and give new relish to the oft-
repeated feast; vessels of burnished gold and silver, wrought into

every exquisite form of vase, and dish, and goblet; guns, swords, pistols, and patent engines of destruction; screws and irons for the crooked, clothes for the newly-born, drugs for the sick, coffins for the dead, and churchyards for the buried – all these jumbled each with the other in the rich light that showed the goldsmith's treasures, pale and pinched faces hovered about the windows where was tempting food, hungry eyes wandered over the profusion guarded by one thin sheet of brittle glass – an iron wall to them; half-naked shivering figures stooped to gaze at Chinese shawls and the golden stuffs of India.

It was not merely the windows that had to be prepared for a shop's opening. Immense amounts of goods were exhibited outside. In order to show a wide range of articles, they would be hung above the windows and around the doors, hoisted into place by apprentices armed with long hooked poles. This laborious process would, of course, have to be gone through in reverse at closing time.

Once the displays were ready, shop assistants would await the public, often dressed by this time in white ankle-length aprons. Apart from a short lunch-break, they could expect to remain on duty for 12 hours or more. If they worked in an establishment that catered to the gentry (known as the 'carriage trade') they could not, when the day came to an end, chivvy a customer who showed no sign of wanting to leave, on the grounds that the shop was closing. They must continue to pull out samples, or wait while garments were tried on, until the client had made a decision and concluded their business.

Quality Stores

The smart shops of the West End were a world apart. The most expensive items often required the most skilled men and women to make them. The staff of these establishments thus formed an aristocracy of labour, while the customers were a separate aristocracy of wealth and taste. A mutual respect existed between the two and there were accepted rituals that took place when a client arrived at one of the gorgeous West End emporia. A memoir by Frederick Willis recalled how, in Piccadilly:

The shops and people radiated quality. The reputation of this
area was owed to the fact that the best tradesmen plied their
trades there and the 'quality' went there to patronize them.
The gleaming carriage and high-spirited horses pulled up at
the entrance, the coachman sat rigidly to attention, the tiger [a
groom or footman, so-called because of his badge-of-office striped
waistcoat] jumped nimbly down and opened the carriage door with
a flourish. First he removed the opulent rugs that were essential
to protect the precious burden from the rude breath of Boreas,
then he stood aside, holding the door open with one hand and
bearing the rugs over his unoccupied arm, an incredible figure,
with his spotless fawn coat, top boots, white doeskin breeches and
top hat decorated with a cockade. My lord and lady then alighted
and sailed across the pavement to the obsequious doorman who
swung open the door for them to enter. If the weather was wet
the doorman advanced with a huge umbrella to escort them across
the pavement, and he also carried a curved wicker protector to
place over the carriage wheel in case my lady's voluminous dress
should be fouled by contact with it while alighting. All this was
done as naturally as you or I would drink a cup of tea.

The carriage and the servants would remain at the kerbside until her
ladyship had completed her purchases, the footmen taking charge of
any packages that were required at once (the rest would be sent to her
home). The men probably enjoyed these outings, for they would be
waiting in the company of other servants and could beguile the time
with gossip. If their employer's errand was at Howell and James, one of
the large Regent Street stores, they could even descend the steps into
the 'area' where bread and cheese and beer were provided for them,
at no cost. Inside, whatever the lady was buying, it is likely she would
have been served by men. Visitors to London had commented since the
previous century on the fact that feminine items, such as perfumes, lace,
ribbons and gowns, were commonly sold by men. They were considered
more polite, more patient and more attentive to female customers than
members of their own sex would have been.

The shopping arcades off Piccadilly had no facilities for carriage-borne
customers, but were fashionable places in which to stroll. Protected

from the weather by glass roofs and guarded by beadles (as Burlington Arcade still is) who kept at bay the peddlers and beggars and advertising-board men of the open streets, the arcades were filled with small and exquisite shops. Above these were even smaller rooms in which the shopkeepers were intended to live. In fact, a number of them were used for assignations by local prostitutes. Sala commented on the ephemeral nature of the goods and services offered by the shops of Burlington Arcade, which he described as:

> A booth transported bodily from Vanity Fair. I don't think there is a shop in its enciente where they sell anything that we could not do without. Boots and shoes are sold there, to be sure, but what boots and shoes? Varnished and embroidered and be-ribboned figments, fitter for a fancy ball or a lady's chamber ... than for serious pedestrianism. Paintings and lithographs for gilded boudoirs, collars for puppy dogs, and silver-mounted whips for spaniels, pocket handkerchiefs, in which an islet of cambric is surrounded by an ocean of lace, embroidered garters and braces, filigree flounces, firework-looking bonnets, scent bottles, sword-knots, brocaded sashes, worked dressing-gowns, inlaid snuff-boxes, and falbalas of all descriptions ... To the end of time, I perpend, we shall have this hankering after superfluities ...

This era of vast capital, huge spending-power and swift communication, which facilitated the transport of goods from producers to stores, saw the beginnings of a number of businesses that continue to flourish today. Some were already old by the middle of the 19th century, such as James Lock, the hatter's in St James's Street (1676), its neighbour the wine-merchant Berry Brothers and Rudd (1696), Fortnum & Mason (1707), Hamley's toyshop (1760), and the bookseller's founded in 1797 by 29-year-old John Hatchard with the words: 'This day, by the Grace of God, the Goodwill of my Friends and £5 in my pocket I have opened my shop in Piccadilly.' Flint & Clark, now Debenham's, opened in 1778. Benjamin Harvey, whose shop would become Harvey Nichols, began trading in 1813.

A number of other establishments now joined them; some have since expanded while others have remained small, but all can still be found in

London, if only in name. As well as those already mentioned there were James Smith, the cane and umbrella makers (1830); the Scotch House (1838); D.R. Harris, the apothecary (1790); the wallpaper firm Sanderson (1860); Whiteley's (1863); John Lewis (1864); and Barker's (1870). The dairyman John Sainsbury opened his first shop in Drury Lane in 1869.

The firm of William Henry Smith had begun as a 'stationer and newsman' in 1792. From their premises in the Strand, William Smith and his brother, the founder's sons, set out to speed up the distribution of newspapers to the main provincial centres. Newspapers were usually sent out of London on the slower night-mail coaches, but the Smiths ensured that their papers always went by day. Their own men collected papers from the presses and delivered them direct to the coaches. When important events occurred and newspapers would be urgently awaited, the Smiths bypassed the transport system altogether by hiring their own relays of horses. The coming of the railways enabled them to improve this system even further, and as well as distributing papers they began to sell them at railway stations. The first of their station-platform shops was opened at Euston in 1848. It was the seed from which a mighty empire was to grow.

The World of the Bazaar

The large stores of Dickensian London had grown from the city's bazaars. This type of indoor market had been known to Londoners since the 17th century, when Exeter 'Change had been built in the Strand. Now there were several similar establishments, largely staffed by women. The 1851 guidebook *London as it is Today* gave an idea of how they were laid out and what they offered:

Soho Bazaar: Formed in 1815, and much frequented. An establishment for the sale of light goods. It consists of several rooms, hung with red cloth and fitted up with mahogany counters, divided into stands, which are occupied by upwards of two hundred females. The nature of the mart, and the variety of goods exhibited, daily attract numerous visitors, and render it quite a fashionable lounge.

At the west end of the Strand was Lowther Arcade, which specialized in toys. These were known as 'knick-knacks' and thus a toy-shop was called a 'knick-knackatory'. The guidebook informed tourists that:

> This pleasing bazaar-like avenue, which forms an acute angle with the Strand, leading to the back of St Martin's Church, was built in 1831 and consists of 25 small but neat shops. The shops in the interior are designed to have the appearance of one great whole, but as the goods are principally displayed in the front of the windows, the effect intended is altogether destroyed. This, the most noted toy-mart in London, is much frequented by visitors.

This place exerted over Victorian children the same magic that Hamley's store still has for later generations. Sala, discoursing on the subject of buying toys for children, provides a useful description of the type of 'whim-whams' that could be bought in a bazaar, alongside the usual dolls, toy soldiers, kites and rocking-horses:

> I fear the price of the merchandize which the pretty and well-conducted female assistants at the stalls have to sell. I have been given to understand that incredible prices are charged for India-rubber balls, and that the quotations for drums, hares-and-tabors, and Noah's arks are ruinously high ... It frequently happens that I feel slightly misanthropic and vicious in my toy-dealing excursions, and that my juvenile friends have sudden fits of naughtiness, and turn out to be anything but agreeable companions. Woe betide the ill-conditioned youngsters who cause me to assume the function of a vicarious 'Bogey!' But I serve them out, I promise you ... I 'warm' them by taking them into toy shops and buying them ugly toys. Aha! My young friends, who bought you the old gentleman impaled on the area railing while in the act of knocking at his own street door, and who emitted a dismal groan when the pedestal on which he stood was compressed? Who purchased the monkey with the horrible visage, that ran up the stick? Who the dreadful crawling serpent, made of the sluggishly elastic substance – a compound of glue and treacle,

I believe – of which printers' rollers are made, and that unwound himself in a shudderingly, reptile, life-like manner on the parlour carpet? Who bought you the cold, flabby toad, and the centipede at the end of the India-rubber string, with his heavy chalk body and quivering limbs ...? This is the best method I know for punishing a refractory child.

The largest and best-known bazaar was the Pantheon in Oxford Street. It stood on a site now occupied by one of Marks & Spencer's major London stores, and was a place that people visited (just as they do shopping-centres today) not only to inspect the wares but to kill time, see their friends or eat and drink. The guidebook praised the Pantheon's facilities:

The visitor to the metropolis may derive much pleasure from an inspection of the fancy articles tastefully displayed on endless ranges of well-disposed stalls. Over the entrance-hall is a suite of rooms devoted to the display for sale of a collection of paintings, modern English artists, many of which are of great merit.

As so often, Sala took a more cynical view. He imagined following some female relations on a visit to the Pantheon in their carriage:

They have alighted beneath the portico of the Pantheon. The affable beadle (whose whiskers, gold-laced hat-band, livery buttons and general deportment are as far superior to those the property of the beadle of Burlington Arcade, as General Washington to General Walker) receives the ladies with a bow ...
    So into the Pantheon, turning and turning about in that Hampton Court-like maze of stalls, laden with pretty gimcracks, toys, and papier maché trifles for the table, dolls and children's dresses, wax flowers and Berlin and crochet work, prints, and polkas, and women's ware of all sorts. Up into the gallery, where you look down on a perfect little ant-hill of lively industry. And, if you choose, into that queer picture-gallery, where works by twentieth-rate masters have been quietly accumulating smoke and dust for some score years. They have lately added, I believe, a

photographic establishment to the picture-gallery of the Pantheon, but I am doubtful of its success. It requires a considerable amount of moral courage to ascend the stairs, or to go into the picture department at all. The place seems haunted by the ghosts of bygone pictorial mediocrities. It is the lazar-house of painting – a hospital of incurables in art.

A highly popular aspect of the Pantheon was a conservatory in which shoppers, or those waiting for them, could sit surrounded by plant and bird-life:

Pass the refreshment counter, where they sell the arrowroot cakes, which I never saw anywhere else, and let us enter the conservatory – a winter garden built long ere Crystal Palaces or Jardins d'Hiver were dreamt of, and which to me is as pleasant a lounge as any that exists in London: a murmuring fountain, spangled with gold and silver fish, and a good store of beautiful exotic plants and myriad-hued flowers. The place is but a niche, a narrow passage, with a glass roof and a circle at the end, where the fountain is, like the hub of a thermometer; but to me it is very delightful. It is good to see fair young faces, fair young forms, in rainbow, flitting in and about the plants and flowers, the fountain and the gold fish.

I really must shut my ears in self-defence against the atrocious, the intolerable screeching of the parrots, the parroquettes, the cockatoos, and the macaws, who are permitted to hang on by their wicked claws and the skin of their malicious beaks to the perches round the fountain. The twittering of the smaller birds is irritating enough to the nervously afflicted; but the parrots! Ugh!

His departure enables us to see that even the rear entrance had dignity:

As we entered by Oxford Street, with its embeadled colonnade, it becomes our bounden duty to quit the building by means of that portal which gives egress into Great Marlborough Street. I can't stand the parrots, so I slip through the conservatory's crystal

precincts, inhale a farewell gust of flower-breeze, pass through a
waiting-room, where some tired ladies are resting till their carriages
draw up, and am genteelly bowed out by affable beadle No. 2.

The Department Store

Whiteley's, which awarded itself the title 'the Universal Provider,' was
the first shop to expand the notion of the indoor market into that of
the fully fledged department store. Sales assistants had traditionally
been apprentices, who lived in the shop and were often regarded as part
of the owner's family. As the big stores developed, it naturally became
impossible to treat employees in this way and the solution was to house
them in what were effectively barracks. 'Living-in' was commonplace
and had, from an employer's point of view, the advantage that no
member of staff could ever be late for work. Since many staff were not
native to London, and did not have friends or relations with whom they
could stay, the arrangement had advantages for them, too. London was
both expensive and dangerous. There was no cheap public transport, and
living in dormitories spared them the necessity of making lengthy and
(after dark) risky journeys.

This convenience came at a heavy cost, however. Privacy was almost
unknown. Men and women, though segregated, had to share rooms
and often to sleep several to a bed. There were no common rooms or
leisure facilities. Though their meals were provided on weekdays, they
received nothing on Sundays and indeed were commonly locked out of
their accommodation for the duration of the Sabbath – a day on which
virtually nothing in London was open, except churches. During Dickens'
lifetime these conditions did not improve. The only gesture toward
ameliorating the lot of shop assistants was the Early Closing Association,
founded in 1842. This sought to establish the practice of shutting at 2pm
on Saturdays, and by the 1860s some West End stores were doing so.
Many shopkeepers were opposed to any curtailment of opening times,
for the end of the day was busy and profitable. The products of this harsh
environment sometimes went on to make their own mark in the world
of commerce; two of them – John Barker and Arthur Lasenby Liberty
– were to establish highly successful stores of their own.

Necessities

It was through London's shops that attempts were made to answer a long-felt need: the creation of public lavatories. There had been facilities of this type in London since the Romans, but they had never been organized by the city authorities. The first such experience that many people had was during the Great Exhibition, when retiring rooms were provided. Building on this success, an attempt was made to establish permanent facilities in the central shopping area. The moving spirit was, surprisingly, the Royal Society of Arts, which suggested that ladies' and gents' lavatories should be situated within shops whose business was particularly oriented toward one sex or the other. *The Times* reported the deliberations that preceded the opening of the first rooms near the Strand:

The Council of the Society of Arts on the 14th of May requested ... a committee for establishing forthwith a certain number of model water-closets and urinals in public thoroughfares with the object of proving that these public conveniences, so much wanted, may be self-supporting.

The Committee consider that the following regulations should be adopted in commencing this experiment:–
1. That these conveniences be established on a moderate scale, in connexion with shops, in some public thoroughfares, and be called 'Public Waiting-rooms'.
2. That the public waiting-rooms for men and women be established in distinct shops, on different sides of the street.
3. That in each shop there be a waiting-room, having two classes of water-closets and urinals, for the use of which a penny and two pence should be charged.
4. That each set of waiting-rooms be provided with a lavatory for washing hands, clothes' brushes, &c., at a charge of two pence and three pence.
5. That each set of waiting-rooms have a superintendent and two attendants.
6. That the charge for the use of the lavatories, water closets, and urinals should include all attendance, and be publicly offered in the shop.

7. That the police should be requested to cause these
establishments to be visited from time to time.

The Committee recommend that the Council should
undertake to lease several ground floors in the Strand, Holborn
and Cheapside ... that no time should be los[t] in inviting
respectable persons holding shops in public thoroughfares, who
may be desirous of connecting the proposed public waiting-
rooms with them, to inform the secretary, Mr. G. Grove, of the
accommodation which their premises offer for the purpose. The
shops which appear to be most suitable for waiting-rooms for
ladies are staymakers', bonnet makers', milliners', &c. Those most
suitable for gentlemen's waiting-rooms are hairdressers', tailors',
hatters', taverns, &c.

Small Shops

Outside the fashionable areas, shops remained small and functional.
When Oliver Twist was taken on by Sowerberry, the undertaker, his
employer's wife showed him the corner in which he would live:

'Then come with me,' said Mrs Sowerberry, taking up a dim and
dirty lamp, and leading the way; 'your bed's under the counter.
You don't mind sleeping among the coffins I suppose? But it
doesn't much matter whether you do or don't, for you can't sleep
anywhere else.'

In fact, this was not an unusual arrangement. Ebenezer Scrooge and his
fellow apprentice, Dick Wilkins, were employees of the jovial Mr Fezziwig
and lived in his shop-cum-warehouse. At the end of the Christmas ball:

The cheerful voices died away, and the lads were left to their
beds, which were under a counter in the back shop.

In Dickens' lifetime, Great Britain was the world's richest country.
It also had a middle class that was growing in prosperity. These facts
are reflected in a 'Boz' essay on a small and out-of-the-way street off

Whitehall that had recently lost its dowdy atmosphere and acquired
pretentions. The street was Scotland Yard – in those days not a police
headquarters – but the description would fit scores of neighbourhoods:

> What is Scotland Yard now? How have its old customs changed;
> and how has the ancient simplicity of its inhabitants faded away!
> The old tottering public house is converted into spacious and
> lofty 'wine vaults'; gold leaf has been used in the construction of
> the letters which emblazon its exterior. The tailor exhibits in his
> window the pattern of a foreign-looking brown surtout, with silk
> buttons, a fur collar, and fur cuffs ...
>   At the other end of the little row of houses a bootmaker
> has established himself in a brick box, with the additional
> innovation of a first floor; and here he exposes for sale, boots
> – real Wellington boots – an article which a few years ago, none
> of the original inhabitants had ever seen or heard of. It was but
> the other day, that a dressmaker opened another little box in the
> middle of the row; and when we thought that the spirit of change
> could produce no alteration beyond that, a jeweller appeared,
> and not content with exposing gilt rings and copper bracelets out
> of number, put up an announcement, which still sticks in his
> window, that 'ladies' ears may be pierced within'. The dressmaker
> employs a young lady who wears pockets in her apron; and the
> tailor informs the public that gentlemen may have their own
> materials made up.

Apprentices and 'shopmen' worked six days a week and for very long
hours, for it was not usual to 'put up the shutters' until 10 or 11pm.
A great deal of business would be done in the evenings, especially in
the chandler's shop (a general merchant that was the counterpart of
the present-day 'mini-market'), selling to customers who had not been
released from their own work until after 8pm. Sala mentioned in passing
that at 10pm:

> The children of the poor do not dream of bed. They are toddling
> in and out of chandlers' shops in quest of ounces of ham and
> fragments of Dutch cheese.

Dickens, as 'Boz', examined the scene at the end of the day:

> **The little chandler's shop with the cracked bell behind the door,
> whose melancholy tinkling has been regulated by the demand
> for quarters of sugar and half-ounces of coffee, is shutting
> up. Flat-fish, oyster, and fruit vendors linger hopelessly in the
> kennel [gutter], in vain endeavouring to attract customers; and
> the ragged boys who usually disport themselves in the streets,
> stand crouched in little knots under the canvas blind of a
> cheesemonger's, where great flaring gas-lights, unshaded by any
> glass, display huge piles of bright red and pale yellow cheeses,
> mingled with little fivepenny dabs of dingy bacon, various tubs of
> weekly Dorset, and cloudy rolls of 'best fresh'.**

The opening of shops on 'red letter days' appears to have been common.
When Scrooge woke up on Christmas morning and sent a passing boy
to buy the prize turkey, no one was surprised that the poulterer's shop
was open. Yet in almost the same year, a young man just arrived in
London from the country was astonished to find the shops closed on a
weekday, and discovered that this was because it was Good Friday. On
regular secular occasions – well-known instances were Greenwich Fair
and any of the periodic days of public hangings – shops might also close.
Otherwise, they remained open all day and far into the evening, as many
London shops owned by people of Indian or Chinese extraction still
do: the whole family is involved and lives to a large extent in the shop;
their work and play, social and commercial lives are intertwined, and
they appreciate the opportunities for attracting customers. And although
opening hours became a good deal shorter for much of the 20th century
they have, since the 1980s, been extended. Our weekday shopping
habits are now becoming more like those of Dickens' generation.

Attracting Attention

In a city full to bursting with shops, it was necessary to advertise
extensively. The traditional way of doing this was to have a sign, and
the streets abounded in them (they were necessary at a time when house

numbering was unreliable). Some became landmarks for the young
Dickens as he explored the streets. He would remember them all his life
and, in some cases, mention them in his novels. One was a brass-and-
wood sign on an ironmonger's shop, which he saw in the Borough as he
walked to and from the Marshalsea Prison:

> My usual way home was over Blackfriars Bridge and down that
> turning on the Blackfriars Road which has Rowland Hill's chapel
> on one side, and the likeness of a golden dog licking a golden pot
> over a shop door on the right.

Another old friend was the small wooden statue seen outside the shop of
a nautical instrument maker. This was the 'little Midshipman', a figure
dressed in the uniform of Nelson's navy, in the act of taking a compass
reading. It is described in *Dombey and Son*:

> A dry day covered him with dust, and a misty day peppered
> him with little bits of soot and a wet day brightened up his
> tarnished uniform.

Some types of shop had little scope for individuality, for the symbol of
their trade was well known. Tobacco shops that sold Scottish rather than
English snuff often had a wooden statue of a Highlander standing by
the door (one can still be seen outside a tobacconist in Charing Cross
Road). The following description is found in *Little Dorrit*:

> The business was of too modest a character to support a life-
> size Highlander, but maintained a little one on a bracket on
> the doorpost, who looked like a fallen cherub that had found it
> necessary to take to a kilt.

Windows would also display the prices of the shop's wares, as Dickens
relates in *Little Dorrit*:

> Nothing would serve Maggy but that they must stop at a grocer's
> window, short of their destination, for her to show her learning.
> She could read after a sort; and picked out the fat figures in the

tickets of prices, for the most part, correctly. She also stumbled, with a large balance of success against her failures, through various philanthropic recommendations to Try our Mixture, Try our Family Black, Try our Orange-flavoured Pekoe, challenging competition at the head of Flowery Teas; and various cautions to the public against spurious establishments and adulterated articles. When he saw how pleasure brought a rosy tint into Little Dorrit's face when Maggy made a hit, he felt that he could have stood there making a library of the grocer's window until the rain and wind were tired.

Another means of attracting attention was by generous use of gas lighting. Expensive though this undoubtedly would have been, it seems to have been effective. Max Schlesinger was astonished to find that a garishly lit edifice he came across proved, on closer inspection, to be not an important public building, as he had supposed, but a tailor's shop:

Holborn is illuminated with gas-light, but the brightest glare bursts forth exactly opposite to us. Who, in the name of all that is prudent, can the people be who make such a shocking waste of gas? They are 'Moses and Son', the great tailor and outfitters, who have lighted up the side-front of their branch-establishment. All round the outer walls of the house, which is filled with coats, vests and trousers to the roof, and which exhibits three separate side-fronts towards three separate streets, there are many thousands of gas-flames, forming branches, foliage and arabesques, and sending forth so dazzling a blaze that this fiery column of Moses is visible to Jews and Christians at the distance of half a mile, lighting up the haze which not even the clearest evening can wholly banish from the London sky. Among the fiery flowers burns the inevitable royal crown, surrounding the equally unavoidable letters V.R. To the right of these letters we have Moses and Son blessing the Queen in flaming characters of hydro-carbon: God bless the People.

What do they make this illumination for? This is not a royal birthday, or the anniversary of a great national victory. Motives of loyalty, politics or religion have nothing to do with the great illuminations executed by Messrs. Moses and Son. The air is calm, there is not even a breath of wind; it's a hundred to one that Oxford Street and Holborn will be thronged with passengers; this is our time to attract the idlers. A heavy expense this, burning all that gas for ever so many hours, but it pays somehow.

Extensive lighting undoubtedly enhanced the beauty and allure of the items in shop windows, though it seems that the public could become jaded by the sight of these commercial riches. In *Nicholas Nickleby*, Dickens depicts a night-time crowd passing the wares on display:

The noisy, bustling, crowded streets of London, now displaying long double rows of brightly-burning lamps, dotted here and there with the chemist's glaring lights, and illuminated besides with the brilliant flood that streamed from the windows of the shops, where sparkling jewellery, silks and velvets of the richest colours, the most inviting delicacies, the most sumptuous articles of luxurious ornament, succeeded each other in rich and glittering profusion. Streams of people apparently without end poured on and on, jostling with each other in the crowd and hurrying forward, scarcely seeming to notice the riches that surrounded them on every side.

Also ubiquitous, and necessary, were the men who tramped the streets day after day carrying signs or sandwich-boards, or even samples of products. 'It pays to advertise' was as true in Dickens' time as it is in ours, and both manufacturers and retailers sought to keep their products in the public eye as relentlessly as possible. If passers-by had become used to the sight of one man with a placard advertising a product, the manufacturer would employ ten. Schlesinger was impressed by the thinking, both subtle and brash, behind these techniques:

Twelve men, out at elbows, move in solemn procession along the opposite pavement, each carrying a heavy wooden pole with a large table affixed to it, and on the table there is a legend in large scarlet letters, 'MR FALCON REMOVED'. It appears that Mr Falcon, having thought proper to remove from 146 Holborn, begs to inform the nobility, the gentry, and the public generally, that he carries on his business at 6 Argyle-street.

Mr Falcon does not send his card-bearers, with the news of his removal, through the whole of London. Why should he? Perhaps he sold cigars, or buttons, or yarns, in Holborn; and it is there he is known, while no one in other parts of the town cares a straw for Mr Falcon's celebrated and unrivalled cigars, buttons, or yarns. His object is to inform the inhabitants of his own quarter of his removal, and of his new address.

The twelve men with the poles and boards need not go far. From early dawn till late at night they parade the site of Mr Falcon's old shop. They walk deliberately and slowly, to enable the passengers to read the inscription at their ease. They walk in Indian file to attract attention, and because in any other manner they would block up the way. But they walk continually, silently, without ever stopping for rest. Thus do they carry their poles, for many days and even weeks, until every child in the neighbourhood knows exactly where Mr Falcon is henceforward to be found, for the moving column of scarlet-lettered boards is too striking; and no one can help looking at them and reading the inscription.

There is no other town in the world where people advertise with so much persevering energy – on so grand a scale – at such enormous expense – with such impertinent puffery – and with such distinguished success.

Naturally only wealthy shops could afford to advertise in this way. The majority could rely only on the loyalty of local customers and the possibility of passing trade. In *Sketches by Boz*, Dickens charted the downward progress of a modest commercial premises in the north London suburbs that he knew. Significant are the variety and the esoteric nature of some of the businesses that occupy it, and the poverty and pathetic optimism of some of the tenants who pass through:

A handsome shop, and on the shutters were large bills, informing the public that it would shortly be opened with 'an extensive stock of linen-drapery and haberdashery'. It opened in due course; there was the name of the proprietor 'and Co.' in gilt letters, almost too dazzling to look at. Such ribbons and shawls! And two such elegant young men, each in a clean collar and white neckerchief, like the lover in a farce. As to the proprietor, he did nothing but walk up and down the shop, and hand seats to the ladies, and hold important conversations with the handsomest of the young men, who was shrewdly suspected by the neighbours to be the 'Co.' We saw all this with sorrow; we felt a fatal presentiment that the shop was doomed – and so it was. Its decay was slow, but sure. Tickets gradually appeared in the windows; then rolls of flannel, with labels on them, were stuck outside the door; then a bill was pasted on the street-door, intimating that the first floor was to be let unfurnished; then one of the young men disappeared altogether, and the other took to a black neckerchief, and the proprietor took to drinking. The shop became dirty, broken panes of glass remained unmended, and the stock disappeared piecemeal. At last the company's man came to cut off the water, and then the linen-draper cut off himself, leaving the landlord his compliments and the key.

New occupants – The shop – not a large one at the best of times – had been converted into two: one was a bonnet-shape maker's, the other was opened by a tobacconist, who also dealt in walking-sticks and Sunday newspapers; the two were separated by a thin partition, covered with tawdry striped paper.

The tobacconist was a red-faced, impudent, good-for-nothing dog, evidently accustomed to take things as they came, and to make the best of a bad job. He sold as many cigars as he could, and smoked the rest. He occupied the shop as long as he could make peace with the landlord, and when he could no longer live in quiet, he very coolly locked the door, and bolted himself. From this period, the two little dens have undergone innumerable changes. The tobacconist was succeeded by a theatrical hair-dresser, who ornamented the window with a great variety of 'characters', and terrific combats. The bonnet-shape maker gave way to a green-grocer, and the histrionic barber was succeeded, in his turn, by a tailor. When we last passed it, a 'dairy' was established in the area, and a party of melancholy-looking fowls were amusing themselves by running in atthe front door, and out at the back one.

Street Vendors

Besides these respectable shops were hundreds of scruffy, insalubrious
establishments in which secondhand and stolen goods could be
purchased. Monmouth Street, near Seven Dials in the notorious district
of St Giles, was synonymous, for instance, with old clothes. Many other
small traders had no premises at all, but were street vendors, who walked
through the capital every day, selling commodities that they carried on
their backs and their heads. Some made a relatively comfortable living
and looked tidy. Others were in ill-health and in rags and were only one
step removed from outright begging.

They sold an astonishing variety of goods, and there were legions
of them in the city's main thoroughfares. Until the beginnings of the
Welfare State in the early 20th century, the gutters of a main street
such as Ludgate Hill were crowded with an almost continuous line of
men selling objects from trays. These might be cheap toys, needles and
ribbons, matches or any other easily transported goods, for those offering
them were frequently elderly and no longer fit for any other work (the
introduction of the old-age pension enabled many of them to retire).

While these were 'static' traders who worked from a pitch, many
others moved through the streets, calling their wares. Some might
be buying and selling cast-off clothing. Others were sellers of flowers,
ballads, stationery, brooms, cat's meat, milk, pies, fruit, footstools, sieves,
saucepans – in fact anything that a householder, or a peckish passer-by,
might need. Max Schlesinger described some of them:

Men with cocoa-nuts and dates, and women with oranges
surrounded us with their carts. One man recommended his dog-
collars of all sizes, which he had formed in a chain round his
neck; another person offered to mark our linen; a third produced
his magic strops; others held out note-books, cutlery, prints,
caricatures, exhibition-medals – all – all – all for one penny. It
seemed as if the whole world were on sale at a penny a bit. And
amidst all this turmoil, the men with advertising boards walked to
and fro; and the boys distributed advertising bills by the hundred,
with smiles of deep bliss, whenever they met a charitable soul
who took them.

Henry Mayhew, in his seminal study of London's poor, interviewed many of these men and women. Most of them had come to their particular trades by accident, and many went from selling one commodity to another as fashion, or the seasons, changed. One man recounted how he came to deal in umbrellas, and then moved into a field that he found more congenial: 'tin-ware', or kitchen and household utensils. He was clearly above the average, seeing and taking opportunities and carefully costing each enterprise, and was thus a born survivor. He was good with his hands and, since he could make household articles as well as sell them, he found a market and a relatively steady living:

I recollected having seen a person selling rings at a penny each; I made up my mind to try the same. I laid out 5 shillings in a tray and stock; after arranging the goods to the best advantage I sallied into the streets. The glittering baubles took for a while, but when discoloured were useless. Having once a considerable stock of these soiled rings, I was prompted to begin 'lot selling'. After calculating the profits, I commenced selling in that line. As this continued for seven weeks I managed to get a living. The system then became general; every street in the metropolis contained a lot seller, so I was determined to change my hand. One day in the street I saw a girl with a bundle of old umbrellas going towards a marine store shop; I asked if the umbrellas were for sale; she replied in the affirmative; the price she asked was 4d.; I became a purchaser.

With these old umbrellas I commenced a new life. I bought some trifling tools necessary for repairing umbrellas, and, after viewing well the construction of the articles I commenced operations. I succeeded, and in a little time could not only mend an old umbrella, but make a new one. This way of living I followed three years. In one of my walks through the streets crying old umbrellas to sell, I saw a street tinker [a mender of pots and pans] repairing a saucepan; he looked so very comfortable with his fire-pan before him, that I resolved from that moment to become a tinker, and for that purpose I bought a few tools, prepared a budget, and sallied into the streets with as much indifference as if I had been at the business since my birth. After a little practice I fancied I was fit for better things than mending old saucepans, and flattered myself that I was able to make a new one. This I resolved to attempt, and succeeded so well, that I at once abandoned the rainy-day system, and commenced manufacturing articles in tin-ware, such as are now sold in the streets, namely funnels, nutmeg-graters, penny mugs, extinguishers, slices, save-alls, &c. I soon became known to the street-sellers and swag-shop proprietors. The prices I get are low, and I am deficient in some of the tools necessary to forward the work, with the required speed to procure returns adequate to my expenses; but thanks to the Lord I am better off than ever I expected to be, with the difference only of a somewhat shattered constitution.

It is worth remembering that many of his customers – domestic servants and poor housewives – simply did not have the time or opportunity to go shopping for necessary items. To them the itinerant seller, whose cry in the streets would announce his arrival and who usually made regular visits, was a godsend. He would come to know his regular customers, and would not only sell new items but mend old ones. An immense amount of the buying and selling of household commodities was carried out in this way. People could not afford to throw things away as they do today, and before the invention of plastic many domestic goods were much more expensive than they would be now. The mending of articles was therefore a highly important factor in household economy. A tinker would come to the servants' entrance and be shown into the scullery, where he might spend half an hour patching saucepans and mending toasting forks or ladle handles. No doubt he would be given a seat by the kitchen fire and a glass of something afterwards, and could regale the maids with gossip from the other houses he had visited – a much more agreeable way to equip and maintain one's kitchen than making a trip to a hardware store.

Despite the Industrial Revolution and the advent of mass production, despite the rise of the department store and the arrival of mass retailing, Dickens' contemporaries depended for many of the items in their homes and their lives on individual men and women who sold their wares in the streets, just as tradesmen had since time immemorial.

City and CLERK

In the mid-19th century London had hordes of clerical workers who commuted each day to the counting-houses of the City, the legal offices of Chancery Lane and the government departments of Whitehall. Only with the coming of the railway and the suburban tram systems would people of this sort be able to live long distances from their place of work. Prior to that their homes would, of necessity, be within an hour's walk or drive. The wealthy would travel to work in their own vehicles; the well-off would take an omnibus, perhaps perching back-to-back on the rooftop seats of a 'knife board'. The remainder would walk, travelling (as contemporary slang put it) by the 'marrowbone stage'.

On six mornings a week, Monday to Saturday, streams of men would trudge in from the suburbs beyond the edge of the city, crossing fields and skirting dust-heaps, brickworks or market gardens to reach the streets of London proper. It was an entirely male procession, for only with the invention (after Dickens' time) of the telephone and the typewriter would women be added to the urban workforce. They might stroll or saunter but most men walked with purpose, as preoccupied as commuters are today, not glancing at their surroundings, for every detail of topography was imprinted on their minds by unending repetition. They would similarly ignore those around them; the need for privacy and 'personal space' that foreigners still notice in Londoners was equally evident in 1835, when Dickens wrote in an article for *The Morning Chronicle* this vivid description of the morning rush hour:

> The early clerk population of Somers and Camden Towns, Islington and Pentonville, are fast pouring into the City, or directing their steps toward the Inns of Court. Middle-aged men, whose salaries have by no means increased in the same proportion

as their families, plod steadily along, apparently with no object in view but the counting-house; knowing by sight almost everybody they meet or overtake, for they have seen them every morning (Sundays excepted) during the last twenty years, but speaking to no one. If they do happen to overtake a personal acquaintance, they just exchange a hurried salutation, and keep walking on, either by his side or in front of him, as his rate of walking may chance to be. As to stopping to shake hands, or to take the friend's arm, they seem to think that as it is not included in their salary, they have no right to do it. Small office lads in large hats, who are made men before they are boys, hurry along in pairs, with their first coat carefully brushed, and the white trousers of last Sunday plentifully besmeared with dust and ink. It evidently requires a considerable mental struggle to avoid investing part of the day's dinner-money in the purchase of the stale tarts so temptingly exposed in dusty tins at the pastrycooks' doors; but a consciousness of their own importance and the receipt of seven shillings a week, with the prospect of an early rise to eight, comes to their aid, and they accordingly put their hats a little more on one side, and look under the bonnets of all the milliners and stay-makers' apprentices they meet – poor girls! – the hardest-worked, the worst-paid, and too often the worst-used class of the community.

Two decades later, and somewhat higher up the scale of wealth and status, the ancestors of flamboyant 21st-century City traders and comfortably salaried civil servants were also on their way to work. George Sala watched them from the vantage point of Ludgate Circus:

If the morning be fine, the pavement of the Strand and Fleet Street looks quite radiant with the spruce clerks walking down to their offices, governmental, financial, and commercial. These are the dashing young parties who purchase the pea-green, the orange, and the rose-pink gloves; the crimson braces, the kaleidoscopic shirt-studs, the shirts embroidered with dahlias, death's heads, race-horses, sun-flowers and ballet-girls. There are some of these gay clerks who go down to their offices with roses in their button-holes, and with cigars in their mouths; there are some who wear

peg-top trousers, chin-tufts, eye-glasses, and varnished boots.
These mostly turn off in the Strand, and are in the Admiralty or
Somerset House. As for the government clerks of the extreme
West-end – the patricians of the Home and Foreign Offices – the
bureaucrats of the Circumlocution Office – they ride down to
Whitehall or Downing Street in broughams or on park hacks.
Catch them in omnibuses, or walking on the vulgar pavement,
forsooth! You may, as a general rule, distinguish government from
commercial clerks by the stern repudiation of the razor, as applied
to the beard and moustaches, by the former ... You may know the
cashiers in the private banking houses by their white hats and buff
waistcoats; you may know the stock-brokers by their careering up
Ludgate Hill in dog-carts, and occasionally tandems, and by the
pervading sporting appearance of their costume; you may know
the sugar-bakers and the soap-boilers by the comfortable double-
bodied carriages with fat horses in which they roll along; you may
know the Jewish commission agents by their flashy broughams,
with lapdogs and ladies in crinoline beside them; you may know
the Manchester warehousemen by their wearing gaiters, always
carrying their hands in their pockets, and frequently slipping
into recondite city taverns up darksome alleys, on their way to
Cheapside, to make a quiet bet or so on the Chester Cup or the
Liverpool Steeplechase; you may know, finally, the men with a
million of money, or thereabouts, by their being ordinarily very
shabby, and by their wearing shocking bad hats, which have
seemingly never been brushed, on the backs of their heads.

Wandering further east, Sala came to the Bank, the hub of the City, and
watched a fleet of omnibuses delivering the clerks:

The vast train of omnibuses that have come from the West and
the East with another great army of clerk martyrs outside and
inside, their knees drawn up to their chins, and their chins
resting on their umbrella handles, set down their loads of cash-
book and ledger fillers. What an incalculable mass of figures
must be collected in those commercial heads! What legions of
L.s.d. [money]! What a chaos of cash debtor, contra creditor,

bills payable, and bills receivable; waste-books, day-books, cash-books and journals; insurance policies, brokerage, dock warrants and general commercial bedevilment! They file off to their several avocations, to spin money for others, poor fellows, while they themselves are blest with meagre stipends. They plod away to their gloomy wharves and hard-hearted counting-houses, where the chains from great cranes wind round their bodies, and they dance hornpipes in bill-file and cash-box fetters, and the mahogany of the desks enters into their souls. So the omnibuses meet at the Bank and disgorge the clerks by hundreds; repeating this operation scores of times between nine and ten o'clock.

Central London, before the later Victorians removed whole sections of it in the interests of progress, or the even more wholesale clearance caused by 20th-century bomb damage, was a closely packed world of narrow streets and dingy buildings. Many wealthy and successful enterprises were conducted from cramped and mean offices, difficult for visitors to find amid a warren of courts and passageways. Sunlight too had difficulty in finding its way in, even before London put on its daily black covering of smoke, and many buildings had angled mirrors fixed outside their windows to trap daylight and reflect it inside. The office from which Ebenezer Scrooge ran his business was by no means untypical, though his miserly nature would naturally have increased the sense of gloom:

The city clocks had only just gone three, but it was quite dark already: it had not been light all day: and candles were flaring in the windows of the neighbouring offices, like ruddy smears upon the palpable brown air. The door of Scrooge's counting-house was open that he might keep an eye upon his clerk, who in a dismal office beyond, a sort of tank, was copying letters. Scrooge had a very small fire, but the clerk's fire was so much smaller that it looked like one coal. But he couldn't replenish it, for Scrooge kept the coal box in his own room; and so surely as the clerk came in with the shovel, the master predicted that it would be necessary for them to part. Whereupon the clerk put on his white comforter, and tried to warm himself at the candle, in which effort, not being a man of strong imagination, he failed.

Also typical of Dickens' time was the small size of many firms. It was not unusual, as in Scrooge's case, for a businessman to have only one employee, and some of his contemporaries might manage without any at all. Mr Tulkinghorn, the lawyer in *Bleak House*, committed to memory the details of all his clients' cases rather than having them written out by subordinates; as his creator put it, he 'wanted no clerks'. Though huge corporations as we know them now did not exist, there were a few multinational banking houses (Rothschild's is the best example) and, at the opposite end of the scale from Scrooge and Marley's modest establishment, a sizable organization like the Hudson's Bay Company (which, at a time when all men who could afford it wore beaver hats, made vast profits from the fur trade) or, head and shoulders above all others, the immense East India Company, which not only held a monopoly of trade with Asia but had its own army and navy, minted its own coinage, and governed the subcontinent of India.

The Heart of Commerce

Even more important than these palaces of commerce was the Royal Exchange, in which the sharpest financial minds of the world's wealthiest nation, as well as crowds of merchants from other countries, could be seen on every trading day strolling, cogitating, conferring or arguing. The Exchange had been central to the life of the City for nearly three centuries. The first building was destroyed in the Great Fire, and its 17th-century successor was also burned down, in 1838, but it was reopened six years later by Queen Victoria. She was commemorated by a marble statue that stood in the midst of the bustling throng.

The new building, designed by William Tite, was considered magnificent: 'It is an honour to the city, and one of the finest structures which the present age has yet produced,' said one commentator. Like its predecessor, it had been inspired by the palaces of Italy, with a courtyard open to the sky and a surrounding colonnade that enabled traders to conduct their business in the open air, despite the fact that the raw chill of an English winter and the soot-filled air of London frequently made this something of a nonsense. The busiest time of day was between 2 and 4pm. George Sala recorded the scenes of a typical afternoon:

Three o'clock strikes – or rather chimes – from the bell-tower of Mr Tite's new building. The quadrangle of the exchange is converted into an accurate model of the Tower of Babel. The mass of black-hatted heads – with here and there a little white one, like a fleck of foam on the crest of a wave – eddies with violence to and fro. Men shout, and push, and struggle, and jostle, and shriek bargains into one another's ears. A stranger might imagine that these money and merchandise dealers had fallen out, and were about to fight; but the beadle of the Exchange looks on calmly; he knows that no breach of the peace will be committed, and that the merchants and financiers are merely singing their ordinary paean of praise to the great god Mammon. Surely – if there be not high treason in the thought – they ought to pull down Mr Lough's statue of Queen Victoria, which stands in the centre of the quadrangle, and replace it by a neat effigy of the golden calf.

Immediately across the street was the Bank of England, one of the most significant buildings in Britain. Founded in 1694 by a Scotsman, its premises had expanded, reflecting the Bank's increasing responsibilities, until it occupied an entire and invulnerable block. A contemporary guidebook declared:

The vast range of building has the great advantage of being quite detached, though closely surrounded, by other buildings. The destruction of its near neighbour, the Royal Exchange, in 1838, and the alterations consequent on the re-erection of that edifice, have had the effect of still more isolating the Bank and improving the architectural features of the neighbourhood. The vaults in which the bullion, coin, bank notes &c are deposited, are also indestructible by fire ...

The affairs of the Bank are regulated by a governor, deputy-governor and twenty-one directors, who are annually elected. The court-room, the pay-hall, the different offices, the vestibule, the governor's apartments, directors', cashiers', and the necessary offices, employ eleven hundred clerks; and the annual charge for salaries, pensions, house expenses &c. may be stated at about £250,000.

Max Schlesinger's indefatigable curiosity naturally led him there:

> We cross a small court-yard, and mount a few steps and, all of a
> sudden we are in a large saloon. This saloon is an office, but it
> makes not a disagreeable impression. There's a vast deal of good
> society in this office: at least a hundred officials and members of
> the public. The officials have no official appearance whatsoever;
> they are simple mortals, and do their business and serve their
> customers as if they were mere shopboys in a grocery shop. There
> is in them not a trace of dignity! Not an atom of bureaucratic
> pride! It is exactly as if to serve the public were the sole business
> of their lives. And the public too! Men, women and boys, with
> their hats on! Walking arm in arm as if they were in the park.
> They change money, or bring it, or fetch it, as if they had looked
> into a neighbour's shop for the purpose. Some of them have no
> business at all to transact. They stand by the fire in the centre of
> the room, and warm their backs!

His visit coincided with one of the twice-yearly occasions on which
those who had invested in government securities came to collect the
accrued dividend, which was handed to them in gold. The result was a
great deal of commotion, a crowd that alternated between good nature
and ill-temper, and a number of less aggressive people having to wait
hours, or days, for service:

> Ranged in long rows along the walls the Bank clerks sit writing,
> casting up accounts, weighing gold, and paying it away over the
> counter. In front of each is a bar of dark mahogany, a little table,
> a pair of scales, and a small fraction of the public; each waiting
> for his fare. The business is well-conducted, and none of them are
> kept waiting any length of time.
>   The saloon just by is more crowded. We are in the middle of the
> year, and the interest on the three per cents is being paid. What
> crowding and sweeping to and fro. At least fifty clerks are sitting
> in a circle in a high vaulted saloon, well provided with a cupola and
> lanterns. They do nothing whatever but pay and weigh, and weigh
> and pay. On all sides the rattling of gold as they push it with little

brass shovels across the tables. People elbowing and pushing in order to get a locus standi near the clerks, the doors are continually opening and shutting. What crowds of people there must be in this country who have their money in the three per cent Consols!

Strange figures are to be seen in this place. An old man with a wooden leg sits in a corner waiting, and Heaven knows how long he has been waiting already. He looks at his large silver watch – it is just twelve – puts his hand in the pocket of his coat, and pulls out a large parcel. Sandwiches! He spreads them out, and begins to eat. He makes himself perfectly at home. I daresay this is not the first time he has waited for his dividends. The young lady on our left is getting impatient. She has made several attempts to fight her way to one of the clerks; she tried to push in first on the right, then on the left, but all in vain. John Bull is by no means gallant in business, or at the theatre, or in the streets: he pushes, and kicks, and elbows in all directions. Poor pretty young lady, it's no use standing on your toes and looking over people's shoulders. You'd better come again tomorrow.

The little boy down there gets much better on. A pretty fair-haired fellow that, with a basket in his hand. Perhaps he is the son of a widow, who cannot come herself to get her small allowance. The boy looks as if about to cry, for he is on all sides surrounded by tall men. But one of them seizes him, lifts him up, and presents him to one of the clerks. 'Pray pay this little creditor of the public; he'll be pressed to death in the crowd!' And they all laugh, and everybody makes room for the boy; for it ought to be said to John Bull's credit, he is kind and gentle with children at all times. 'Well done, my little fellow! Now be careful that they don't rob you of your money on the way. How can they ever think of sending such a baby for their dividends!'

Life as a Clerk

Half an hour's walk westward was the country's administrative centre, Whitehall, in which hundreds of other clerks worked in conditions similar to those of their counterparts in the City. Nepotism had a great deal to do with appointment to the higher, lucrative and comfortable positions: the ludicrous 'Barnacle Junior' whom Arthur Clennam met at the Circumlocution Office in *Little Dorrit* was probably recognized at once by Dickens' original readers. Nevertheless, life for even the humblest government clerk would have been agreeable. Hours were extremely short – 10am to 4 or 5pm, with a generous lunch break – in comparison with those in other professions. It was not, of course, a job into which anyone could just drift. The ability to read well and to write clearly (the stately 'court hand' of practised scribes could be achieved later) were naturally essential, but it was also necessary to enter as a young man and serve a form of apprenticeship. They would have been groomed for this occupation from their early teens.

The patronage necessary to start a career in this field need not come from a well-placed relative. In the previous century a young man, William Brummell, had written for his father a card advertising 'Apartments to Let,' which was placed in the window. A tenant appeared, attracted by the beauty of the handwriting. This man was soon appointed Secretary of the Treasury, and he took with him the son of the house as his clerk. Brummell went on to have a successful career in Whitehall, just as his own son, 'Beau' Brummell, was to enjoy success in the world of fashion.

Clerks of the day sat high off the ground on stools which usually had no backs, bent over their work at narrow, sloping desks (years spent in this highly uncomfortable posture made many of them noticeably stoop-shouldered and prone to back pain). Alternatively, several clerks might sit at a single long desk. Light was provided by candles, evil-smelling oil or gas lamps, or whatever daylight could filter through the often small and inadequate windows. Heating depended on fireplaces, with junior employees farthest removed from the benefit of the coals (though they were likely to have the task of refilling the coal-scuttle). Communication with other rooms or buildings was facilitated by messengers, invariably old men or young boys, who hung about all day, waiting to be summoned by the tinkling of a handbell and sent on errands. Without machinery, offices were a good deal quieter than they are today – more like the reading-room of a library. Until the steel-nibbed pen became widespread, clerks cut their own writing implements from goose feathers, and throughout the century inkwells were a ubiquitous part of every office landscape. The staple and the paper-clip had not been invented, and sheaves of paper were joined together with ordinary pins. In a world without photocopiers, clerks like Bob Cratchit spent countless hours copying letters and invoices. The work was extremely monotonous, but it offered the compensations of comradeship and relative security. To visitors, it might often look as if the clerks spent their lives in thoughtful inactivity. In *Great Expectations*, Pip visited his friend Mr Pocket at the counting-house in the City where he worked:

> I often paid him a visit in the dark back-room in which he consorted with an ink-jar, a hat-peg, a coal-box, a string-box, an almanac, a desk and stool, and a ruler; and I do not remember that I ever saw him do anything else but look about him. If we all did what we undertake to do as faithfully as Herbert did, we might live in a Republic of the Virtues. He had nothing else to do, poor fellow, except at a certain hour of every afternoon to 'go to Lloyd's' – in observance of a ceremony of seeing his principal, I think. He never did anything else in connection with Lloyd's that I could find out, except come back again. When he felt his case unusually serious, and that he positively must find an opening, he would go on 'Change at a busy time, and walk in and out, in a kind of gloomy country-dance figure, among the assembled magnates.

Not all clerks were involved in legal or financial business, nor did they spend their days in quietness. The paperwork necessary for the manufacture and sale of goods was often processed in counting-houses that were shaken by the noise of machinery and filled with the smells of industry. Arthur Clennam knew such an office, and found it congenial, as Dickens recounted in *Little Dorrit*:

> The little counting-house reserved for his own occupation was a room of wood and glass at the end of a long low workshop, filled with benches, and vices, and tools, and straps, and wheels; which when they were in gear with the steam-engine, went tearing round ... The noises were sufficiently removed and shut out from the counting-house to blend into a busy hum, interspersed with periodical clinks and thumps. The patient figures at work were

swarthy with the filings of iron and steel that danced on every bench, and bubbled up through every chink in the planking. The workshop was arrived at by a step-ladder in the outer yard below, where it served as a shelter for the large grindstone where tools were sharpened. The whole had at once a fanciful and practical air in Clennam's eyes and, as often as he raised them from his first work of getting the array of business documents into perfect order, he glanced at these things with a feeling of pleasure in his pursuit that was new to him.

'Boz' described the habits of a member of the clerical class, and his working environment in a counting-house:

The dingy little back office into which he walks every morning ... taking off that black coat which lasts the year through, and putting on the one which did duty last year, and which he keeps in his desk to save the other. There he sits till five o'clock, working on ... only raising his head when someone enters the counting-house.

... About five, or half-past, he slowly dismounts from his accustomed stool, and again changing his coat, proceeds to his usual dining-place ... He orders a small plate of roast beef, with greens, and half-a-pint of porter ... and bespeaks the paper after the next gentleman ... Exactly at five minutes before the hour is up, he produces a shilling, pays the reckoning ... and returns to the office, from which, if it is not foreign post night, he again sallies forth, in about half an hour. He then walks home, at his usual pace, to his little back room at Islington, where he has his tea.

Assisting the Law

Scribes were a highly important part of the legal profession. Their task was to copy out on parchment the elaborate and decorative documents required by lawyers, and the best examples of this type of work were magnificent. They enjoyed little status, security or remuneration. The work of Captain Hawdon in *Bleak House*, scraping a meagre living copying documents for a firm of law stationers, was typical. The nature, structure and pitfalls of this branch of the clerk's life were vividly evoked in a pamphlet, *Scribes Ancient and Modern (Otherwise Law Writers and Scriveners)*, written by W. Warrell in the 1880s but looking back at the profession 50 years earlier. Unusually, apprentices received wages:

> **Law Stationers employ men on their premises to engross Deeds, Affidavits, copy Writs, Summonses, and all kinds of work. It is to learn these forms, and the peculiar style of writing, and what words to text, and upon what kind of paper the work is to be written, that boys are apprenticed. The term is usually 5 years. The pay is chiefly for piece-work. For engrossing a Deed on parchment a Scribe receives 1 shilling for every nine folios of 72 words. For engrossing a Deed he receives 1 shilling for every 10 folios. For copies of Deeds he receives 1 penny for every folio.**
>
> **The conditions are that apprentices either live on the premises and are termed indoor apprentices – taking their meals with the master and his family – or live at home with their parents. Of course the indoor apprentices' wages are very low. The 'outdoor' apprentice receives 5 shillings per week for the first year, 7 shillings the second, 9 shillings the third, 12 shillings the fourth and 15 shillings the fifth year. The hours 40 or 50 years ago were from 8 a.m. till 8 p.m., and in many instances til 9 p.m., Saturdays included.**

Warrell provided a list of all the necessities that an apprentice would have to acquire. Though some of these items continue to be used by specialist calligraphers today, in Dickens' time many of them were the commonplace tools of office life. It is worth noticing that a ruler was not flat, like its modern counterpart, but cylindrical:

> **Text pens made from turkey quills of various sizes.**
> **Penknife for cutting out on parchment and scratching out on paper, with a smooth clean bone handle to rub down the rough surface occasioned by scratching out.**
> **A piece of pumice-stone for rubbing down a rough skin [parchment] – this is generally needed when engrossing a Deed by endorsement. An endorsed deed is generally known as a 'dolly'.**

Pounce-box, and pounce rubber – The pounce is necessary for parchment. It consists of thoroughly dried whiting, with a slight admixture of resin. The rubber is generally a long strip of cloth about 2" wide, wound round and round in the shape of a pill-box, fastened off at the end by a pin to prevent it unrolling, and surmounted by a coat of wax to hold it together. If the skin is greasy (as all skins are, more or less) the pounce renders it fit to write upon.

Tin roller – A piece of tin rolled in such a manner that when the skin is inserted in the roller, it rolls the Deed up. A very useful article when a large skin is being used on a small desk.

Pencil – To tick mistakes in engrossments and fair copies discovered either on examination, or when copying, and for the purpose of marking the number of folios on the work when completed.

Ruler – A good straight round ruler for underscoring and underlining prominent words and ruling up endorsements and titles.

An Apron – To keep the pounce from his clothes. Some Scribes wear [protective] sleeves, made of the same material as the apron.

French Chalk – This is, in default of pumice-stone, a good substance to use instead of pounce on a rough skin.

Pen-case – Many Scribes carry a case, about 6 or 8" in length, made of parchment to hold their text and other pens.

Guides – Each Writer should provide himself with a leaden weight to place on his work to prevent him leaving out a line.

As regards Runners – The Scribe does not furnish these. Each Law Stationer keeps a set of runners and a ruling piece, viz. a flat leaden disc. A runner is an instrument composed of a revolving wheel with teeth. It is used to run down the edge of the paper or parchment, giving so many perforations in a given space … The Scribe who runs his work, places the right hand edges of his work together, and then runs the runner down the edge of the paper, the teeth perforating both sides at once. He can then, on opening the sheet, connect each perforation by a pencil line.

It was the practice of a Law Stationer to give his apprentices a roll of 60 skins to rule in slack time. The skins were 25" by 29". This size is used for what are termed 'Indentures.'

The Pattern of Work

Paid holidays for workers were not instituted until the 1930s, and millions dreaded the times of year during which work stopped. Because the legal world observed three 'terms' per year, with vacations in between, there were slack times in which no work was available. The result was weeks of unemployment and hardship. Groups of dejected men might be seen hanging about the street corners near Chancery Lane through the long summer days. Sometimes there were opportunities to work in agriculture as a means of tiding over, as Warrell explained:

> The Vacation is what all Scribes dread. The Vacation inflicts misery on Lawyers and Barristers who are not blessed with many clients; it is starvation to the Scribe; it means the workhouse for many. Some pass a few weeks earning a scanty livelihood in the counties of Surrey & Kent picking hops, for hop-picking falls due about the time when the Vacation sets in.

When term began again, the rush of work drove them to the other extreme. It was very common for scribes to have to take work home, and many documents were completed at kitchen tables, in the early hours of the morning, by men dropping with fatigue. Frequently, the men also had to work through their day off – Sunday – regardless of the claims of respectability. Warrell defined the function of the legal scribes:

> When the Courts open the Scribes are pretty busy. Each night, as long as a case lasts, they write in lithographic ink on prepared paper the whole of the current day's evidence. It is then taken to the litho printers & printed & tied up, ready for delivery to Counsel at 9 o'clock next morning. This evidence is called 'Shorthand Notes' & runs for 200 to 600 copies per day.
>
> ... In the present age it is the custom of Solicitors or their Clerks to bring the work (which they have prepared in the form of a Draft) to the Law Stationer & to say: 'How long will it take to run off 2, 3, or 4 copies of this?' or 'I must have 3 copies of this in a quarter of an hour without fail!' The work is given to the Manager, who splits it up into sheets, & if you entered a large

office, where there were perhaps a dozen writers, you would hear
3 or 4 voices all dictating at once. What cannot be written in the
office is taken out to some outside writers. By this means many
hundreds of folios (a folio is 72 words) are copied in one hour.

Solicitors prepare many drafts of Leaves, Conveyances,
Mortgages, Settlements, Wills & other instruments during the
day, & at night send the Drafts to the Law Stationer. This work
is distributed amongst the men, whose hours are, as a rule, from
9 in the morning till 7 or 8 in the evening. Each writer will take,
perhaps, from 60 to 120, or more, folios at night. This, of course,
means very little rest for the Scribe. On an average Scribes do not
exceed 12 folios per hour. True, there are some who can continue
for several hours together at the speed of 15, 16, 17 or even 18
folios per hour, but these are exceptions.

Solicitors, or their clerks, have a habit of ordering their work
(which they send at night) 'by 9 or 9.30 or 10 o'clock' next
morning whether they require the work or not. In many cases
when the work is sent home it lies in the Solicitor's office till
the afternoon.

The human side of the profession was also illustrated:

It is not a libel to say that Law Writers or Scribes are far
from being total abstainers. It would be a wonder if they were
teetotallers, for they are daily hurried and worried & their
nerves strained to the utmost pitch, to be succeeded by
nervous exhaustion.

It is generally believed that the constant anxiety occasioned by
hurrying off work & working so much at night has a debilitating
effect upon the nerves & eyesight of Scribes. And it is to these
causes, coupled with the sedentary nature of their occupation,
that their failing regarding drink is undoubtedly to be traced.

One of the most remarkable incidents in the history of Scribes
was the 'Railway Mania' in the 3rd decade of this century. Many
Bills were presented to Parliament, & the evidence required in
support was extremely voluminous. Many of the Law Stationers
offices were open day & night. The work was written on brief

paper, & the pay to the Scribe was 8 pence per sheet. Some of the Scribes, in their eagerness to make money, widened out the writing terribly. Whole sheets with short lines with simply 'yes' or 'no' were passed, & in some cases plain sheets of brief were put in the job & charged for at 8 pence per sheet. Some Scribes made 10s per hour, others made £10, £12 or even £15 per week.

Despite the serious nature of the work in which they were engaged, the standard was often extremely low because of the circumstances in which they worked:

... The less said about the specimens of writing the better. Many of the writers never went to bed; when they became tired they slept at the desk until refreshed, & then, awakening, proceeded with the merry game of coining money.

In spite of their poverty and the difficulty of keeping up with deadlines, the scribes seem to have had the option of simply giving up on work without serious consequences:

The word 'to chuck' means to take a quantity of work which is wanted at a given time & to bring it back untouched or incomplete. A 'royal chuck' means to bring it back completely untouched – not even unrolled. Some Scribes have chucked to the extent of taking home a settlement, wanted next day at 10.00 for signature by the parties before a marriage ceremony. A messenger has been sent to the Scribe's home & the Scribe was found drunk in bed. It would take pages to describe the many kinds & degrees of chucks – from the little chuck, where the man is ½ hour late – to the chuck royal.

The pamphlet concludes with a list of the most commonly used excuses for failure to complete work. Though some have a distinctly period feel, others are still doing duty today:

... took home some open skins to engross, & left them on the table; his child scribbled over the skin & made it dirty & greasy.

The clock-weight unfortunately in its downward course rested on the back of a chair, which happened to be underneath it, and thus stopped the clock.

'The lamp went out and I found that we had no oil in the can' has been frequently given.

Wives' confinements cause many 'chucks,' as well as the death of a grandmother, uncle, aunt, sister &c.

A row with the wife.

The train was late.

The inkpot got upset & spoiled the paper, so there wasn't enough paper.

Couldn't read the Draft, it was so rough.

The skin was so rough.

The paper was so greasy.

Didn't take enough paper.

So cold I couldn't hold the pen.

Met a friend last night.

When I got home I found some friends & I couldn't get on, they hindered me.

A query as to the reading of the Draft.

Left the Draft at the office.

A fire.

A fog on the line.

The snow stopped the train.

So hot I couldn't work.

Thought the work was not wanted.

When I got home no one was at home, & I couldn't get in for 2 hours.

Got home very late just ripe for working all night, but the sons of the landlord refused me admittance, & threw my work out in the street; consequently had to walk about all night.

Though clerks might be at work in the counting-houses until well into the evening, much of the City's business was done by six o'clock. It was at that hour that the Post Offices closed. By the time the clocks chimed the hour, a vast accumulation of letters, parcels and packets, as well as innumerable bundles of newspapers bound for the mail-trains and the provinces, had to be brought to the Post Offices and deposited through the windows that served the different districts, counties and countries. Such was the rush to deliver items before the windows were closed precisely on the hour, that in the evenings (especially on a Friday) a stampede could be witnessed as office boys, clerks, private citizens and, most conspicuously, newspaper men and boys arrived with their burdens. This was particularly true of the biggest Post Office of all: the GPO in St Martin's-le-Grand. Such was the fame of the spectacle that it was the subject of a painting by the genre artist George Elgar Hicks. His canvas, entitled *The General Post Office, One Minute to Six* and painted in 1860, was based on Sala's published account of the same scene:

> The newspaper boys are, of course, in immense array at the six o'clock fair on Friday evening. They are varied, as currants are by sultanas in a dumpling, by newspaper men, who, where the boys struggle up to the window and drop in their load, boldly fling bags full, sacks full, of journals into the yawning casement. There is a legend that they once threw a boy into the window, newspapers and all. But at six o'clock everything is over – the window is closed – and newspaper fair is adjourned to the next Friday.

The painting captures the tension of the jostling, urgent crowd, their faces betraying anxiety, determination – or relief as they saunter away having 'beaten the clock.' The men from newspaper offices, for whom this ritual is a daily occurrence, carry their bundles on their heads, and the air is filled with flying packages as boys hurl them into the sorting-room. The artist was criticized for the fact that the characters looked unnaturally clean: 'The faces are painted up to the pink of doll-like perfection, and not to the dingy reality of London life.' Max Schlesinger visited a City Post Office and described a similar scene:

> On either side there are numbers of office windows and little tablets. They are so many sign-posts, and direct you to all the quarters of the world; to the East and West Indies, to Australia, China, the Canary Islands, the Cape, Canada, etc. Every part of the globe has its own letter box; and the stranger who, about six o'clock p.m., enters these halls, or takes up his post of

observation near the great City Branch Office, in Lombard Street, would almost deem it that all the nations of the world were rushing in through the gates, and as if this were the last day for the reception and transmission of letters.

Breathless come the bankers' clerks, rushing in just before the closing hour; they open their parcels, and drop their letters into the various compartments. There are messengers groaning under the weight of heavy sacks, which they empty into a vast gulf in the flooring; they come from the offices of the great journals, and the papers themselves are sorted by the Post Office clerks. Here and there, among this crowd of business people, you are struck with the half comfortable, half nervous bearing of a citizen.

And once the clock has struck:

Now the wooden doors are closed; the hall is empty as if by magic, and the tall columns throw their lengthened shadows on the stone flooring. This is the most arduous period of the day for the clerks within. All that heap of letters and newspapers which has accumulated in the course of the day is to be sorted, stamped and packed in time for the various mail-trains. Clerks, servants, sorters and messengers hurry to and fro in the subterraneous passage between the two wings of the building. Clerks suspended by ropes mount up to the ceiling and take down the parcels which, in the course of the day, were deposited on high shelves. And the large red carts come rattling in and receive their load of bags, and rattle off to the various stations; the rooms are getting empty; the clerks have got through their work; the gas is put out, and silence and darkness reign supreme.

In Perspective

Those in a secure position might look forward to the prospect, enjoyed by comparatively few, of a pension and thus a comfortable retirement. The essayist Charles Lamb, himself the son of a lawyer's clerk, worked for the East India Company for 36 years. His colleagues were pleasant and the work was undemanding but he longed to be free to spend his remaining years doing the things he loved. In 1825 he seized an opportunity to take 'early retirement'. In an article written after his departure, he recalled the euphoria with which he gave up his old life. It could easily have been written in our own times:

Independently of the rigours of attendance, I have ever been haunted with a sense of incapacity for business. This, during my latter years, had increased to such a degree that it was visible in all the lines of my countenance. My health and my good spirits flagged. Besides my daylight servitude, I served over again all night in my sleep, and would awake with terrors of imaginary false entries, errors in my accounts, and the like. I was fifty years of age, and no prospect of emancipation presented itself.

On the 5th of last month, L—, the junior partner in the firm, calling me on one side, directly taxed me with my bad looks, and frankly enquired the cause of them. So taxed, I honestly made confession of my infirmity, and added that I was afraid I should eventually be obliged to resign his service. He spoke some words to hearten me, and there the matter rested.

On the evening of the 12th April, just as I was about quitting my desk to go home (it might have been eight o'clock) I received an awful summons to attend the presence of the whole assembled firm in the formidable back parlour. L—, I could see, smiled at the terror I was in, which was little relief to me – when to my utter astonishment B—, the eldest partner, began a formal harangue to me on the length of my services, my very meritorious conduct during the whole of the time. He went on to descant on the expediency of retiring at a certain time of life (how my heart panted!) and asking me a few questions as to the amount of my property, ended with the proposal, to which his three partners nodded a grave assent, that I should accept from the house, which I had served so well, a pension for life to the amount of two-thirds of my accustomed salary – a magnificent offer! I do not know what I answered between surprise and gratitude, but it was understood that I accepted their proposal, and I was told that I was free from that hour to leave their service. I stammered out a bow, and at just ten minutes after eight I went home – for ever.

Like many others, Lamb returned a few weeks later to see his former colleagues, his 'co-bretheren of the quill', and was torn between nostalgia and relief:

Not all the kindness with which they received me could quite restore to me that pleasant familiarity which I had heretofore enjoyed among them. We cracked some of the old jokes, but methought they went off but faintly. My old desk; the peg where I hung my hat, were appropriated to another. I knew it must be, but could not take it kindly. D—l take me if I did not feel some remorse at quitting my old compeers, that smoothed for me with their jokes and conundrums the ruggedness of my professional road. But my heart smote me. I shall be some time before I get quite reconciled to the separation.

He was highly fortunate. It was Bob Cratchit rather than Charles Lamb whose experience reflected the lives of many clerks. Had Scrooge not undergone his famous transformation, his employee might have had nothing more to look forward to than continuing in his position until infirmity and failing eyesight put him in the workhouse.

Transport and TRAVEL

'Journeys are very perilous,' said Quilp, 'especially outside the coach. Wheels come off, horses take fright, coachmen drive too fast, coaches overturn.'

Dickens, as we have seen, travelled to London by coach, and for just over a decade after his arrival from Kent in 1822 the mail coach was unchallenged as the fastest and most glamorous form of transport. As sleek as greyhounds, these vehicles could travel at up to 16 miles an hour. To us this naturally seems unremarkable – a bicycle can easily go that fast – but to anyone seated high on the roof of a speeding coach, clinging to their hat in the slipstream and watching the team of straining horses ahead, hearing the rattle and jingle of wheels and harness, the braying of the guard's horn and the crack of the coachman's whip, the experience would have been highly exhilarating. It was little wonder that small boys dreamed of becoming coachmen, or that rich young men in the Regency period made a hobby of taking over the reins and doing the driving themselves.

The mail coaches were one of the wonders of Britain, admired by natives and foreigners alike, as well as by those who operated them (one coachman called them 'the most perfect system of road travelling the world has ever seen'). They were part of a transport structure that was certainly faster, better organized and thus more efficient than that of any other country in Europe. They had been established only in 1784, so that barely four generations of men were to work with them before the coming of the railways finally put them out of business by the 1860s. The Wellers in *Pickwick Papers* are an instance of family involvement: Tony, the father, was a coachman and his son Sam an ostler, but by the time Sam reached middle age the stage coach would be gone.

Mail coaches looked magnificent. They had originally been painted black and yellow, but by Dickens' time they were maroon and black. The wheels were crimson. The royal cipher and coat of arms gave them an aristocratic flourish. They were cleaned regularly and their paintwork, like the brass and steel of the harness, sparkled in the sun. With their teams of four sleek horses they were the epitome of elegance and, on roads dominated by slow-moving wagons, the passing of a coach would bring people running to watch them. Their names – 'Comet', 'Meteor', 'Telegraph', 'Swiftsure', 'High-Flyer' – increased the sense of dash and speed. They were expensive to travel in and beyond the means of many.

By the start of the 19th century, coach travel was becoming noticeably faster and more efficient. This was due partly to the extensive road-building undertaken by the engineer Thomas Telford and the improvement in road surfaces brought about by the Scotsman John Macadam, and partly to the growth of the turnpike trusts, which administered stretches of highway, collecting tolls for the use of sections of road and keeping them in repair. The coaches, too, were efficiently maintained, as a driver, Edward Corbett, recalled:

As the business became more and more matured, spare coaches were put on the roads, so that each one on arriving in London should have two days for repair. As each came into London it was sent to the factory at Millbank, nearly five miles off, to be cleaned, greased, and examined, for which the charge of one shilling was paid for each coach. Before this arrangement was made, it was nothing unusual for passengers to be kept waiting for a couple of hours, while some repairs were being done, which were only discovered to be necessary just as the coach was about to start, and then the work was naturally done in such a hasty manner that the coach started in far from good condition.

The same commentator described the improvement in speed:

The mail from London to Chester and Holyhead, which started from the General Post Office at eight o'clock on Monday evening, arrived at Chester at 25 minutes past twelve on the morning of the following Wednesday, thus taking about 28 hours and a half to perform a journey of 180 miles. The 'Bristol' occupied 15 hours and three-quarters on her journey of 120 miles, whilst that to Shrewsbury, which at that time ran by Uxbridge and Oxford, consumed 23 hours in accomplishing the distance of 162 miles. This shows a speed of nearly 8 miles an hour which, if kept, was very creditable work.

By the year 1825, some considerable acceleration had taken place. The Shrewsbury mail, which had then become the more important Holyhead mail, performed the journey to Shrewsbury in 24 hours and a half, and was again accelerated in the following year. A few years later the time was reduced to 16 hours and a quarter, and she was due at Holyhead about the same time as, a few years previously, she had reached Shrewsbury, or 28 hours from London; and thus, owing in a great degree to the admirable efficiency of Mr Telford's road-making, surpassing by 6 hours the opinion expressed by him in 1830, that the mail ought to go to Holyhead in 34 hours.

Coach travel became cheaper during the 1820s, when prices were standardized for long journeys at £2 for an outside passenger and £4 for those inside. It thus became less exclusive and brought hitherto fashionable destinations within reach of the less wealthy. Some regular visitors to Brighton, for instance, complained that the tone of the place had been lowered by hoi polloi who could now afford the journey (a close parallel with the cheap flights of our own day). The case for coach travel as an indulgence for the rich must not be overstated, however, for passengers could include the lowest elements in society, as Pip explained in *Great Expectations*. He was awaiting the start of a journey when told that there would be some unusual travelling companions:

At that time it was customary to carry convicts down to the dockyards by stage-coach. As I had often heard of them in the capacity of outside passengers, and I had more than once seen them on the high road dangling their ironed legs over the coach roof, I had no cause to be surprised when Herbert, meeting me in the yard, came up and told me there were two convicts going down with me.

The two men were to sit in the front seat outside with their guard.
A gentleman complained at having to share the seat with them:

'Don't take it so much amiss, sir,' pleaded the keeper to the angry
passenger, 'I'll sit next you myself. I'll put 'em on the outside of
the row. They won't interfere with you, sir. You needn't know
they're there.'

'And don't blame me,' growled the convict I had recognized, **'I**
don't want to go. I am quite ready to stay behind. As far as I am
concerned, anyone's welcome to my place.'

'Or mine,' said the other gruffly, **'I wouldn't have incommoded**
none of you, if I'd had my way.' Then they both laughed, and
began cracking nuts, and spitting the shells about – as I really
think I should have liked to do myself, if I had been in their
place, and so despised.

Mail coaches (they were called stage coaches because they made
scheduled stops at specified places, just as their motorized descendants do
today) were a world in microcosm. As well as conveying the Royal Mail
to all parts of the kingdom, they carried newspapers. They were therefore
often the first to bring important news and if significant events were in
the offing their arrival would be eagerly awaited. They were the only link
that many small communities had with London and the wider world and
so the sight of an approaching vehicle would always arouse excitement
and curiosity. They also brought more material items, such as books,
clothing or foodstuffs ordered from London shops: the coach offices of
taverns were crowded with parcels awaiting dispatch or collection. Lock,
the St James's Street hatter, for example, sent his products to distant
clients by this route. The coach might return to town with a few brace of
pheasant, a goose or some rabbits hanging from the roof.

A coach carried six passengers inside. They sat in threes, facing each
other, on leather-covered horsehair cushions, and clean straw would
be put on the floor. Though protected from the elements, the swaying
motion of the vehicle would still be unpleasant for those prone to sea-
sickness. Up to ten sat on the roof, on wooden benches with iron rails
to stop them falling off, were exposed to all weathers. They had to be
agile enough to climb several rungs on the side of the coach to take

their seats. If the coach lost a wheel and tipped over, as sometimes happened, they faced the prospect of a nasty spill that would leave them with broken bones. At night, or in winter, they had to be bundled in blankets, capes and scarves, with hats pulled over their eyes. They arrived wet, stiff and frozen at the coach's periodic stops, to be revived with coffee or brandy-and-water.

The passengers would have been a motley collection of people going up to London to see the shops, to visit their lawyers, to attend weddings or funerals, to seek employment. Thrust together in a small vehicle for hours, or even days, they would have no choice but to get to know each other and the result might be a Chauceresque exchange of stories. For a young man like Dickens, gifted with imagination, memory and a talent for mimicry, the long hours spent on a coach roof listening to the conversation of others must have been a useful opportunity, furnishing him with material for his writings and his theatricals.

Coaches that ran at night left the GPO in Lombard Street at 8pm precisely; their departure – the noisy loading of mail bags, the yells of the drivers, slamming doors, the bellow of horns from the scarlet-coated guards and the clatter of hooves on the cobbles as the great vehicles wheeled out of the gates – would cause an interested crowd to gather.

The long-range mail coaches had regular places – either inns or coffee houses – at which they picked up and set down passengers. Northbound coaches, for instance, departed from the Bull and Mouth (a name derived from 'Boulogne Mouth', referring to Henry VIII's siege of Boulogne's harbour) in St Martin's-le-Grand by St Paul's. Piccadilly had become the terminus for services from the west of England, and one of its inns – confusingly also called the Bull and Mouth – was right on Regent (Piccadilly) Circus, on a site later occupied by Swan & Edgar's department store. It was here that the Shropshire mails arrived. The White Horse cellar, further down Piccadilly (on the site of the Ritz), was the destination of coaches from Bath and Exeter. The Gloucester Coffee House was the point of arrival and departure for the Portsmouth coach.

The accommodating, provisioning and servicing of the coaches and their passengers was a major undertaking. William Chaplin, owner of the curiously named Swan With Two Necks, a coaching-inn opposite the GPO, had 1,800 horses and nearly 2,000 employees. This workforce prepared the horses, fitted them into the shafts, roused the passengers (the earliest departure was at 5am), cleaned their rooms, served their meals, booked their tickets, loaded their luggage and polished their boots – like Sam Weller when he is first introduced to readers of *Pickwick Papers* – as well as driving and maintaining the vehicles.

The Travel Experience

South of the river, in the Borough, were several large and ancient coaching inns. The White Hart, at which Mr Pickwick first met Weller, was one of these (another, the Tabard, from which Chaucer's pilgrims had set off for Canterbury 500 years earlier, survived until 1874). Although it was possible to sail to mainland Europe from the Thames, it was from these inns that the coaches had always set off for the Kent coast and the Channel ports. For many people, therefore, the Borough High Street would have had the same sense of excitement that an international airport has today – that of the place where adventurous foreign journeys begin. In *Pickwick Papers*, the accommodation in which travellers stayed the night before a dawn start is described:

> A double tier of bedroom galleries, old clumsy balustrades, ran around two sides of a straggling area, and a double row of bells to correspond, sheltered from the weather by a little sloping roof, hung over the door leading to the bar and coffee room.

Dickens analysed the process of arranging and then setting off on a coach journey, from the Golden Cross at Charing Cross, in one of his early Boz essays. First, the booking had to be made in advance:

> You enter a mouldy-looking room, ornamented with large posting-bills; the greater part of the place enclosed behind a huge lumbering rough counter, and fitted up with recesses that look like the dens of the smaller animals in a travelling menagerie, without the bars. Some half-dozen people are 'booking' brown-paper parcels, which one of the clerks flings into the aforesaid recesses with an air of recklessness. Porters, looking like so many Atlases, keep rushing in and out, with large packages on

their shoulders. One of the clerks, with his hat half off his head, enters the passengers' names in the books with a coolness which is inexpressibly provoking; and the villain whistles – actually whistles – while a man asks him what the fare is outside, all the way to Holyhead! Your turn comes at last, and having paid the fare, you tremblingly enquire 'What time will it be necessary for me to be here in the morning?' – 'Six o'clock,' replies the whistler, carelessly pitching the sovereign you have just parted with, into a wooden bowl on the desk, 'Rather before than arter.'

The next day the passengers assembled in the pre-dawn chill:

You arrive at the office, and look wistfully up the yard for the Birmingham High-Flier, which, for aught you can see, may have flown away altogether, for no preparations appear to be on foot for the departure of any vehicle in the shape of a coach. You wander into the booking-office, which with the gas-lights and blazing fire looks quite comfortable. There stands the identical book-keeper in the same position as if he had not moved since you saw him yesterday. He informs you that the coach is up the yard, and will be brought round in about a quarter of an hour.

The first stroke of six peals from St Martin's church steeple. The coach is out; the horses are in, and the guard and two or three porters are stowing the luggage away. The place, which a few minutes ago was so still and quiet, is now all bustle; the early vendors of the morning papers have arrived, and you are assailed on all sides by shouts of 'Times, gen'lm'n, Times,' 'Herald, ma'am'. The inside passengers are already in their dens, and the outsides, with the exception of yourself, are pacing up and down the pavement to keep themselves warm.

'Take off the cloths, Bob,' says the coachman, who now appears for the first time, in a rough blue great-coat. 'Now, gen'lm'n,' cries the guard, with the waybill in his hand. 'Five minutes behind time already!' Up jump the passengers. The thin young woman is got upon the roof, by dint of a great deal of pulling and pushing, and helping and trouble, and she repays it by expressing her solemn conviction that she will never be able to get down again.

'All right,' sings out the guard at last, jumping up as the coach starts, and blowing his horn directly afterwards, as proof of the soundness of his wind. 'Let 'em go, Harry, give 'em their heads,' cries the coachman – and off we start as briskly as if the morning were 'all right,' as well as the coach.

This essay was written only a few years before the demise of the mail coach as a means of long-distance travel. It is often assumed that the horse reigned supreme until displaced by the steam railway engine, but this was not entirely true. Steam-driven road vehicles were also tried. The first demonstration of a steam coach in London had been given by Richard Trevithick, the railway pioneer, as early as 1803. It was not until 1826, however, that a boiler suitable for use with a coach was invented. This had a series of U-shaped tubes, filled with water and heated by a fire that used a combination of coke and charcoal. It had a two-cylinder engine. The driver sat low down (below the feet of the passengers) at the front and steered with a tiller, while the passengers were seated more than 2m/6ft above the ground. The three funnels through which the steam was expelled were above the boiler at the rear. The coach ran for a few years on a regular service from London to Bath. Its inventor, Sir Goldsworthy Gurney, also created a chain-driven, steam-powered carriage with a chimney at the rear. In 1829 it gave a display in which it hauled a four-wheeled vehicle containing the Duke of Wellington.

Gurney's boiler was used to power a coach that provided a regular service between Gloucester and Cheltenham for about four months in 1831. The vehicle could carry 18 passengers (six inside and a dozen outside), but suffered a number of teething difficulties, particularly with its steering. In 1827 another engineer, Walter Hancock, had invented a boiler that could drive a coach. He built a carriage, 'The Infant', with which he began a passenger service, also in 1831, between London and Stratford-by-Bow in Essex; two others, 'The Enterprise' and 'The Autopsy', were soon in operation between Paddington and the Bank. These travelled at ten miles an hour and could carry 14 passengers, who paid sixpence each. Hancock's service continued for about a decade, but the public did not take to steam carriages. A well-publicized accident in Scotland, in which an exploding boiler killed five passengers, seriously damaged their credibility. They were also unpopular with other road users (the owners of horse-drawn buses were suspected of strewing the roads with stones to disable the temperamental steam vehicles) and the parallel development of the railway attracted more funding and public support. Nevertheless, the steam coach would have been a familiar sight to many of Dickens' fellow Londoners. Its chugging progress and belching smoke may have been a novelty for a few years, but it had neither the sleek grace of the horse-drawn mail coach nor the efficiency of the railway. By the middle of the century it was a dead letter.

The Railway Arrives

The railway came to London on 14 December 1837. In that year, after considerable publicity and argument, a stretch of track was opened between Greenwich and a terminus on the edge of London at Spa Road (it was later extended to London Bridge). The line was largely built on arches and initially went only to Deptford. A contemporary report related by John o' London gave an account of the opening:

> The directors having arrived at the London terminus were shown to their seats by ushers in waiting, and the band of music having taken up its position on the roof of the carriage, the official bugler blew the signal for the start, and the train steamed off amidst the firing of cannon, the ringing of church bells, and the cheers of an excited crowd. Spa Road, the only intermediate station, was filled to excess with almost the multitude there assembled, was reached with almost the swiftness of a discharged rocket, and afterwards Deptford, where a vast concourse, in carriages and on foot, awaited the visitors, with a second band of music, which then took the place of the first on the return journey.

The eight-carriage train carried 256 passengers and took 14 minutes to complete the journey. Over the following nights the track was illuminated with lanterns, and for several weeks bands were stationed at both ends of the line to 'play in' the trains. Pedestrians were permitted, for a small payment, to walk along the track when trains were not running on it. Next to Spa Road Station the Bridge House Hotel was

opened for passengers en route to Greenwich, which was the starting-
point for cross-Channel steamers before Dover Harbour was built.
Some 20,000 people travelled on the line in the first week, and this
increased to an average of 32,000. Trains ran every 15 minutes from 8am
until 10pm. The locomotives, named *Royal William* and *Royal Adelaide*
after the King and Queen, were 4.5m/15ft long and had four wheels.
Like all early locomotives, they had unsheltered footplates: the crew
worked entirely in the open.

The following year the more important line from London to
Birmingham opened. This involved the building of a station at Euston
Square after it was realized that the original terminus, at Chalk Farm, was
too far from the centre. In 1851 a guidebook described Euston Station:

> **The passenger station near Euston Square occupies an area of
> about 12 acres, in which the operations necessary for dispatch
> and reception of not less than 18 trains each way per day are
> carried on with so little noise, confusion, or semblance of bustle,
> that it would almost seem that these complicated arrangements
> acted of their own accord. The entrance to the station is through
> the gigantic and very absurd Doric Temple [the Euston Arch was
> a well-loved London landmark until it was demolished in 1961]
> placed in the centre line of Euston Square. Facing it is a large,
> plain range of buildings containing the offices, waiting-rooms, and
> board and meeting rooms of this Company. Passing firstly into
> an immense and beautiful hall, with a ludicrous cage for the sale
> of refreshments in the centre. The booking-offices are very fine
> specimens of architecture, but the waiting-rooms are far from
> corresponding with them in magnificence.**
>
> **The 'out' trains of the main line leave upon the rails next the
> waiting-rooms on the east side. The 'in' trains all arrive on the
> line on the extreme east of the station, where there is a platform
> and a road for public and private conveyance to transport the
> crowds who arrive. The whole of the operations connected with
> the reception and dispatch of the trains are thus carried on under
> a shed of immense superficial extent, but too low, or at least
> without sufficient ventilation, to allow of the rapid escape of the
> steam from the locomotives. On the west of the lines leading**

from the station are the shops where the carriage repairs for the London end of the line are effected.

By the time the London termini were in operation, the railway had ceased to be a novelty. People had also begun to get used to the colossal scale of the stations and the technological marvels that they represented. William Tayler, who walked over to Paddington to see the new buildings, probably spoke for many when he said: 'The works are really wonderful for any human beings to have done.' The first passenger line – the Stockton and Darlington Railway – had opened in 1830, and since then many millions of people had experienced the thrill of this form of travel. One of them, Fanny Kemble, recorded the sensation of crossing countryside without following the contours of the ground, going through cuttings and along embankments:

> You can't imagine how strange it seemed to be journeying on thus, without any visible cause of progress other than the magical machine, with the flying white breath and rhythmical unvarying pace. When I reflected that these great masses of stone had been cut asunder to allow our passage thus far below the surface of the earth, I felt as if no fairy tale could ever be half so wonderful as what I saw. Bridges were thrown from side to side across the top of these cliffs, and the people looking down upon us from them seemed like pygmies standing in the sky. You cannot conceive what that sensation of cutting the air was. I could either have read or written; and, as I was, I stood up and with my bonnet off 'drank the air before me'. This sensation of flying was quite delightful, and strange beyond description.

Unlike stage coach passengers, railway travellers had the choice of three 'classes' of accommodation. First class carriages were based on the design of the mail coach, with three compartments containing sets of face-to-face seats, six passengers in each. Second class coaches were plainer but also seated 18. Third class had wooden seats and, like the driver and fireman, passengers were entirely exposed to wind and rain. Some railways did not even provide seats for this class of passengers. On the London and Greenwich Railway these carriages were called 'standups'

or 'standipedes'. When passengers complained, the company tartly
retorted that 'if people would insist on travelling at so cheap a rate, it
was only reasonable they should pay the penalty in a certain amount
of discomfort.' Only in 1844, with the passing of an Act of Parliament,
were railway companies obliged to run trains with roofed third class
carriages – though only once a day. It was further stipulated that the
trains must run at 12 miles per hour and that passengers would pay a fare
of a penny a mile.

Other railway companies built stations around the edges of the city
centre during the following two decades. There were almost innumerable
small companies, often with grand and pompous names, that ran single
routes from one corner of the suburbs to another: the West End of
London and Crystal Palace Junction Railway, the East and West India
Docks and Birmingham Railway, the Victoria Station and Pimlico
Railway, the West End Railway. The Great Western Railway established
the London end of its line to Bristol at Paddington. Unlike the other
systems, on which the rails were less than 1.5m/5ft apart, the Great
Western was built on a gauge of over 2.1m/7ft, and continued to run
trains of this width until 1892. Paddington, like Euston, was beyond
the limits of London and thus inconvenient for travellers to use. As a
result, plans were made for a 'city railway' that would bring trains right
into the heart of the metropolis, with a central terminus at Farringdon.
Although the scheme was not realized, this was to be the beginning of
the Metropolitan Railway – the London Underground.

As railway fever gripped the country in the 1840s and 1850s and
the resistance of landowners and civic authorities was overcome, lines
sprouted everywhere. Once-quiet lanes on the outskirts filled with the
hooting of engine whistles, the chuffing and clanking of locomotives,
the hiss of boilers and the thudding of trains over points. People living
next to the tracks, whose walls shook and windows rattled every time
a train went by and whose washing hung out to dry was blackened
by the smuts from passing engines, came to accept the railway as a
necessary evil, its speed and convenience compensating for its noisy
intrusiveness. The Duke of Wellington had objected to the railways on
the grounds that they would encourage the lower orders to move about.
They did indeed do so. The advent of this cheap form of travel (there
were special workmen's trains into London every morning) meant that

not only middle-class clerical workers but also manual labourers could live beyond walking distance of the city. The result was growth and development of the suburbs on a scale not previously seen.

George Sala caught a morning train from Euston in order to observe his fellow passengers in the wooden-seat discomfort of a third class carriage (at least they had roofs by this time). There were few middle class travellers about:

> The seven o'clock travellers are not exactly of the class who drink sherry and play cards; they are more given to selling walnuts than to eating them. They are, for the most part, hard-faced, hard-handed, poorly-clad creatures; men in patched, time-worn garments; women in pinched bonnets and coarse shawls, carrying a plenitude of baskets and bundles, but very slightly troubled with trunks and portmanteaus. You might count a hundred heads and not one hat-box; of two hundred crowding round the pay-place to purchase their third-class tickets for Manchester, or Liverpool, or even further north, you would look in vain for the possessor of a railway rug, or even an extra overcoat. Swarming about the pay-place, which their parents are anxiously investing, thirteen-and-fourpence or sixteen-and-ninepence in hand, are crowds of third-class children. I am constrained to acknowledge that there are few handsome children, well-dressed children, even tolerably good-looking children. It is a long way to Liverpool, a long way to Manchester; the only passengers by the seven o'clock train who can afford to treat the distance jauntily are the Irish paupers, who are in process of being passed to their parish, and who will travel free.
>
> But hark! The train bell rings; there is a rush, and a trampling of feet, and in a few seconds the vast hall is almost deserted. Let us follow the crowd of third-class passengers on to the vast platform. There the train awaits them, puffing, and snorting, and champing its adamantine bit. But what a contrast to the quietude of the scarcely-patronized first and second class wagons are the great hearse-like caravans in which travel the teeming hundreds who can afford to pay but a penny a mile! What a hurly-burly; what a seething mass; what a scrambling for place; what a

shrill turmoil of women's voices and children's wailings. What a motley assemblage of men, women, and children, all marked with the homogenous penny-a-mile stamp of poverty! Sailors with bronzed faces and those marvellous tarpaulin pancake hats; squat, squarely-built fellows, using strange and occasionally not very polite language, much given to 'skylarking' but full of a simple, manly courtesy to all the females; railway navvies going to work at some place down the line, and obligingly franked thither for that purpose by the company; pretty servant-maids going to see their relatives; Jew pedlars; Irish labourers in swarms; soldiers on furlough, proceeding to Weedon Barracks ... journeymen mechanics with their tool-baskets; charwomen, servants out of place, stablemen, bricklayers' labourers, and shopboys; and a low-browed, bull-necked, villainous-looking gentleman, who has taken a remote corner, between two stern guardians, and who, strive as he may to pull his coat-cuffs over his wrists, cannot conceal the presence of a pair of neat shining handcuffs.

By the time this was written, in 1858, the stage coach had long been relegated to a role as a local conveyance, and the train had no competitor in providing long-distance transport. The travelling public, which had abandoned the horse for the first time in history, quickly came to take the railway for granted.

The London Omnibus

The development of London's outer reaches was driven by the advent of the railway, but it had been triggered by another form of public transport: the omnibus. In 1825, stage coaches had begun making short journeys to the suburbs, but they were too slow and expensive to provide a viable service: it was complained that they took three hours to get from Paddington to the City, and charged 2 shillings for an outside seat and 3 shillings for inside ones.

The situation was changed by the starting of a cheaper transport service along precisely that route, from the village of Paddington to the Bank, in July 1829. The man who began it, George Shillibeer, was a coach-builder. He had worked in Paris, where English coaches were highly fashionable, and had seen a similar system of public transport there. Jacques Lafitte, the man behind the Parisian vehicles, had actually commissioned Shillibeer to design two of them. Using this experience on his own account in London, he built a single-deck vehicle that was entered by a door at the back and had benches facing each other along the sides. The driver sat at roof level to control a team of three horses, walking abreast. The first journey was made on 4 July from a public house at Paddington called the Yorkshire Stingo, and a crowd gathered to watch its departure. It travelled along the New Road (Euston and Marylebone Road) carrying 22 passengers for a fare of one shilling.

Shillibeer's conveyance (which can still be seen in the London Transport Museum) had tremendous style and was instantly popular with Londoners. It was painted dark green and curved elegantly at the front. The wheels were bright yellow and the horses were matching bays. Shillibeer had been a midshipman in the Royal Navy and he dressed his conductors in short blue nautical jackets. The first two he employed were the sons of naval officers, and brought the traditional courtesy of the Senior Service to their task. They helped to give the new conveyance a sense of dignity and a touch of luxury, as did Shillibeer's habit of providing his passengers with free periodicals. Painted in gold on the side of the vehicle was the word 'Omnibus' – a term borrowed from its Parisian forerunners and meaning simply a repository for many things – but the word took some time to enter the public consciousness and for a time the vehicles were called 'Shillibeers'.

The omnibus was so successful that it was immediately imitated. In less than a year Shillibeer had 12 in service throughout London, and the vehicles of other operators were soon plying routes all over the capital, so that by 1837 there were over 400; the major reason for the widening of the Strand in 1835 was the increased traffic of omnibuses. They had a crew of two: driver and conductor, the latter standing on a platform at the rear. His job was not only to sell tickets but also to tout for custom. He continually called out to pedestrians and often bullied them into travelling in his vehicle. Rivalries quickly developed between different operators and a contemporary *Punch* cartoon shows two conductors fighting over the custom of a stout woman; one has seized her child, the other has her luggage, and both are trying to drag her aboard.

For those who travelled voluntarily, there were no specific boarding-places. Unlike their predecessor the short-stage coach, omnibuses had no fixed stops. They could be hailed – and would stop – anywhere, and a journey might therefore be interrupted a dozen times in the course of a single street. By the same logic, they set down passengers anywhere, doing so not at the kerbside but in the middle of the road, leaving them to win their way through the traffic to the safety of the pavement.

Only the middle class could afford to travel regularly by omnibus and this was reflected in the upholstered interiors of many of the vehicles, but the demand became so great that more space was soon created by putting seats on the roof. These were of the so-called 'knife-board' variety – a bench running fore-to-aft with a single back-rest. Passengers sat along both sides, with their backs to each other. Naturally, only men had clothing practical enough to enable them to climb the rungs on to the roof. Indeed, with the arrival of the crinoline it became very difficult for women to travel in an omnibus at all. However, the knife-board seats were the most popular, as Francis Wey, visiting from France, discovered:

We had heard so much about the London omnibuses, with their velvet upholstery and veneered panelling, that we were anxious to see these wonderful conveyances. So our amazement was great on boarding one in the Strand to find it narrow, rickety, jolting, dusty and extremely dirty. The only advantage of these vehicles is that they are closed by a door. The conductor stands outside on a small footboard, incessantly hailing passers-by. The custom, anyhow, is never to go inside an omnibus, even when it rains, if there is an inch of space unoccupied outside; women, children, even old people, fight to gain access to the top.

Sala explained why safety, as well as fashion, suggested avoiding the interior of the vehicle:

Never ride inside an omnibus. A friend of mine once had his tibia fractured by the diagonal brass rod that crosses the door; the door itself being slammed violently to, as is the usual custom, by the conductor. Another of my acquaintance was pitched head foremost from the interior, on the mockingly fallacious cry of 'all right' being given – was thrown on his head, and killed. Inside an omnibus you are subjected to innumerable vexations and annoyances. Sticks or parasols are poked in your chest and in the back of your neck, as a polite reminder that somebody wants to get out, and that you must seize the conductor by the skirt of his coat, or pinch him in the calf of the leg, as an equally polite request for him to stop; you are half suffocated by the steam of damp umbrellas; your toes are crushed to atoms as the passengers alight or ascend; you are very probably the next neighbour to persons suffering under vexatious ailments; it is ten to one that you suffer under the plague of babies; and five days out of the seven, you will have a pickpocket for a fellow-passenger. The rumbling, the jumbling, the jolting – the lurking ague in the straw when it is wet, and the peculiar omnibus fleas that lurk in it when it is dry, make the interior a place of terror and discomfort; whereas outside all is peace. You have room for your legs; you have the fresh air; you have the lively if not improving conversation of the driver and conductor, and you have the inestimable advantage of surveying the world in its workings as you pass along.

Max Schlesinger appreciated the importance that this relatively new institution had already assumed in British life, commenting that:

Among the middle classes of London, the omnibus stands immediately after air, tea, and flannel, in the list of the necessities of life.

Schlesinger's description of a typical specimen is somewhat at odds with that of the French visitor quoted above:

The outward appearance of the London omnibus is very prepossessing. It is always neat and clean, the horses strong and elegant; the driver is an adept at his art; the conductor is active, quick as thought, and untiring as the perpetuum mobile.
    The vehicle itself is an oblong square box, painted green, with windows at the sides and a large window in the door at the back. Many omnibuses are named after their chief stations.

Others luxuriate in names of a more fantastic description, and
the most conspicuous among them are the Waterloos, Nelsons,
Wellingtons, Taglionis, Atlases, etc.

Now the crew appears:

A man with an opera-hat, a blue, white-spotted cravat, coat of
dark-green cloth, trousers and waistcoat of no particular colour; his
boots are well polished, his chin is cleanly shaved. There is a proud
consciousness in the man's face; an easy, familiar carelessness
in his movements as he ascends. He takes his seat on the box,
and looks to right and left with a strange mixture of hauteur and
condescension, as much as to say: 'You may keep your hats on,
gentlemen.' He produces a pair of stout yellow gloves; he seizes the
reins and the whip – By Jove! It's the driver of the omnibus!
    Immediately after him ... another individual, whose bearing is
less proud. He is thin, shabbily dressed, and his hands are without
gloves. It is the conductor.

The vehicle sets off and it is clear that both men are actively in search of
prey. The conductor:

... makes a descent upon the pavement, lays hands on the maid
of all work that is just going home from the butcher's, and invites
her to take a seat on the 'bus'. He spies an elderly lady waiting at
the street-corner; he knows at once she is waiting for an omnibus,
but that she cannot muster resolution to hail one. He addresses
and secures her. Another unprotected female is caught soon after,
then a boy, and after him another woman. Our majestic coachman
is meanwhile quite as active as his colleague. He is never silent,
and shouts his 'Bank! Bank! Charing-cross!' at every individual
passenger on the pavement. Any spare moments he may snatch
from this occupation are devoted to his horses. He touches them
up with the end of his whip, and exhorts them to courage and
perseverance by means of that particular sound which holds
the middle between a hiss and a groan, and which none but the
drivers of London omnibuses can produce.

The driver explains that dealing with the traffic and the distraction of hunting for passengers are reflexes that can be learned:

'The city,' said he, 'is a training-school for carriage-osses and for any gent as would learn to drive. As for a man who isn't thoroughly up to it, I'd like to see him take the ribbons, that's all! 'specially with a long heavy 'bus behind and two osses as is going like blazes in front. I see many a country fellow in my time as funky [scared] as can be, sweating, cause why? He felt himself in a fix. And an oss, too, as has never been in the city afore, gets giddy in its head, and all shaky-like, and weak on its legs. But it's all habit, that's what it is with men and osses.'

Schlesinger was impressed not only with the skill of the driver but also with the detailed planning that went into the flow of this omnibus traffic. Elsewhere in his wanderings he came across the following scene:

Just look at that lumbering omnibus, thundering along at a sharp trot. It has reached the brink when the horses are stopped for a second; and at that moment a fellow makes a rush at the omnibus, bending his body almost under the wheels, and moving forward with the vehicle, which still proceeds, he unhooks the drag [a wooden wedge, used as a brake] and puts it to one of the hind-wheels. This done, he calls out 'All right!' The horses, sagacious creatures, understand the meaning of that sentence as well as the driver; they fall again into a sharp trot down the hill. At the bottom there is another human creature making a neck-or-nothing rush at the wheels, taking the drag off and hooking it on again. 'All right!' The horses stamp the pavement to the flying-about of sparks, the driver makes a noise which is half a whistle and half a hiss, and the omnibus rushes up the opposite bank.

    Those two men save the omnibus exactly one minute in each tour down Holborn Hill, for one minute each of them would lose if they were to stop to put on the drag. But one minute's loss to the many thousands who daily pass this way represents a considerable capital of time.

Competing with the hordes of buses on London's streets were even greater numbers of cabs. The 'hackney carriage' (a catch-all term for any form of public coach or hired vehicle) had been in use since the 17th century. By Dickens' time these four-wheeled carriages were called 'growlers'. There was also the two-wheeled cabriolet. The Dickensian cabriolet had a covered seat for the passenger, protected by an 'apron' (a mudguard screen) and a curtain, while the driver sat to his right, exposed to wind and rain. It was about one of these that Dickens wrote his essay on 'The Last Cab-Driver':

> His cabriolet was gorgeously painted – a bright red; and wherever we went, City or West End, Paddington or Holloway, there was the red cab, bumping up against the posts at the street corners, and turning in and out, among hackney-coaches, and drays, and carts, and wagons, and omnibuses, and contriving by some strange means or other, to get out of places which no other vehicle could have contrived to get into at all.
>
> It was omnipresent. You had only to walk down Holborn, or Fleet Street, or any of the principal thoroughfares in which there is a great deal of traffic. You had hardly turned into the street, when you saw a trunk or two lying on the ground: an uprooted post, a hat-box, a portmanteau, and a carpet-bag, and a horse in a cab standing by, looking about him with great unconcern.
>
> 'What's the matter here?'
>
> 'O'ny a cab, sir.'
>
> 'Anyone hurt?'
>
> 'O'ny the fare, sir. I see him a turnin' the corner, ven hump they cums agin the post, and out flies the fare like bricks.'
>
> Need we say it was the red cab; or that the gentleman with the straw in his mouth, who emerged so coolly from the chemist's shop nearby and philosophically climbing into the little dickey, started off at full gallop, was the red cab's licensed driver?

Cab-drivers were, as they are now, colourful London characters, and Dickens used them a number of times in his novels (the 'Pugnacious Cabman' is one of the first characters whom readers meet in *Pickwick Papers*). They were noticeably uncivil, especially when examining the

PLATE 1. St Paul's Cathedral and Queenhithe, seen from Southwark Bridge, c.1859. Before the creation, in 1870, of the Victoria Embankment – a granite quay and a broad avenue linking the City of London with Westminster – London's river front was a random collection of wharves, warehouses, moorings and stairs. Drawing on his youthful experiences in a riverside factory, Dickens used this setting to great effect in several novels.

PLATE 2. The Thames from Waterloo Bridge, 1842, depicting the river as a place of work and industry. Today the Houses of Parliament stand in the middle of this scene. London's low skyline is dominated by Westminster Abbey and, left of it, the turreted roof of St John's Church, Smith Square. The brewery at left is on the site of the London Eye. The statue of a lion, just visible on its roof, now stands at the foot of Westminster Bridge.

PLATE 3. A London street scene, 1835. Improved technology brought an explosion in printed advertisements to public spaces. The posters here tout the pleasures of Astley's Amphitheatre, Vauxhall Gardens, a masked ball and a concert by the renowned singer, Liza Vestris – a striking illustration of the varied entertainments offered by the capital.

PLATE 4. The Strand, looking east, 1824. The church of St Mary-le-Strand, like St Clement's behind, is still there. All else has changed. The large building at left is Exeter 'Change, a shopping arcade whose upper floors were occupied by a menagerie. The roaring of lions was often audible to passers-by.

PLATE 5. At the Dinner Table, 1860s. The development of photography made it possible to record domestic life with a level of detail previously unknown. This scene is highly posed, but it nonetheless conveys the atmosphere of comfort that characterized the homes of better-off Victorians.

PLATE 6. A gin shop, 1848. Water was often unsafe to drink and gin – at twopence a pint – offered a cheap narcotic. With no age limit on its sale, drunkards could include the very young. Unlike most public houses, this establishment is not dominated by men; here there is a wide mix of ages and sexes. As was usual, almost everyone wears their hat indoors.

PLATE 7. Street Breakfast, 1825. Stalls at which pedestrians could stop for an early morning repast could be found on many street corners, providing coffee and rolls. The woman wears a shawl and poke bonnet, some men still wear knee-breeches and most have top hats. The soldier has no civilian clothes to wear off duty. The man at left is a market porter, as can be seen from his headdress.

PLATE 8. Burlington Arcade opened in 1819. A covered passage with small shops that specialized in costly luxuries, its offerings included scented hair oil, silver dog collars and embroidered gloves. The trade in these items reflected the increasing spending power of the upper and middle classes. It retains its exclusive character today.

PLATE 9. Covent Garden Market, 1864. Originally the site of Westminster Abbey's market garden (Covent is a corruption of 'Convent', meaning, however, a monastery) this was the city's biggest vegetable market, but the congested site ultimately proved impractical and it was relocated in 1974. The buildings here, now put to other uses, look much the same as in Dickens' day. The market attracted scavengers looking for food at the end of each day.

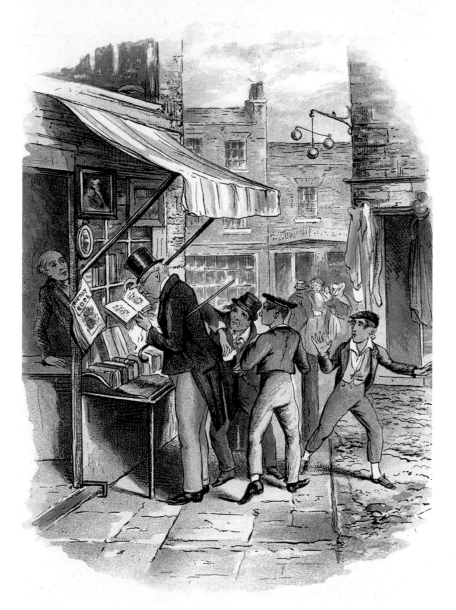

PLATE 10. Many criminals were children who had developed expertise in specialized activities. Here the Artful Dodger steals a handkerchief. The pockets on a cutaway coat were in the tails, which made theft a good deal easier. In the background is a pawnshop, symptomatic of widespread poverty – there were thousands of these throughout London.

PLATE 11. The General Post Office, 1860. This painting by George Elgar Hicks captures the last-minute rush to post letters and newspapers before the office closes at 6pm. The stampede was such a well-known daily event that tourists (seen here at left) came to watch. The artist was criticized for making the messenger boys look too clean.

PLATE 12. The life of an office clerk was relatively secure, but long years spent in cramped and uncomfortable working conditions took their toll, as can be seen in this cartoon. Many thousands commuted on foot every day across fields to the City, to spend the day hunched over tall desks.

PLATE 13. Offices of Dickens' era bore no resemblance to those of today. There were no women, no machines, and very little noise. Clerks sat on tall stools and worked at sloping desks, and the most junior employee would sit furthest from the fire. Many firms had only two or three staff.

PLATE 14. The Elephant and Castle, a south London public house (at centre) that gave its name to the surrounding district. It was, and remains, an important traffic hub, though now altered beyond recognition. This print conveys the sense of speed and bustle as coaches arrive and depart. The coach bringing Pip to London in *Great Expectations* would have come along the Old Kent Road (left).

PLATE 15. An omnibus driver and passenger. The omnibus began as an expensive, middle-class conveyance that provided free morning papers and, in the absence of bus stops, could be hailed and boarded anywhere. Drivers and conductors called out the route as they went along. Fierce competition between companies sometimes led rival conductors to squabble over passengers.

PLATE 16. A Third Class railway carriage. Though overcrowded and clearly uncomfortable, trains like this gave millions of people their first opportunity to journey more than few miles from home, and changed their habits of travel and settlement forever. These passengers, seated on wooden benches, and well-wrapped against draughts, paid a penny a mile.

PLATE 17. The railway network represented the biggest building project since the Egyptian pyramids, and the London stations – like the contemporary Crystal Palace – were the biggest secular buildings Londoners had seen. They began to change the scale of the city, which became a much grander, more imposing and less intimate place. Charing Cross, seen here, was one of the smaller termini.

fare, and Dickens advised his readers, when paying, not to try short-changing a man who can cause them to have an accident as they alight:

> In the event of your contemplating an offer of eightpence, on no
> account make the tender, or show the money, until you are safely
> on the pavement. It is very bad policy attempting to save the
> fourpence. You are very much in the power of a cabman, and he
> considers it a kind of fee not to do you any wilful damage.

As is the case throughout the world, cabs were seen as slow and their drivers as rude or deliberately malign. Pip travelled in a hackney carriage to visit the lawyer, Jaggers:

> Mr Jaggers sent me his address; it was Little Britain, and he had
> written after it on his card, 'just out of Smithfield, and close
> by the coach-office'. Nevertheless, a hackney coachman, who
> seemed to have as many capes to his greasy great-coat as he
> was years old, packed me up in his coach and hemmed me in
> with a folding and jingled barrier of steps, as if he was going to
> take me fifty miles. His getting on his box, which I remember
> to have been decorated with an old weather-stained pea-green
> hammercloth, moth-eaten into rags, was quite a work of time. It
> was a wonderful equipage, with six great coronets outside, and
> ragged things behind for I don't know how many footmen to hold
> on by. I had scarcely time to enjoy the coach and to think how
> like a straw-yard it was [straw was put on the floor for warmth],
> and yet how like a rag-shop, and to wonder why the horses' nose-
> bags were kept inside, when I observed the coachman beginning
> to get down, as if we were going to stop presently. And stop we
> presently did, in a gloomy street, at certain offices with an open
> door, whereon was painted MR JAGGERS.
> 'How much?' I asked the coachman
> The coachman answered, 'A shilling – unless you want to
> make it more.'

The other form of public transport ran on the river. The steamboat, often driven by side-wheels, had arrived in the Thames shortly before

Dickens came to London. From piers along both banks the boats ran a passenger service to Greenwich, Southend, Margate and other far-flung places along the river's north and south shores. They also made regular sailings across the Channel, enabling passengers to travel direct from the heart of London to the heart of Europe. This was, of course, significant to the plot of *Great Expectations*. Pip described the shipping below London Bridge:

> Old London Bridge was soon passed, and Old Billingsgate market with its oyster-boats and Dutchmen, and the White tower and Traitor's Gate, and we were in among the tiers of shipping. Here were the Leith, Aberdeen, and Glasgow steamers, loading and unloading goods, and looking immensely high out of the water as we passed alongside; here were colliers by the score and score, with the coal-whippers plunging off stages and deck, as counterweights to measures of coal swinging up, which were then rattled over the side into barges; here, at her moorings, was tomorrow's steamer for Rotterdam, whose bowsprit we crossed.

When seeking an escape-route for Magwitch, Pip examined the options:

> It had seemed to me, in the many anxious considerations I had given the point, almost indifferent what port we made for – Hamburg, Rotterdam, Antwerp – the place signified little, so that he was got out of England. Any foreign steamer that fell in our way and would take us up, would do. I had always proposed to myself to get him well down the river in the boat: certainly well beyond Gravesend, which was a critical place for search or inquiry if suspicion were afoot. As foreign steamers would leave London at about the time of high-water, our plan would be to get down the river by a previous ebb-tide, and lie by in some quiet spot until we could pull off to one.

On a more mundane level, hundreds used the steamers as a means of commuting to work. Like the omnibuses, they were too costly for anyone below the clerical class to use. They may have been swifter than a wheeled vehicle held up in traffic, but their passage through the noisome waters of the Thames was more unpleasant. In spite of this, the passengers had an opportunity to appreciate the majesty of London's riverfront. Sala witnessed the morning commute:

> On the broad – would that I could add the silvery and sparkling
> – bosom of Father Thames, they have been borne in swift, grimy
> little steamboats, crowded with living freights from Chelsea, and
> Pimlico, and Vauxhall piers, from Hungerford, Waterloo, Temple,
> Blackfriars, and Southwark – straight by the hay-boats, with their
> lateen sails discoloured in a manner that would delight a painter,
> straight by Thames police hulks, by four and six-oared cutters,
> by coal-barges, and great lighters laden with bricks and ashes and
> toiling towards Putney and Richmond; by oozy wharves and grim-
> chimneyed factories; by little, wheezy, tumbledown waterside
> public houses; by breweries, and many-windowed warehouses; by
> the stately gardens of the Temple, and the sharp-pointed spires of
> city churches, and the great dome of Paul's looming blue in the
> morning, to the Old Shades Pier, hard by London Bridge. There
> is landing and scuffling and pushing; the quivering old barges,
> moored in the mud, and swaying and groaning beneath trampling
> feet. Then, for an instant, Thames Street, Upper and Lower,
> is invaded by an ant-hill swarm of spruce clerks, who mingle
> strangely with the fish-women and the dock-porters. But the
> insatiable counting-houses soon swallow them up.

For the rest of the century, and throughout the opening years of the next one, the horse continued to co-exist comfortably with the machine as a provider of public transport. Though within a few years of Queen Victoria's death motor-taxis were to challenge the dominance of the hansom cab (a two-wheeled cabriolet that became an icon of the age), and although motor-buses appeared a few years later, it was not until October 1911 that the last horse-drawn passenger vehicle was withdrawn from service by the London General Omnibus Company. The transport revolution was a gradual process.

ENTERTAINMENT

**The sight-showers, we thus see, were in high activity.
We have seen, in some half-quiet thoroughfare of Lambeth,
or of Clerkenwell, a dingy cloth spread upon the road, and a
ring of children called together at the sound of a horn, to behold
a dancing lass in all the finery of calico trousers and spangles,
and a tumbler with his hoop: and on one occasion sixpence was
extracted from our pockets, because the said tumbler had his hoop
splendid with ribbons, which showed him to have a reverence for
the poetry and antiquity of his calling.**

Above the thunder and rattle of traffic, the sound of music was
always audible in Dickens' London. The streets abounded in
performers and musicians of both sexes, all ages and many nationalities.
There were singers of ballads and popular songs who sold copies of the
words and rendered *ad nauseam* the songs of the day; no doubt 'Cherry
Ripe', 'Hot Codlins' or 'Tipitywitchet' got on the nerves of many people
as much as their equivalents do today. In present-day London there are
scores of street performers; in those days there were thousands. They
were impossible to avoid, for, unlike their modern counterparts, they
did not confine themselves to major thoroughfares but brought their
noise and spectacle into residential areas, if only in the hope of being
paid to go away.

As well as singers, there were instrumentalists creating a host of
different sounds. In the city centre or the quieter streets and squares of
the outskirts could be heard the blare of trumpets, the crash of cymbals,
the shriek of a penny-whistle, the nasal whine of a hurdy-gurdy, the
boom of a drum, the shrill of pan pipes or the shimmer of a harp. Barrel
organs, almost always operated by Italians, were so commonplace that

Thomas Carlyle, who hated them, had to seek refuge in a soundproof study. Though some players were beggars, others were professionals with a good deal of ability, both as musicians and managers: investment in expensive instruments, and possibly the employment of assistants, required the skills of a businessman.

For the many who had some form of disability, their talent was their lifeline. Henry Mayhew interviewed a man, blind from birth, who had been a street musician for 23 years. He played the violin, but had contrived an ingenious wooden frame that enabled him simultaneously to play a cello with his foot. His statement that 'My parents were poor, but managed to have me taught music' must have reflected a common experience, for it guaranteed at least modest earning power for as long as one could endure to work out of doors.

As well as individuals, there were entire bands to be heard on street corners. They might be members of a theatre orchestra, who were free during the daytime. And, like so many of the capital's street performers, they could have been foreigners. Throughout the 19th century and until the First World War, German bands were a common sight, often dressed in quasi-uniform.

Music was also the required accompaniment to another popular entertainment: the Punch and Judy show. Though now associated mainly with the seaside, it was then a favourite London attraction. Originally from Italy, it had been a staple of English childhood since the 17th century, and in Dickens' time was as popular as ever. Staged, as today, in a portable tent just large enough for one person to sit in, working the glove puppets above their head, the show required a second person – perhaps the puppeteer's wife – to draw in the audience and collect the money. The stage and equipment might be transported in a small donkey-cart, pushed in a barrow, or simply carried on the backs of the proprietors. A show would often be accompanied by the music of pan pipes (a useful instrument because it could be tucked into the waistcoat and played without using the hands, leaving them free to play something else, such as a drum or a tambourine), and a trumpet fanfare or the banging of a drum would announce that the performance was about to begin. In *The Old Curiosity Shop*, Dickens created the characters Codlin and Short, who travelled the country with a Punch and Judy show:

Short blew a blast upon the brazen trumpet and carolled a fragment of a song in that hilarious tone common to Punches and their consorts. If the people hurried to the windows, Mr Codlin pitched the temple, and hastily unfurling the drapery and concealing Short therewith, flourished hysterically on the pipes and performed an air. Then the entertainment began as soon as might be; Mr Codlin having the responsibility of deciding on its length and of protracting or expediting the time for the hero's final triumph over the enemy of mankind, according as he judged that the after-crop of halfpence would be plentiful or scant. When it had been gathered in to the last farthing, he resumed his load and on they went again.

From the 1820s, this form of entertainment was joined by a rival: 'Fantoccini', another Italian import, which used a similar portable booth. It was, likewise, a two-person operation, accompanied by the same drums, pipes and trumpets, but with string puppets to perform the plays. There were other variations on the marionette theme. A character interviewed by Henry Mayhew recalled his career as one of three operators of a mechanical puppet show. His account hints at two important difficulties that faced street performers: the prospect of lean times during the winter months, when audiences would not want to linger out-of-doors, and the possibility that, with changes in fashion, the public would lose interest in what had once been an exciting novelty:

I took up with a foreigner named Green, in the clock-work figure line. The figures were a Turk called Bluebeard, a sailor, a lady called Lady Catarina, and Neptune's car, which we called Nelson's car as well; but it was Neptune's car by rights. These figures danced on a table, when taken out of a box. Each had its own dance when wound up.

First came my Lady Catarina. She, and the others of them, were full two feet high. She had a cork body, and a very handsome silk dress, or muslin, according to the fashion, or the season. Black in Lent, according to what the nobility wore. Lady Catarina, when wound up, danced a reel for seven minutes, the sailor a hornpipe, and Bluebeard shook his head, rolled his eyes, and moved his

sword, just as natural as life. Neptune's car went straight or
round the table, as it was set.

We showed our performances in the houses of the nobility, and
would get ten or twelve shillings at a good house, where there
were children. I had a third share, and in town and country we
cleared fifty shillings a week, at least, every week, among the
three of us, after all our keep and expenses were paid.

A month before Christmas we used to put the figures by, for the
weather didn't suit; and then we went with a galantee [shadow
puppet] show of a magic lantern. We showed it on a white sheet,
or on the ceiling, big or little, in the houses of the gentlefolk, and
the schools where there was a breaking-up. It was shown by way
of a treat to the scholars. There was Harlequin, and Billy Button,
and such-like. We had ten and sixpence and fifteen shillings for
each performance, and did very well indeed. I have that galantee
show now, but it brings in very little. Green's dead, and all in
the line's dead, but me. The galantee show don't answer, because
magic lanterns are so cheap in the shops. When we started, magic
lanterns wasn't so common.

Those who were unable to buy instruments and equipment, or who did
not belong to a troupe of performers, had to be clever to survive. The
fact that some were foreigners who barely spoke English must have made
the challenge they faced as jobbing entertainers even greater. One of
the most intriguing men whom Mayhew discovered was an Italian from
Genoa, a former soldier who had lost a leg fighting against the Austrians
in an elite sharpshooter regiment. Dubbed the 'Gun-Exercise Exhibitor',
his only talent was for reciting the manual of arms (in French) while
performing the drill movements of the Piedmontese Army (as well as
his wooden leg would allow) using his crutch in place of a rifle. He
yelled the orders to himself as if he were addressing a company, and
went smartly through the motions with his makeshift firelock, loading,
ramming in the shot, presenting and firing. It is difficult to imagine this
earning much money, but he was apparently able to feed himself and pay
for lodgings. The only thing that threatened his slender livelihood, he
confessed, was the fear that his voice was suffering from years of shouting
in cold weather.

Another ex-serviceman who walked the streets was a sailor who carried on his shoulders a model of a fully rigged warship. This, and a small child (presumably his daughter) whom he strapped on his back in a wooden box, rendered him so conspicuous that he was sketched by George Scharf in 1840 and interviewed by Mayhew in the 1850s. The new satirical magazine, *Punch*, described him in its first volume in 1841:

Jack [the generic term for any British sailor] with a cheerful heart goes forth into the highways and byways to sing 'the dangers of the sea' and to collect from the pitying passers-by the coppers that drop 'like angel visits' into his little oil-skin hat.

The most remarkable specimen of the class may be frequently seen about the streets of London, carrying at his back a good-sized box, inside which, and peeping through a sort of port-hole, a pretty little girl of some two years old exhibits her chubby face. Surmounting the box, a small model of a frigate, all a-taut and ship-shape, represents 'Her Majesty's frigate Billy-Ruffian' [the nickname of HMS *Bellerophon*, famous in the Napoleonic wars] on board o' which the exhibitor lost his blessed limb.

Jack's songs, as we have remarked, all relate to the sea – he is a complete repository of old ballads and fo'c'sle chants. 'Tom Bowling', 'Lovely Nan', 'Poor Jack' and 'Lash'd to the Helm', but 'The Bay of Biscay' is his crack performance ... Having chosen a quiet street, where the appearance of mothers with babies in the windows prognosticates a plentiful supply of coppers, Jack commences by pitching his voice uncommonly strong, and tossing Poll and the Billy-Ruffian from side to side, to give an idea of how Neptune serves the Navy ...

A more common form of street entertainment for those without musical or acting ability was the exhibiting of 'Happy Families': collections of dogs, cats and mice, or dogs and rabbits, that sat peacefully together. These could be extensive. The owner of one collection told Mayhew:

Mine, that is the one I have the care of, is the strongest – fifty-four creatures. The others will average forty each, or 214 birds and beasts. Our only regular places now are Waterloo-bridge and the

> National Gallery. The expense of keeping my fifty-four is 12s. a-week, and in a good week we take 30s; and in a bad week, not 8s. It's only a poor trade, though there are more good weeks than bad.

There were innumerable other clockwork, sleight-of-hand or peep-show attractions. Londoners had an insatiable need for diversion. Any unusual spectacle or ability could earn money, but those involved could only expect to earn pennies, and it took a great many of these to make a living.

There was a perception among Dickens' contemporaries that, as the century reached its midpoint, the rambunctious street entertainments of the Georgians were in decline and that the Great Exhibition, as well as marking a shift toward respectability in public attitudes, had brought a seriousness to public pleasures that had previously been lacking. The publisher and commentator Charles Knight clearly saw this, and welcomed it, when he wrote:

> Take an example from the man who, when the planets are shining brightly out of a serene heaven, plants a telescope in Leicester Square or St Paul's Church Yard, and finds enough passengers who are glad to catch glimpses of worlds unseen to the naked eye, and forget for a moment the small things which surround us here. Open the great books of Nature, of Science, and of Art to the people; and they will not repine that the days of conjurors, and puppet-shows, and dancing bears have passed away.

Advertised Amusement

The miniature street spectacles had to compete for the attention of the public with the new phenomenon of advertising, which was an entertainment in itself. Men paraded the streets carrying placards describing products, exhibitions, medicines and forthcoming events, often with extraordinary costumes or props (Warren's blacking firm employed men to walk in single file wearing giant blacking-jars). There were also huge, clumsy vehicles, which attracted notice by their ability to stop the traffic. Max Schlesinger, walking one night in the neighbourhood of Great Russell Street, encountered some of these:

Crowds of advertising monsters move about in various shapes, to the right and to the left, walking, rolling on wheels, and riding on horseback. Behold, rolling down from Oxford Street, three immense wooden pyramids – their outsides are painted all over with Egyptian hieroglyphics and with monumental letters in the English language. These pyramids display faithful portraits of Isis and Osiris, of cats, storks, and of the Apis; and amidst these old-curiosity-shop gods, any Englishman may read an inscription, printed in letters not much longer than a yard, from which it appears that there is now on view a panorama of Egypt – one more beautiful, interesting and instructive than was ever exhibited in London.

The pyramids advance within three yards from where we stand, and, for a short time, they take their ease in the very midst of all the lights, courting attention. But the policeman on duty respects not the monuments of the Pharoahs; he moves his hand, and the drivers of the pyramids, though hidden in their colossal structures, see and understand the sign; they move on.

But here is another monstrous shape – a mosque, with its cupola blue and white, surmounted by the crescent. The driver is a light-haired boy, with a white turban and a sooty face. There is no mistaking that fellow for an Arab; and, nevertheless, the turban and the soot make profound impression. On the back of the mosque there is an advertisement, which tells us that Dr Doem is proprietor of a most marvellous Arabian medicine, warranted to cure the bite of mad dogs and venomous reptiles generally; even so, that a person so bitten, if he but takes Dr Doem's medicine, shall feel no more inconvenience than he would feel from a very savage leader in the *Morning Herald*. The mosque, the blue crescent, the gaudy colours, and the juvenile Arab from the banks of the Thames, have merely been got up to attract attention. There need be no very intimate connexion between the things puffed and the street symbolics which puff them.

Hark! A peal of trumpets! Another advertising machine rushes out of the gloom of Museum Street. In this instance the Orient is not put in requisition. The turn-out is thoroughly English.

Two splendid cream-coloured horses, richly harnessed; a dark green chariot of fantastic make, in shape like a half-opened shell,

and tastefully ornamented with gilding and pictures; on the
box a coachman in red and gold, looking respectable and almost
aristocratic, with his long whip on his knee; and behind him the
trumpeters, seated in the chariot, and proclaiming its advent.
In this manner have the people of London of late months been
invited to Vauxhall – to that same Vauxhall which, under the
regency, attracted all the wealth, beauty and fashion in England
– which, to this very day, still attracts hundreds of thousands.
Even Vauxhall – the old and famous – makes no exception to the
common lot; it is compelled to have its posters, its newspaper
advertisements, and its advertising vans.

In no other town would such tricks be necessary conditions
of existence; but here, where everything is grand and bulky
... where every hour has its novelty – even the most solid
undertakings must assume the crying colour of charlatanism.

The same may be said of great institutions of a different kind;
of fire and insurance companies; of railways and steamers; and
of theatres – from Punch's theatre in the Strand, upwards to the
Royal Opera, which ransacks Europe for musical celebrities and
which, nonetheless, must condescend to magnify its own glory on
gigantic many-coloured posters, though it has managed, up to the
present day, to do without the vans, trumpets and sham Nubians.

Panoramic Pleasure

The Egyptian Panorama touted by those wooden pyramids was typical
of a more genteel and instructive form of entertainment, aimed at those
with shillings rather than pennies to spend on pleasure. Panoramas were
a relatively new notion in the middle of the century, equivalent, perhaps,
to the television travelogue of our time. They gave superficial glimpses of
other lands and, more importantly, in an era in which many people were
illiterate, they offered education to those who could not learn about the
world in any other way. They were based on drawings, made *en route* by
travellers and turned into large-scale paintings by a team of artists, so
their authenticity depended on the accuracy of the original sketches,
and the painters' imaginations sometimes over-embellished the scenes.

Clever use of sound and lighting enabled the seas and rivers to roll, storms to break and the sun and moon to rise and set. There were several panoramas in London, for they enjoyed a tremendous vogue in the first half of the century. *London as it is Today*, published in 1851, informed the public about what they might expect to see:

> From America, we have received the idea of the Moving Panorama, which by a motion imparted to the canvas, the opposite from that of a person supposed to travel in a boat or carriage, exhibits a succession of objects to the extent of hundreds of miles, with little fatigue or inconvenience, and what is equally important in these times of economy, at very little expense to the spectator. Thus in a few hours we have explored the whole navigable shores of the Mississippi in a few days, and for a few shillings, we have been able to see the whole course of the Nile, from above ancient Thebes, with its vast wrecks of olden magnificence, through the desert to grand Cairo and the sea; besides the varied and lengthened route of the overland mail to India, and the beauties and majesty of Constantinople, the Dardanelles, and the Bosphorus, and even to visit the remote shores of New Zealand, and the still more estranged and wondrous regions of the North Pole – by summer and winter. The panorama of New Zealand is chiefly interesting to emigrants anxious to catch a distant, faint anticipation of their land of promise. The school-master and his pupils; parents, philosophers, and the rising generation, are all interested in the success of these pictorial illustrations; travellers returning from the several depicted regions will, with pleasure, recognize the scenes of their past exertions, if they are correct, and criticize severely where otherwise; and the inexperienced, about to visit foreign lands, may from them acquire a certain fund of knowledge of their future destiny.

But reviewers could be unforgiving of inconsistencies and mistakes:

> It is an accurate representation as far as could be by artists in England working from faithful sketches by another hand, and under the direction of the gentleman who made those sketches:

it is very cleverly painted, and exhibits a variety of buildings, jungle, and effects. But whilst we praise the amount of skill and talent, we object strongly to the abuse of both; shifting scenes and dioramic effects, instead of modestly assisting nature and art, are made, in many instances, to out-step them, and destroy all faith and illusion; sometimes in defiance of common sense, as in the beautiful moon-light scene, where the reflected light moves on the flowing waters – exaggeration represents the river as running at the rate of three hundred or four hundred miles an hour, and the boats and other objects in front of the scene are immovably still, while the distance appears to move. We are severe on these inconsistencies and clap-traps, because they tend to corrupt public taste, and to bring into contempt and disrepute an otherwise valuable and commendable mode of imparting knowledge.

The best-known panorama was the Colosseum in Regent's Park. A copy of the Pantheon in Rome, it was an important architectural landmark and added to the classical dignity of the stuccoed terraces around the Park. It has long since vanished, but is resurrected by this detailed description in the same guidebook:

It was erected in 1824, from the designs of Mr Decimus Burton, and is 130 feet in diameter by 110 feet in height; it is polygonal in form, and is surmounted by an immense glazed cupola. In front is a grand portico, with six large fluted columns of the Grecian-Doric order, supporting a bold pediment. The entrance to the building is from the Regent's Park; on descending a broad staircase, the doorway of the Museum of Sculpture is on the left hand; and on passing through it the spectator is immediately within a noble rotunda, lighted by an entire dome of richly cut glass, to the extent of several thousand feet. The frieze is enriched with the entire Panathenic procession from the Elgin Marbles, over which are twenty allegorical subjects in fresco painting, on panels. On the floor around, in recess, and in the room are numerous admirable specimens of sculpture, by several of the most eminent artists of Europe, consisting of colossal statues, minor figures beautifully wrought, and busts of eminent persons; and round the room are

couches covered with embroidered velvet, for the convenience
of visitors. In the centre of this apartment is an immense organ,
performances on which during the afternoon and evening add
greatly to the gratification of the company. Beneath this instrument
is the entrance to the staircase leading to the admirably executed
Panorama of LONDON BY DAY. This admirable work, exhibiting
a panoramic view of London, taken from the top of St Paul's, was
painted by Mr E.T. Paris, from sketches made by Mr Horner, and
presents the rare combination of minute detail, with a truth of
effect absolutely amounting to deception. This painting, which
is exhibited during the day, is in the evening followed by the
extraordinary panoramic view of PARIS BY NIGHT, a work
of great power. Standing on a lofty eminence, the spectator sees
spread around him a mighty city, the gay inhabitants crowding
the marts of commerce, or the numerous places of fashionable
resort. It well supports the high position in public favour which
this establishment has obtained, it being one of the most important
exhibitions in the metropolis, alike unequalled for the magnitude of
its resources, and the taste which is displayed in their development.

Another example of the species was to be found in Leicester Square.
This one, the brainchild of Thomas Burford, had been opened 30 years
earlier than the Colosseum. The guidebook explained what it offered:

This gentleman's ever active pencil places before our view, in
rapid succession, every spot celebrated in ancient or modern
history, or deriving éclat from recent passing events. One of
the present subjects is a painting of the Arctic Regions, from
drawings taken by Lieutenant Browne, R.N. of HMS Enterprise,
and presented to Mr Burford by the Admiralty: also the Lakes of
Killarney, and the Ruins of Pompeii. The views are open from ten
o'clock till dusk, all the year round. Admission, one shilling each
view; or two shillings and sixpence for the three.

Yet another establishment offered views of far-flung places, and again
the result appeared to be a combination of breathtaking artistry and
sloppiness – in this case the fact that the work was not quite finished:

The Polyrama comprises views of two hundred miles of scenery, it approaches more to the full appearance of the real proportions, and in several instances astounds us by the effect of unexpected vastness; executed in a bold, sometimes hasty, dashing manner, it arrives at its object almost without any assistance from dioramic effects, by its own force of light and shade, and a masterly use of knowledge and perspective; and, above all, by an untampered truthfulness, the natural consequence of the same person working the painting from his own sketches from nature, with all the vivid recollections of circumstances. It blazes in sun-shine, and frowns in a majesty that partakes largely of the historical character, but we see no reason why the adjuncts of dioramic effects, more general finish, more softening of troubled skies, and here and there the obliteration of a patch of uncovered canvas which, though not larger than a fan, detracts from the illusion, may not be attended to.

Even more ambitious, perhaps, was an attraction that enabled the public to see the entire planet at once:

Mr Wylde's Model of the Globe. In the centre of Leicester Square, is situated in an octagonal brick edifice of unpretending exterior, but of considerable size, topped by a metal-covered cupola. The visitor passes into the interior of the Globe, and there gains a view of the whole world.

The Globe existed for only a decade, but while it lasted was one of the best-known attractions of London. The public ascended a series of levels, which involved them in a tour of the earth, and at each level there were guides to explain the significant features.

All the splendours of entertainment that London could offer were overshadowed by the Crystal Palace, a colossal glass-and-iron structure erected in Hyde Park to house the Great Exhibition of arts and industries, which was held between May and October 1851. The building became, overnight, one of the splendours of Europe, and attracted six million visitors from Britain and overseas. Dickens ignored it in his writings though his contemporary, William Thackeray, called it 'The vastest and sublimest popular festival that the world has ever witnessed.' It housed an exhibition of 19,000 items of machinery and technology, manufactured goods, art and curiosities. When it was opened, in a magnificent ceremony at which Queen Victoria presided, *The Times* boasted:

> The edifice, the treasures of art collected therein, the assemblage and the solemnity of the occasion, all conspired to suggest something even more than sense could scan, or imagination attain. Around [the important guests], amidst them, and over their heads, was displayed all that is useful or beautiful in nature or in art. Above them rose a glittering arch far more lofty and spacious than the vaults of even our noblest cathedrals. Some saw in it the second and more glorious inauguration of their Sovereign; some a solemn dedication of art and its stores.

When the Great Exhibition ended, it was decided to preserve the structure that had been built for it; three years later, greatly enlarged, the Crystal Palace reopened on a site on the top of Sydenham Hill, south of London, as a venue for musical concerts, exhibitions and festivals. When this scheme had been proposed, one of those involved had echoed Charles Knight's earlier comments on the rising tone of public entertainment:

> If for the mass of our population we could provide some more refined amusements than those of Greenwich [Fair] or, worse than all, the gin-palace or the saloon, we would go a great way towards advancing the character of the English nation. What was wanting for the elevation of our working classes was that very description of refinement which it might be hoped would be affronted by contemplating the marvels of nature and art in a palace. If the palace be made worthy of the people in England, the people of England would flock in millions to it.

Its sheer scale dwarfed all the other attractions, and its elaborate interiors, including re-creations of Egyptian, Greek, Roman and Renaissance monuments as well as a fountain made of crystal, provided generations of visitors with a potted history of world culture. In its grounds were fountains rivalling those at Versailles, as well as a funfair, an exhibition of life-sized models of dinosaurs (which are still there) and a weekly firework display. It remained a very popular place of resort until well into the following century, but financial difficulties and changing public taste led to its decline. The building was destroyed by fire in 1936.

Entertaining Animals

For those interested in the animal kingdom, there were collections of wild beasts to admire. The Zoological Gardens in Regents Park were opened in 1828 at the instigation of Sir Stamford Raffles, who almost a decade earlier had founded the city of Singapore. The gardens superseded the menagerie that had existed at the Tower of London since the Middle Ages (the creatures from this, and from another collection at Windsor, had been incorporated into it) and were a welcome contrast to the indoor menagerie at Exeter 'Change in the Strand. Described as 'probably the most beautiful lounge in the metropolis', the zoo was laid out as a garden, in which were set the various buildings containing the animals. An 1851 guidebook provides a picture of the scene:

> From the rustic entrance lodges runs a broad terrace walk, bordered with a choice variety of flowers, and continued over the lower ground at the same level for some distance by a handsome viaduct; beneath which is a long range of roomy cages, forming one of the most striking objects in the gardens, and in which will be found an extensive collection of carnivorous animals. To the right of the terrace walk, immediately on entering, is a shaded winding path, an opening in the foliage of which discloses a fine view of the park; and in the foreground graze several rare ruminant animals. Dispersed throughout the grounds with a view to producing as picturesque an effect as possible will be found numerous graceful buildings, admirably adapted for the wants of their various inmates.

As for the creatures living in this setting:

The collection of rare and beautiful specimens is large: on the 1st of January, 1850, it consisted of 1,361 living animals: 354 mammalia, 853 birds and 154 reptiles, amongst whom we would point out as most particularly worthy of the attention of the visitor, a remarkably fine specimen of the rhinoceros; an immense white polar bear; the graceful giraffes; the fierce aurochs; the sacred Brahmin bull; the spotted leopard; the intelligent-looking seal; the patient llama; and an immense land tortoise, the gift of Her Majesty; the kingly vultures; the soaring eagles; the swift ostrich; the fine collection of owls; the terrific pythons; and the deadly cobra capello, or hooded snake; but during the last few months the hippopotamus, and his Nubian keeper, have been the reigning favourites. The various animals are exhibited in paddocks, dens and aviaries, suited to their several habits.

Four of the giraffes had arrived in 1836 from the Sudan, where they had been purchased by the Society for £700, and with them came three Arab attendants. They had made a magnificent entrance into London by walking all the way to Regent's Park from their landing-place at Blackwall. The effect of this apparition can easily be imagined.

The zoo was the subject of tremendous public interest. The introduction of a new exhibit was often a major event, announced in the newspapers and guaranteeing crowds of curious visitors. This notice in *The Times* on 2 February 1852 was typical of the excitement generated:

Zoological Gardens, Regent's park – the Hippopotamus, presented by His Highness the Viceroy of Egypt, the Elephant Calf and many recent additions are Exhibited daily. Admission 1 shilling, Mondays 6d.

London Zoo was not the only place in the city in which exotic animals could be seen. South of the river, in Walworth, were the Surrey Zoological Gardens. Opened in 1831, these became the new home of the animals removed from Exeter 'Change and, with a 6ha/15-acre site that included a lake, gave them a far more appropriate setting than their cramped quarters in the Strand. This collection also included giraffes, with Nubian attendants, as well as elephants, llamas, reindeer and a giant tortoise on which children were able to ride. Like its rival in Regent's Park, it received gifts of animals, such as a pair of dromedaries from Egypt's Ottoman ruler. The guidebook stated that:

> The avenues to the several buildings are planted with upwards of two hundred varieties of the most choice and hardy forest trees, of this and other countries, forming a complete arboretum, all of which are clearly labelled. In the centre is a large circular lake, three acres in extent, in which are numerous aquatic birds. On the right of the lake is a large, well-planned and well-ventilated, circular, glazed building, having four entrances; in the centre are places of the carnivori. The collection of animals, birds, and reptiles is large, and is continually receiving new accessions; altogether forming a most interesting and instructive resort. The panoramic views introduced on the borders of the lake, and which are changed annually, and are much admired; and with the fireworks form great objects of attraction during the summer season.

A visit from Queen Victoria and her consort, Prince Albert, in 1848 enabled the Surrey Zoological Gardens to be styled 'Royal'. The zoo closed only eight years later but, because of its setting and facilities, the place was reinvented as a major concert venue and flourished in this role until two years after Dickens' death, when the site was sold for building.

A short distance across the fields from Walworth was an even more eminent place of entertainment, 'Astley's Royal Equestrian Amphitheatre' in Lambeth. Dating from 1768 and rebuilt almost continually following periodic fires, it had been founded by Philip Astley, a former cavalry soldier who demonstrated horsemanship in a sawdust-strewn ring, originating the form that the circus has followed ever since. It was constructed largely from ships' timbers and had a canvas ceiling. In 1824 it was sold by Astley's family and the new owner, Andrew Ducrow, expanded its repertoire from simple equestrian displays to elaborate horseback performances that included acrobats, clowns and mock battles. Because it was exciting, amusing and respectable, Astley's was extremely popular with families, particularly celebrating children's birthdays or in school holidays. Adding to the affection in which it was held was the fact that many children's parents had themselves been taken there in their youth. A favourite haunt of Dickens, it was mentioned in *Bleak House* and *The Old Curiosity Shop* (in which Kit Nubbles took his family there four times a year). It was also the subject of one of the *Sketches by Boz*. Through Dickens' descriptions we can sense the excitement that its very name conjured up – the scent of straw and sawdust, gas-jets and greasepaint and horses – that would have thrilled the generations who watched its performers:

> There is no place which recalls so strongly our recollections of childhood as Astley's. It was not a 'Royal Amphitheatre' in those days; but the whole character of the place was the same, the pieces were the same, the clown's jokes were the same, the riding-masters were equally grand, the comic performers equally witty, the tragedians equally hoarse, and the 'highly-spirited chargers' equally spirited. Astley's has altered for the better – we have changed for the worse ...
>
> We defy anyone who has been to Astley's two or three times, and is consequently capable of appreciating the perseverance with which the same jokes are repeated night after night, and season after season, not to be amused with one part of the performance at least – we mean the scenes in the circle. For ourself, we know that when the hoop, composed of jets of gas, is let down, the curtain drawn up, the orange peel cleared away and the sawdust shaken, with mathematical precision, into a complete circle, we feel as much enlivened as the youngest child present; and actually join in the laugh which follows the clown's shrill shout of 'Here we are!' just for old acquaintance' sake. Nor can we quite divest ourself of our old feeling of reverence for the riding-master, who follows the clown with a long whip in his hand, and bows to the audience with graceful dignity.

The adult Dickens' love of this place is evident in this scene from *The Old Curiosity Shop*:

> Dear, dear, what a place it looked, that Astley's! with all the paint, gilding, and looking-glass; the vague smell of horses suggestive of coming wonders, the curtain that hid such gorgeous mysteries;

the clean white sawdust down in the circus; the company coming
in and taking their places; the fiddlers looking carelessly up at
them while they tuned their instruments, as if they didn't want
the play to begin, and knew it all before hand! What a glow was
that which burst upon them all, when that long, clear, brilliant
row of lights came slowly up; and what feverish excitement when
the little bell rang and the music began in good earnest, with
strong parts for the drums, and sweet effects for the triangles!
Well might Barbara's mother say to Kate's mother that the gallery
was the place to see from, and wonder it wasn't much dearer than
the boxes, and well might Barbara feel doubtful whether to laugh
or cry, in her flutter of delight.

Outings

There were many other opportunities for family expeditions. *The Times*
of 2 February 1852 listed two of them, one of which was a troupe of
performing fleas:

> Russian fleas – 200 of these little creatures are Exhibiting daily,
> from one till 10, at 5 Leicester-square. Their performances
> astonishing all beholders. Fleas of all nations, giving their varied
> entertainment, stage-coach and omnibus conveyance &c. Kossuth
> on four Austrian fleas; Louis Napoleon on the Russian flea
> Hercules, 5 years old. Admission 1 shilling.

Another was an attraction that is still part of many visitors' experience
of London:

> Kossuth, the Hungarian exile [involved in the 1848 revolution
> against Austrian rule, he had had to flee to Turkey, but was a
> much talked-about figure] is now added to Mme Tussaud & Son's
> exhibition, and five beautiful varieties of the Bloomer Costume,
> by which the public may judge if this dress can ever become
> popular. Admission – Large Room and Hall of Kings, 1 shilling,
> Napoleon shrine and Chamber of Horrors, 6d.

The famous Tussaud waxworks were created by a young French woman who had come to England in 1802. She had begun her 'career' in prison during the Revolution, modelling the heads of guillotined aristocrats, some of them her friends. The exhibition was established in Marylebone in 1835, occupying part of the Baker Street Bazaar. It was described in *London as it is Today*:

The visitor on entering passes through a small hall, tastefully decorated with casts from the antique, and proceeds by a wide staircase to a saloon at its summit, which is also richly ornamented. Here, at a small table, sits a lady who receives admission money, an office which for so many years was performed by the late Madame Tussaud herself [she died in 1850], and numerous of our readers will doubtless remember her as she sat there, easy and self-possessed, her accent at once proclaiming her gallic origin. Over the principal entrance is an orchestra, in which during the evening exhibitions, appropriate music is performed.

Not quite a museum was the Egyptian Hall near the eastern end of Piccadilly. This large and conspicuous building, its façade an elaborate pastiche of Egyptian architecture and decoration, hosted a number of important exhibitions. In 1816 Napoleon's carriage was displayed there, attracting 10,000 visitors a day. Four years later the Egyptian collection of the Italian archaeologist Belzoni proved another 'blockbuster', as did the displaying in 1844 of the American midget General Tom Thumb, who arrived at the door in his own miniature carriage.

On Display

The capital's (and Britain's) most important repository of curiosities was the British Museum. Opened in 1759, this was housed until the 1840s in Montague House, a 17th-century nobleman's mansion built of stone and red brick in French style on the site of the present museum in Bloomsbury. The building was undeniably elegant, with its soaring chimneys, scalloped roofs and rows of leaded windows, but it was hopelessly unsuitable for the display of the multifarious collections.

The Prussian visitor Prince Pückler-Muskau, for one, was not impressed
by the spectacle:

> ... a strange 'Mischmasch' of works of art, natural curiosities,
> books and models are preserved in a miserable building. At the
> top of the staircase, as you enter, stand two giraffes [in fact there
> were three], in the character of stuffed guards, or emblems of
> English taste.

In those days the museum was hidden from the street by a pilastered
front wall. Visitors entered through a classical gate surmounted by a
cupola, obelisks and porticoes. On either side stood sentry boxes and
Guardsmen, for until the 1860s the British Museum, like the Bank
of England, had a permanent military guard. Inside the gate were a
colonnade and a spacious courtyard. Crossing this, visitors mounted
a short flight of stone steps to the door. Inside there were stone-
flagged floors, monuments (the first thing people saw on entering was
Roubilliac's statue of Shakespeare, which is still on display now in the
British Library), black leather fire-buckets, top-hatted policemen and
uniformed warders. In 1837 the latter were given permission by William
IV to wear the silver-buttoned blue-and-scarlet 'Windsor Livery', as they
still do on important occasions. A walk up the wide staircase with its
wrought-iron banister brought visitors face-to-face with the very giraffes
that had so offended Muskau. Everywhere there was a sense of clutter,
but the variety of exhibits was overwhelming. The principal treasures
were listed in *London as it is Today*:

> In 1772, Parliament purchased Sir William Hamilton's collection
> of Roman vases and curiosities. The Townley Marbles were added
> in 1805, Colonel Greville's minerals were purchased in 1812;
> the Elgin and Phigalian Marbles came in 1815, and in 1823 King
> George IV presented the splendid and very valuable library of his
> father George III, comprising upwards of 70,000 volumes.

The guide went on to describe the natural history exhibits in the
collection, which would be moved to South Kensington in 1883 and
installed in a museum of their own:

The collection of animals has fine specimens of the giraffe, the elephant, the rhinoceros and the hippopotamus, and a truly magnificent collection of birds, including individuals of every known variety, from the majestic condor of the Andes to the diminutive humming-bird of South America, the trogon, the lyre-bird, the sacred ibis and the domestic stork, together with the stormy petrel and the sea-gull of our own coasts.

There were several other museums in the city. One that is long departed but which captured effectively the spirit of the early 19th century – the era of religious revival and the abolition of slavery – was the London Missionary Museum at Moorfields. Its grimacing wooden idols and fearsome-looking weaponry could give children nightmares. The collection was described for visitors as containing:

Idols and other symbols of heathen worship, in the region over which the care of the London Missionary Society extends, but principally from Asia and the South Sea Islands. This museum is particularly interesting on account of all the materials for its formation having been collected by the most pious and indefatigable missionaries, dispersed at various periods over the most distant regions of the earth, where they voluntarily undergo the greatest privations for the sake of promoting Christianity among the heathen. Many of the objects in the collection not only particularly illustrate the religious worship of the people among whom they were stationed, but many of them also display the ingenuity of the savages in the manufacture of articles before their intercourse with Europeans; and others, again, the great advantages they have gained in the progress of the arts and civilization from the partial labours of the missionaries. There is also an extensive collection of Hindoo, Chinese and Burmese idols, and a collection of miniature portraits of many of the missionaries and their no less enterprising and estimable wives.

Those who wanted further glimpses of the exotic could visit the East India Company's museum, at its headquarters in Leadenhall Street. The artefacts there were of historical importance as well as mere curiosity value. A Regency guide entitled *Description of London* explained what could be seen:

> The interior is well worth visiting. The Company's Sale Room
> and the Museum must be particularly mentioned: the latter
> contains models of Hindoo and Gentoo idols; Chinese gardens in
> ivory; all kinds of curiosities from the British Empire in India;
> some highly finished Indian and Chinese views; Tippoo Sultan's
> library, his armour, the golden lion's head which stood at the foot
> of his throne, his canopy, &c.

A generation later, *London as it is Today* described one of the Company's most sensational possessions:

> The East India Museum, Leadenhall Street. This valuable collection
> is principally devoted to curiosities or articles of vertu, from the
> east, including many of the trophies that graced the arms of the
> troops of the Honourable East India Company, especially those
> taken at the siege of Seringapatam; one of the most singular of
> which is a curious musical instrument, invented for the diversion
> of the Sultan Tippoo Saib, on the principle of an organ, which is
> built to resemble a tiger, killing and devouring a British officer,
> the sound of the music being intended to imitate his dying cries.
> Daggers, swords, and matchlocks, used by Indian heroes and Persian
> warriors, are also exhibited in great numbers, with a variety of
> implements used in the households of social life. Open to visitors on
> Tuesdays and Thursdays, by order of any director of the Company,
> and on Saturdays, from ten till four o'clock, without any restriction.

'Tippoo's Tiger', a life-sized mechanical toy, had been given to the Sultan by the French and was brought back to London after his defeat by the British in 1799. It was by far the most popular artefact at East India House. It was kept not in the Company's museum but in the reading room of the library, to the great irritation of those who went there to work – or sleep – because visitors were constantly cranking the handle to hear the noise it made. Eventually this misuse seems to have broken it. In 1843 one observer complained that:

The machine or organ is getting much out of repair and does not altogether realize the expectation of the visitor.

Some years later a journal, *The Athenaeum*, mentioned that:

Luckily a kind fate has deprived him of his handle, and stopped up, we are happy to think, some of his internal organs, and we do sincerely hope he will remain so, to be seen and to be admired, if necessary, but to be heard no more.

This wish has since been fulfilled. The tiger, repaired but kept out of reach in a glass case, is now in the Victoria and Albert Museum. The East India Company was disbanded in 1858, following the Indian Mutiny, and its collections were dispersed.

Outdoor Pursuits

In summer, when Londoners sought their relaxation out of doors, a place of enduring popularity was the pleasure garden. Vauxhall, on the south bank of the Thames, was a relic of the 18th century that still exerted a strong appeal. The attractions were the same as in Vauxhall's Georgian heyday and they were night-time pleasures: the gardens were illuminated by thousands of lamps, which were a spectacle in themselves. There were discreet alcoves for dining, and flirting, grouped around a central pavilion in which bands played and famous singers performed. Dark avenues offered further opportunity for flirtation, and there were fireworks and balloon ascents. Once Victoria came to the throne and morals began to become more rigid, the gardens suffered from their association with the wilder days of the Georges. They closed in 1859 and their site was covered by buildings and railway lines. Dickens visited them by day in the 1830s. Though they looked unimpressive in the glare of sunlight, his description helps to recreate this lost London institution:

We paid our shilling at the gate, when we saw for the first time that the entrance, if there had been any magic about it at all, was now decidedly disenchanted, being, in fact, nothing more

or less than a combination of very roughly-painted boards and
sawdust. We glanced at the orchestra and supper-room as we
hurried past – we just recognized them, and that was all. We
bent our steps to the firework-ground; there, at least, we should
not be disappointed. We reached it, and stood rooted to the spot
with mortification and astonishment ... the Moorish tower – that
wooden shed with a door in the centre, and daubs of crimson and
yellow all round, like a gigantic watch case! ...

We walked about, and met with a disappointment at every
turn; our favourite views were mere patches of paint; the
fountain that had sparkled so showily by lamp-light presented
very much the appearance of a water-pipe that had burst; all the
ornaments were dingy, and all the walks gloomy. There was a
spectral attempt at rope-dancing in the little open theatre. The
sun shone upon the spangled dresses of the performers, and their
evolutions were about as inspiring and appropriate as a country-
dance in a family vault.

A variation on this theme was the tea garden or pump room. Small
health resorts, a sort of Bath or Buxton in miniature, had been opened
all over the outskirts of London during the 18th century in places where
medicinal springs had been found. In an age of heavy drinking, and
overeating by the better-off, these establishments offered a painless and
sociable way of restoring one's health. To entertain those who were
'taking the waters', the gardens provided music, dancing and other mild
exercise such as skittles. Many of them were simply the grounds attached
to a public house, tidied up and prettified in order to attract the custom
of families. They aped in a modest way the delights of the great Georgian
pleasure-grounds at Vauxhall, Cremorne and Ranelagh. In *Sketches by
Boz*, Dickens portrayed the clientele of one of these places:

The heat is intense this afternoon, and the people, of whom
there are additional parties arriving every moment, look as warm
as the tables which have been recently painted, and have the
appearance of being red-hot. What a dust and noise! Men and
women – boys and girls – sweethearts and married people – babies
in arms, and children in chaises – pipes and shrimps – cigars and

periwinkles – tea and tobacco. Gentlemen in alarming waistcoats
and steel watch-guards, promenading about, three abreast, with
surprising dignity (or as the gentleman in the next box facetiously
observes, 'cutting it uncommon fat!') – ladies, with great, long,
white pocket-handkerchiefs like small table-cloths in their
hands, chasing one another on the grass in the most playful and
interesting manner, with the view of attracting the attention of
the aforesaid gentlemen – husbands in perspective ordering bottles
of ginger-beer for the objects of their affections, with a lavish
disregard of expense; and the said objects washing down huge
quantities of shrimps and winkles, with an equal disregard of their
own bodily health and subsequent comfort – boys, with great
silk hats just balanced on the top of their heads, smoking cigars,
and trying to look as if they liked them – gentlemen in ink shirts
and blue waistcoats, occasionally upsetting either themselves, or
somebody else, with their own canes.

Some of the finery of these people provokes a smile, but they are
all clean, and happy, and disposed to be good-natured and sociable.
Those two motherly-looking women in the smart pelisses, who
are chatting so confidentially, inserting a 'ma'am' at every fourth
word, scraped an acquaintance about a quarter of an hour ago; it
originated in the admiration of the little boy who belongs to one of
them – that diminutive specimen of mortality in the three-cornered
pink satin hat with black feathers. The two men in the blue coats
and drab trousers, who are walking up and down, smoking their
pipes, are their husbands. The party in the opposite box are a
pretty fair specimen of the generality of the visitors. These are the
father and mother, and old grandmother: a young man and woman,
and an individual addressed by the euphonious title of 'Uncle Bill',
who is evidently the wit of the party. They have some half-dozen
children with them, but it is scarcely necessary to notice the fact,
for that is a matter of course here. Every woman in 'the gardens',
who has been married for any length of time, must have had twins
on two or three occasions; it is impossible to account for the
extent of juvenile population in any other way.

It is getting dark, and the people begin to move. The field
leading to town is quite full of them; the little hand-chaises

are dragged wearily along, the children are tired, and amuse
themselves and the company generally by crying, or resort to the
much more pleasant expedient of going to sleep – the mothers
begin to wish they were at home again – sweethearts grow more
sentimental than ever, as the time for parting arrives – the
gardens look mournful enough, by the light of the two lanterns
which hang against the trees for the convenience of smokers
– and the waiters, who have been running about incessantly for
the last six hours, think they feel a little tired, as they count
their glasses and their gains.

On a number of occasions, tea gardens were the setting for balloon
ascents. The first flight in a balloon had been made in Paris in 1783, and
the following year this new sensation had arrived in London: two men
– a Frenchman and a Neapolitan – made an ascent from the Artillery
Ground, north of the City, where a crowd of 150,000 had gathered to
watch. They were highly successful, for they travelled a distance of
39km/24 miles, taking with them a pigeon and a cat. The cat suffered
greatly in the cold air and, whether from compassion or bravado, the
aeronauts interrupted their journey in order to land and release it.

By the 19th century, ballooning had become an accepted aspect of
London entertainment. Flights were frequent, though the sight of one of
these craft floating above would still be a thrilling experience for most
people. There is an account of an ascent in *Sketches of Boz*, the scene
being Vauxhall Gardens, where a balloonist and his son were to make a
double attempt:

Some half-dozen men were restraining the impetuosity of one
of the balloons, which was completely filled, and had the car
attached; and as rumours had gone abroad that a Lord was 'going
up', the crowd were more than usually anxious and talkative.
One little man in faded black entered into conversation with
everybody: 'He's a rum 'un, is Green; think o' this here being
up'ards of his two hundredth ascent; the man as is ekal to Green
never had the toothache yet, nor won't have within this hundred
year, and that's all about it.' But, he added, 'I don't know where
this here science is to stop, mind you; that's what bothers me.'

Just at this moment all eyes were directed to the preparations which were being made for starting. The car was attached to the second balloon, the two were brought pretty close together, and a military band commenced playing, with a zeal and fervour which would render the most timid man in existence but too happy to accept any means of quitting that particular spot of earth on which they were stationed. Then Mr Green, senior, and his noble companion entered one car, and Mr Green junior and his noble companion the other; and then the balloons went up, and the aerial travellers stood up, and the crowd outside roared with delight, and the two gentlemen who had never ascended before, tried to wave their flags, as if they were not nervous, but held on very fast all the while; and the balloons were wafted gently away, our little friend solemnly protesting, long after they were reduced to mere specks in the air, that he could distinguish the white hat of Mr Green. The gardens disgorged their multitudes, boys ran up and down screaming 'bal-loon'; and in all the crowded thoroughfares people rushed out of their shops into the middle of the road, and having stared up in the air at two little black objects till they almost dislocated their necks, walked slowly in again, perfectly satisfied.

In 1836 Robert Holland, MP, set off with a companion and a supply of provisions and reached Germany within a day. Incredibly, the related activity of parachuting was practised by some balloonists. The first descent had taken place in 1802 and, despite one or two fatalities, this spectacle continued to be seen. An advertisement for the Flora Tea Gardens in Bayswater announced on 1 July 1839 that a Mr Hampton:

... is now making arrangements for his third parachute descent, which will take place in a few days at an altitude of Three Miles, so as to be perfectly visible to the Entire Population of the Metropolis.

The last of the London pleasure-gardens to be opened – it began business only in 1831 – was Beulah Spa. It was set on a hillside overlooking south London, 11km/7 miles south of the city. Its lifespan was to be short, for just over two decades later it would be doomed by the arrival nearby of the Crystal Palace, which boasted much more extensive gardens and more varied entertainments. During its brief existence, however, Beulah was a gathering place for the wealthy and fashionable. It added the word 'Royal' to its title, though it also became popular with the other classes (Gabriel Parsons planned an expedition there in *Sketches by Boz*). Its major attraction was its chalybeate spring, one of many in the neighbourhood. Its beautiful setting, in a bowl-shaped depression that was laid out as a garden, and its commanding views across Kent, Surrey and Middlesex gave it clear advantages over resorts, such as Sadler's Wells, that were in the shadow of London. Its distance from the centre of town did not discourage visitors, for it was served by three coaches a day from Charing Cross. Dickens was not a habitué, but he knew both the locality and the properties of the water that could be found in local springs. He often visited a family nearby whose home, Springfield, had its own well, and he is said to have written some of *David Copperfield* beneath a cedar tree (the only part of the property to survive) in the garden there. An advertisement for the spa listed its attractions:

> Visitors to this fashionable place of summer resort, which is now open every day, will find every convenience there for the enjoyment of a variety of cheerful, elegant, and healthful recreation and amusement amidst landscape scenery of the most splendid description. The gardens contain a most superb variety of floricultural specimens. A new archery ground is in every way to the convenience and enjoyment of this fashionable and healthful recreation. Bows and arrows are provided for the use of visitors. Picnic and gypsy parties are catered for. A brass and quadrille band is in daily attendance. The Beulah Saline Water is forwarded to all parts of the Kingdom at 2 shillings a gallon.

The buildings, which were based around an octagonal thatched edifice that served as both refreshment and 'reading room', were designed, like the Regent's Park Colosseum, by the eminent architect Decimus Burton. The spring itself was concealed inside a curious structure 'built in the form of an Indian Wigwam'. Admission to the grounds cost a shilling, or half-a-crown on special occasions when more elaborate entertainment was provided.

By modern standards, there was little to do. Much of a visitor's time was spent merely strolling about, or sitting at vantage points to admire the views. Vigorous public exercise, other than riding, was not yet customary for gentlemen, and strenuous exercise for ladies was unthinkable. Apart from the archery butts and a maze, the only outlet for surplus energy was provided by music, as there was a lawn for dancing in front of the bandstand. Fortune tellers roamed the grounds (the area had been famous for its gypsy community, which lived in nearby woods), and a strolling minstrel, in a cloak and turban, serenaded visitors with a guitar and expected to be rewarded with silver. If given a copper coin, he would return it with a bow. In the evenings there were firework displays, sometimes coupled with balloon ascents. There were fêtes that attracted thousands and the gardens came into their own on these occasions: on a warm night the air would be filled with the scent of flowers and the lilting sound of waltzes, and the trees would be hung with Chinese lanterns, as the crowds looked up at the colourful flashes and showers above them.

Beulah suffered a steady decline in popularity even before the Crystal Palace caused its demise. In 1845, over a decade before it closed, it was visited by a writer from *Punch*, who left this account of its abandoned and unloved state:

We entered a lodge in the Swiss style; and here a gentleman demanded a shilling from us before we were free of the Spa gardens. They are beautiful. The prettiest lawns, the prettiest flowers, rocks, grottoes, bridges, shrubberies, hermitages, kiosks, and what not; and charming bowers wherein a man might repose by the lady of his heart, and, methinks, be supremely happy. But the company we saw were: three trumpeters dressed in green, blowing 'Souni la tromba' out of a canvas arbour, a most melancholy obligato, a snuffy little old gentleman with two grandsons, one a Bluecoat boy. His yellow stockings glittered like buttercups on the sunshiny grass; a professional gypsy in a dark walk; two pretty servant-maids carrying a small basket and on the look-out for their masters and mistresses, who were straying in some part of their Elysium. When the trumpeters had done, a poor wizened Italian dressed in a hat and peacock's feathers – very like the monkey that accompanies the barrel organs – came up and began warbling, in

rather a sweet feeble voice, the most seedy old love song ... Then
we strayed through shrubberies and rose gardens until we came
to the archery ground. Targets were set up; just for all the world
as in Ivanhoe – and a fellow in Lincoln green came forward and
invited us to the butts. The odious fellow sneered all the while.
'It isn't the harrows that's bad,' said he, sardonically, laughing at
our complaints, '*they're* good enough to shoot with.' Rather to his
discomforture, we called upon him to do so. He levelled his arrow,
he bent and twiddled with his bow, previous to stringing it; he
lifted up to the sight mark and brought it down, he put himself in
an attitude so prodigiously correct that we thought that the bull's
eye might shut up at once. At last, whiz, the arrow went.

It missed. The old humbug could no more shoot than we could.
He took twelve shots at the target and didn't hit once. And so we
left the archery ground with the most undisguised contempt. No
new company had arrived at the Spa during our brief absence.
The little old man was still sunning and snuffing himself on the
bench. The Bluecoat boy and his companion were still clambering
over rustic archways. The two servant-maids had found Master
and Missus and were spreading out a cloth in an arbour. The
band began to blow when this banquet was served – and the poor
minstrel came up, leering and grinning with his guitar, ready to
perform for them. They and we were the only guests of the place
– the solitude was intense. We left them there, of a gorgeous
afternoon, drinking tea and eating shrimps in the sunshine.

Such were the respectable pleasures of the social class to which
Dickens belonged. There was, however, an entire world of sport and
entertainment that was anything but respectable. For centuries, the
baiting of animals had been a widespread and accepted part of English
life in both city and country. Though they were commonplace, these
'sports' were condemned by many contemporary observers as cruel and
mindless violence. Pepys, Evelyn, Defoe and Boswell, commentators
on life in London during the 17th and 18th centuries, had all attended
contests of this type and had, on the whole, disapproved of them. Cock-
fighting, ratting, boxing, cudgels and the baiting of bulls, bears and
badgers were among the traditional amusements of the English. At the

beginning of Dickens' life all of them still flourished. By the time of his death all had been banned, gone out of fashion or, in the case of boxing, been subjected to strict regulations that entirely changed the nature of the sport. Englishmen were learning to appreciate more civilized games; professional football and the heyday of school and university sport would follow in a decade or so, and by the end of the century the old spectacles would seem as barbaric to contemporaries as they do to us.

The baiting of bulls and bears followed the same principle. The beast would be attached to a post by a chain or rope, leaving just enough leeway to strike, or to turn around, and would be set upon by trained dogs, or by men with whips. A bull could kick with its hooves, but its best defence was naturally its horns, which could tear huge gashes in an attacking dog, or toss it considerable distances (there were instances where dogs were thrown into the laps of people in the audience). A bear had sharp teeth, sharp claws and huge strength. Nevertheless neither could, nor was intended to, last long against a pack of dogs or a group of men. Badgers, dangerous animals for their size, were baited with dogs, and so was the harmless and defenceless duck (few realize that the quaint English pub name, 'The Dog and Duck', refers to this practice).

As with so many of the vices of Dickens' world, the need for reform was apparent to much of the public and change was on the way. A 'society for the prevention of cruelty to animals' was set up in 1822; it was to gain royal patronage and wield increasing influence. Both bull- and bear-baiting were banned in 1835. Cock-fighting, an addiction among Londoners and a sport that often surpassed the Turf in the amount of money wagered on it, was prohibited in 1849. Badger-baiting followed in 1850. Needless to say, many ignored the law and continued these activities in secret.

Rat-catching was another blood sport. This was staged in a wooden 'ring' surrounded by a barrier and, like cock-fights and prize-fights, it often took place on the premises of public houses. Hundreds of farm rats, fatter than the sewer variety, would be emptied from sacks on to the floor. There a terrier or other small dog would be set on them and would simply kill as many of them with its teeth as possible, while the rats crowded into the corners or made attempts to bolt from one side to the other. The cornered rats would fight back, so the dog did not have things all its own way. The result was not in doubt, however, and the

dog's prowess was measured by how many rats it killed in a given time.
The most famous, though not the fastest, ratting dog of all was Tiny
the Wonder, a terrier weighing little over 2.2kg/5lb. Renowned for his
ferocity, he drew crowds in the 1840s and 1850s. He once killed 200 rats
in the space of an hour. Large numbers of West End 'toffs' would come to
see these contests.

Boxing was a different matter. It was a sport with more general appeal,
not least because, a generation earlier, it had attracted the interest of
Byron and other glamorous Regency figures. Successful prize-fighters
gained wealth and public adulation, as compensation for the injuries
that often ended their lives in their 20s or 30s. Boxing was 'bare-
knuckle', carried on without gloves or any other protection. There were
no rules against hitting 'below the belt' or gouging the eyes, and nor
was there any limit to the number of rounds fought: the contestants
remained in the ring until one of them collapsed, which might be after a
fight lasting more than two hours.

An agreement between two well-known pugilists indicates how much
money was involved in a major contest and demonstrates that there
were at least some regulations. The contest, when it took place, was held
in a raised ring and not simply in a marked-out space. This not only
made the contestants more visible, but prevented supporters of either
man from striking or impeding his opponent:

> THOMAS WINTER SPRING agrees to fight John Langan for
> three hundred pounds a-side. A fair stand-up fight – half minute
> time to be allowed between each and every round, in a 24 foot
> ring. The fight to take place on 7th January, 1824. Fifty pounds a
> side are now deposited in the hands of Mr H. One hundred and
> fifty pounds a-side are to be made good at Mr Belcher's Castle
> Tavern, Holborn, on the first Monday in December.

The contest itself drew huge crowds. The adversaries and their seconds
sized each other up:

> The John Bull fighter bolted towards the place like lightning, and,
> in a few minutes afterwards, shouts rending the air proclaimed
> the approach of the Irish Champion. He immediately went up

and shook hands with Spring. The latter, with great good nature and manliness, said, 'I hope you are well, Langan.' 'Very well, my boy; and we'll soon be talking to each other in another way.' The men now stripped, when Reynolds went up to Spring, and said, 'I understand you have got a belt on and whalebone in it; if you persist in fighting in such a belt, I shall put one on Langan.' Spring replied (showing a belt such as are worn by gentlemen when riding), 'I have always fought in this and shall now.' 'Then,' replied Reynolds (putting on a large belt, crossed in various parts with a hard substance), 'Langan shall fight in this.' 'No you won't,' said Cribb, 'it is not a fair thing.' 'Never mind,' urged Spring, 'I'll take it off,' which he did immediately. Josh Hudson and Tom Reynolds were the seconds for Langan, and the Irish Champion declared he was ready to go to work. The colours were tied to the stakes; and singular to state, black for Langan; and blue for Spring. 'This is new,' said Josh, 'but nevertheless, the emblem is correct as to milling, it is black and blue; and I'll take one hundred to one, we shall see such colours upon their mugs before it is over.' The time was kept by Lord Deerhurst and a sporting Baronet; and Colonel Berkeley acted as the referee. Two and a half, and three to one on Spring.

First Round – on stripping, the bust of Langan was much admired for its anatomical beauty; his arms also were peculiarly fine and athletic. His legs were thin; his knees very small, and his loins extremely deficient as to strength. It was evident that he had reduced too much in training. Langan did not exceed 12 stone four pounds in weight. The Irish champion was nearly two inches shorter than his opponent. Spring was in fine condition; cool and confident, and more than a stone heavier than his adversary. On placing themselves in attitude, the advantages in point of person were decisively manifest on the side of the English champion, to every unbiased spectator. The combatants kept at a respectable distance from each other; yet both on the look out for an opening. The champion slowly advanced, and Langan kept retreating backwards, till he was near the stake at the corner of the ring. At this instant the position of Langan was not only fine, but formidable; and Spring did not view it with contempt. The latter

let fly right and left and Langan's left ogle received a slight touch.
Spring got away from a heavy body blow. A pause, an exchange of
blows, but no mischief done. Some blows were exchanged rather
sharply, and Tom Reynolds exclaimed, 'first blood!' 'No,' replied
Spring. 'Yes,' urged Hudson, 'it is on your lip.' A long pause.
Some hits passed between the combatants, when they closed,
and severe struggle occurred to obtain the throw; both down,
but Langan uppermost. The round occupied eight minutes. 'This
battle will not be over in half an hour,' said a good judge.

In fact, it lasted 77 rounds and ended when the less experienced fighter,
the Irishman Langan, lost consciousness. He came to shortly afterward
and offered to carry on, but by that time Spring had already been
declared the winner. There was far more blood ('claret') spilled in this
type of boxing than in its modern counterpart, and the injuries looked
terrible. A book on boxing by another champion, Daniel Mendoza,
listed the most telling blows:

The eye-brow, on the bridge of the nose, on the temple arteries,
beneath the left ear, under the short ribs or in the kidneys,
deprives the person struck of his breath, occasions an instant
discharge of urine, puts him in the greatest torture and renders
him for some time a cripple.

This adequately conveys the sheer awfulness of the injuries that boxers
were likely to suffer and, although few actually perished in the ring, a
number of them died of the effects of fights, through serious damage to
brains or kidneys. It may be wondered why anyone would want a career
in pugilism, but these men had the same motives as boxers today: for
those who were successful, the sport paid well and brought celebrity;
there was a genuine desire to outclass one's opponent, and a tremendous
camaraderie among fighters and their hangers-on. It was not necessary, or
indeed possible, to fight very often and some of the greatest boxers took
part in no more than half-a-dozen contests in the course of their careers
('Gentleman' John Jackson, who gave boxing lessons to Byron, fought
only three times in major matches). Some fighters were driven by lack of
opportunity elsewhere: Bill Richmond was black, Daniel Mendoza and

Sam Elias ('Dutch Sam') were Jews. All these men came from groups
that were subject to popular prejudice and discrimination. It is likely
that their early development as fighters was a reaction to street-corner
insults. Sport, as is still the case, offered the poor a way of rising in the
world. By no means all fighters were brutes. Jem Mace, a redoubtable
boxer who was a native Londoner, was also a talented violinist.

Tom Sayers, perhaps the greatest of the bare-knuckle fighters, died
in 1865 at the age of 39, and more than 100,000 people attended his
funeral. Despite this tribute, bare-knuckle fighting had lost its audience.
It had suffered a long decline in popularity as the sporting public,
like the rest of Victorian society, found more refined outlets for its
enthusiasm and energies.

London's annual fairs were another survivor of the wilder Georgian
city. Bartholomew Fair, which had been held in Smithfield in the
shadow of St Bartholomew's church since the 12th century, and
immortalized in a play by Ben Jonson, was a cloth fair (the street next
to the church still bears that name) that had long since become a scene
of general revelry. Much visited by pickpockets and other criminals, it
became so violent and dangerous that it was abolished in 1855. Another
fair was held every Easter at Greenwich. This too had a reputation for
rowdiness, but was marginally more civilized. Dickens wrote of it in one
of the *Sketches by Boz*, as:

> A periodical breaking-out, a sort of spring-rash: a three days'
> fever, which cools the blood for six months afterwards, and at
> the expiration of which London is restored to its old habits of
> plodding industry.

James Grant visited the fair and described its range of attractions:

> Of eatables, of all descriptions, there was a most abundant supply:
> apples, oranges, and nuts, stared you in the face in every direction;
> while gingerbread was presented in an inconceivable diversity
> of forms. Nor was there any lack of liquids: there was an ample
> supply of chalk-and-water, baptized milk; there were little cans of
> table-beer, and ginger-beer, and soda-water. But the weather was
> intensely cold, which is always fatal to the sale of beer of all kinds,

especially in the open air. The shivering persons who stood in the market-place would not have drunk soda-water or ginger-beer had they been paid for doing it. 'Summat to warm us' was the universal motto, and the effects were visible in the scenes of drunkenness and disturbance wherever you turned your eye.

Of showy articles, there was also a most liberal supply. The assortment of dolls was varied and abundant. 'Buy a doll, Sir,' 'Buy a doll, Ma'am,' the article which they were invited to purchase at the same time being thrust in the faces of the men and women. Crackers, scratchers, little drums, sixpenny looking-glasses, watches which never went and never were meant to go, and other articles too tedious to mention, were all exposed to the eye, under the most attractive possible circumstances.

You would have fancied, from the number of caravans, booths, and other places, that the marvels of the whole world had been congregated. The great difficulty was to make a selection. The figures which were daubed on the canvas at the front of the caravans, as is usually the case, far surpassed the things represented. Nothing could exceed the earnestness or the eloquence with which the proprietors praised the articles exhibited. There was 'the Lincolnshire Ox, the most biggest hanimal of the kind as was ever seen'. The next-door-neighbour was 'the most extraordinary sheep with four legs and half of a fifth 'un'. Adjoining the last 'vonderful production' was a 'vonderful pig' – a 'werry extraordinary hanimal' – as was 'so fat as never to rise off the place where she lay.'

In a theatrical booth, the audience heckled a tight-rope walker with cries of 'Vy do you always dance the same thing?' the barracking of the crowd raising more laughter than the clown's antics. Grant continued:

Gambling was carried on at Greenwich Fair to a very great extent, and in every variety and form. There were roulette, hazard, and other games, at which persons might play for stakes of from one shilling to a sovereign, and many were the simpletons these notable hell-keepers victimized on the occasion ...

The last, and assuredly not the least attractions of Greenwich Fair are the dancing booths. By nine o'clock, they began to be tolerably attended: by ten they were full. Most liberally was the light fantastic toe tripped: the girls seemed in perfect ecstasies: they would have danced themselves to death, if necessary. The floor was not cleared until three in the morning. On one side were four or five boxes [booths] where the 'partners' swigged porter or sipped brandy-and-water, by way of refreshing themselves. In some cases, the arms of the beau were to be seen affectionately around the neck of the belle, while in others, all the indications and demonstrations of love were given by the young ladies.

Grand Theatre

Considering the vast extent and wealth of the British capital, it might be expected that it should possess an ample fund of amusement for its enormous population. This, in truth, it does – the theatre, of course, holding the first rank.

'The theatre', in this context, meant only the three large establishments situated in the West End: the Theatre Royal, Covent Garden; the Theatre Royal, Drury Lane; and, most fashionable of all, the Theatre Royal in the Haymarket. The last staged only opera since the other two retained, by virtue of patents granted in 1660 by Charles II, a monopoly of the production of drama. All other playhouses – and there were scores of these, mostly small and unpretentious, throughout the city centre and the suburbs – were thus technically forbidden to stage productions of any serious cultural merit. A senior government official, the Lord Chamberlain, was empowered to enforce this stipulation. He also granted licences to the other playhouses, but issued them only for the performance of music, dancing and pantomime. Every production therefore had to have some sung or orchestral accompaniment in order to keep within the law, and 'straight plays' often had songs inserted for this reason. The monopoly of the patent theatres did not end until 1843.

The grand theatres were undoubtedly magnificent and Londoners were proud of them. Like all playhouses, however, they were extremely vulnerable. The lighting of a large and crowded building with candles, oil-lamps or gaslight was likely to be risky, for the combination of inflammable materials – paint, canvas, wood, dust and accumulated litter – meant that a blaze was virtually inevitable. Within a few months in 1808–9 both Drury Lane and Covent Garden burned down. The latter was to be destroyed again in 1856 and replaced by the present building. A *Description of London*, published in 1824, contained this somewhat fawning description of the glories of Drury Lane:

> **This substantial and superb theatre was rebuilt, in 1811, on the ruins of the former, which had been burnt down in 1809. The grand entrance to the boxes is from Brydges-street, through a spacious hall leading to the boxes and pit. Three large doors lead from this hall into the house, and into a rotunda of great beauty and elegance. The grand saloon is 86 feet long, circular at each extremity, and the ceiling arched; the effect of two massy Corinthian columns at each end, with ten corresponding pilasters at each end, is grand and pleasing.**
>
> **The house is built to afford sitting room for 2,810 persons: 1,200 in the boxes; 850 in the pit; 480 in the lower, and 280 in the upper gallery. The body of the theatre has recently undergone considerable improvements. There is altogether a master-piece of art, and an ornament to the metropolis.**

Similarly, the description of Covent Garden combined factual information with civic pride. Foreign visitors to the capital city of a 'nation of shopkeepers' would have noticed that the writer dwelt not on the cultural attainments of the theatre but on the size of its profits:

> **This theatre was rebuilt in 1809, after the conflagration in 1808, and is, as a building, one of the ornaments of the metropolis, and the completest theatre in Europe. Great exertions have been made to raise its amusements to the highest pitch of scenic splendour and dramatic perfection; accordingly the dresses are more costly, and all the arrangements are on a more expensive scale than were ever known in this metropolis. The interior is gold upon white. The half-price begins at both theatres at the end of the third act**

of a play of five acts, or at the end of the second act of a play of three acts. Each theatre employs, as actors, artists, musicians, and mechanics, from 200 to 250 persons, at salaries from £30 to £2 a week. Each holds, when crowded, [audiences that bring in] about £750; and with a full house, about £650; the nightly expenses are at least £200; hence the proprietors have a clear profit of about £40,000 per annum.

The Haymarket theatre, the third of the London giants, was the equal of Covent Garden in terms of wealth and glamour. The programmes offered there, during the first half of the century, reflected the increasing sophistication of at least the elite London audiences, according to the 1851 guidebook *London as it is Today*:

> Originally established for the performance of Italian operas, to which ballets and divertissements are now always added, and is now one of the most fashionable places of amusement in the metropolis, its only rival being the Royal Italian Opera, Covent Garden, which has recently been established to gratify the increasing taste of the public for exquisite music and dancing. At these two houses, the most celebrated artistes are engaged, and in consequence of their rivalry, at an enormous expense, far exceeding that of any other theatres in the world.

With further boastfulness the account continued:

> The dimensions of the interior are nearly the same as those of La Scala, at Milan. The width of the stage is nearly 80 feet; its depth 62 feet; and from the centre boxes in the grand tier, containing 210 boxes, will hold 1,000 persons, the pit nearly 800, and the gallery the same. The first three tiers of private boxes are the property of the nobility, or of wealthy commoners, and are let at from 150 to 400 guineas the season, according to the situation and size.

Though the best seats in the house appeared to be beyond the reach of most people, there were in fact ways by which access to this privileged world could be obtained:

Persons desirous of admission to the boxes or stalls, may obtain tickets at the shops of some of the respectable booksellers in the vicinity, to whom subscribers when not using their own boxes, are in the habit of entrusting their tickets for disposal. In this way, tickets for the boxes may usually be had for a guinea, to the stalls for 14 shillings and sixpence, and to the pit for 6 shillings.

And men were warned that a dress code was observed:

Visitors to all parts of the theatre, except the gallery, are expected to appear in evening costume – frock coats and coloured trousers and cravats, not being admissible.

For all this sense of exclusivity, the theatre had to be all things to all people. Though opera and ballet were rarefied art forms that attracted an aristocratic and educated audience, theatre could not afford to depend on these classes. Managers were not motivated by a desire to provide a beautiful spectacle, or to educate and uplift: they cared only about turning a profit, and to fill the pits and galleries they had to put on productions that had broad (lowbrow) appeal. Shakespeare's works in their traditional form could not attract audiences large enough and so the Bard was commonly – as we would say – 'dumbed down', with scenes rewritten and endings altered to suit fashion and the taste of a shallow audience. To increase attendance, serious drama might be combined with comedy, pantomime and even acts by performing animals. Queen Victoria attended the Drury Lane pantomime in 1839. Her journal suggests that she was utterly bored by the performance but that 'the lions repaid all'. Her Majesty was much taken with the tricks of the lion-tamer, Isaac van Amburgh, whose cast of 'big cats' included leopards, cheetahs and tigers. The Queen wrote that:

They all seem actuated by the most awful fear of him. He takes them by their paws, throws them down, makes them roar, and lies upon them after enraging them. It's quite beautiful to see, and makes me wish I could do the same!

Patrons could sit through the whole range of offerings or leave after the item they had come to see. David Copperfield recalled an evening at one of the big theatres, in a passage suggesting that, in spite of the distractions, a play could still be a magical experience:

> It was Covent Garden Theatre that I chose; and there, from the back of a centre box, I saw Julius Caesar and the new Pantomime. To have all those Romans alive before me, and walking in and out for my entertainment, instead of being the stern taskmasters they had been at school, was a most novel and delightful effect. But the mingled reality and mystery of the whole show, the influence upon me of the poetry, the lights, the music, the company, the smooth stupendous changes of glittering and brilliant scenery, were so dazzling, and opened up such illimitable regions of delight, that when I came out into the rainy street at twelve o'clock at night, I felt as if I had come from the clouds, where I had been living a romantic life for ages ...

The Audience Experience

The theatre was a bear-pit. London audiences were much less well mannered than they are today. It was not thought necessary to sit quietly during the performance, and actors delivered their lines against a hubbub of noise. The audience in the pit would walk around, shout comments at the stage and leave litter everywhere. Many people attended solely in order to meet acquaintances, show off their clothes or, like David Copperfield, 'live a romantic life' for a few hours amid the plush velvet, the chandeliers and the extravagant scenery. Prince Pückler-Muskau was greatly struck by the behaviour of London playgoers:

> The most striking thing to a foreigner in English theatres is the unheard-of coarseness and brutality of the audiences. The consequence is that the higher and more civilized classes go only to the Italian Opera, and very rarely visit their national theatre. Whether this be unfavourable or otherwise to the stage I leave others to determine.

English freedom here degenerates into the rudest licence, and it is not uncommon in the midst of a tragedy, or the most charming 'cadenza' of a singer, to hear some coarse expression shouted from the galleries in stentor voice. This is followed, according to the taste of the bystanders, either by loud laughter and approbation, or by the castigation and expulsion of the offender.

Whichever turn the thing takes, you can hear no more of what is passing on the stage, where actors and singers, according to ancient usage, do not suffer themselves to be interrupted by such occurrences, but declaim or warble away. And such things happen not once, but sometimes twenty times, in the course of a performance, and amuse many of the audience more than that does. It is also no rarity for some one to throw the fragments of his 'goute', which do not always consist of orange-peels alone, without the smallest ceremony on the heads of the people in the pit, or to shail them with singular dexterity in the boxes; while others hang their coats and waistcoats over the railings in the gallery, and sit in shirt-sleeves.

If these things were true of the great London theatres, they must have been even more in evidence in the lesser establishments. Here too the emphasis was on the performance of multiple short acts and dramas, to give the audience variety. Few of the pieces that entertained Dickensian theatregoers are remembered today. A typical sample, described by George Sala, indicates the sort of stereotype that was in vogue during this era:

What shall I assume the final piece that is to be performed this night will be? Will you have the 'Flowers of the forest', the 'Poor Strollers', 'Sweethearts and Wives', 'Pizarro', the 'Padlock' or a 'Game at Romps'? What do you say to a fine old English comedy, such as 'John Bull', or the 'School of Reform', with a dissipated young squire, a gouty, virtuous tenant-farmer, a comic ploughman, a milkmaid with a chintz gown tucked through the placket-holes, and a song, and a spotless but persecuted maiden.

Aspiring Actors

Such was the attraction of the stage that many could not resist the desire
to tread the boards. There were theatres in which members of the public
could pay the management for a part in the play – the leading roles,
naturally, being the most expensive ('Boz' listed them: 'Duke of Glo'ster,
£2; Earl of Richmond, £1; Lord Stanley, 5s; Lord Mayor of London, 2s
6d). There were also 'private theatres' in which productions were staged
entirely by such amateurs for paying audiences. Dickens made rather
savage fun of these establishments in *Sketches by Boz*, mocking the
pretentions of the would-be thespians as well as the often abysmal acting:

> The principal patrons of private theatres are dirty boys, low
> copying-clerks in attorney's offices, capacious-headed youths from
> city counting-houses, Jews whose business, as lenders of fancy
> dresses, is a sure passport to the amateur stage, shop-boys who
> now and then mistake their master's money for their own; and a
> choice miscellany of idle vagabonds. The proprietor of a private
> theatre may be an ex scene-painter; a low coffee-house-keeper, a
> disappointed eighth-rate actor, a retired smuggler, or uncertified
> bankrupt. The theatre itself may be in Catherine Street, Strand,
> the purlieus of the city, or the neighbourhood of Gray's Inn Lane,
> or the vicinity of Sadler's Wells; or it may, perhaps, form the chief
> nuisance of some shabby street, on the Surrey side of Waterloo
> Bridge. All the minor theatres in London, especially the lowest,
> constitute the centre of a little stage-struck neighbourhood. Each
> of them has an audience exclusively its own.
>   The lady performers pay nothing for their characters, and it
> is needless to add are usually selected from one class of society;
> the audiences are necessarily of much the same character as
> the performers.

Dickens also described the cast, as they prepared in the dressing-room
for a performance of *Macbeth*:

> The characters in the tragedy are all dressed, and their own
> clothes are scattered in hurried confusion over the wooden dresser

which surrounds the room. That snuff-shop-looking figure, in front of the glass, is Banquo; and the young lady with the liberal display of legs, who is kindly painting his face with a hare's foot, is dressed for Fleance. The large woman, who is consulting the stage-directions in Cumberland's edition of *Macbeth*, is the Lady Macbeth of the night; she is always selected to play the part, because she is tall and stout, and looks a little like Mrs Siddons – at a considerable distance. That stupid-looking milksop, with light hair and bow legs, is fresh-caught; he plays Malcolm tonight, just to accustom himself to an audience. He will get on better by degrees; he will play Othello in a month, and in a month more, will very probably be apprehended on a charge of embezzlement. The black-eyed female with whom he is talking so earnestly, is dressed for the 'gentlewoman'. It is her first appearance too – in that character. The boy of fourteen who is having his eyebrows smeared with soap and whitening, is Duncan, King of Scotland; and the two dirty men with the corked countenances, in very old green tunics, and dirty drab boots, are the 'army'.

This seems unnecessarily cruel. The amateur stage, then and now, exists principally to entertain the cast and their friends and makes no pretence of doing more. It is also unfair because Dickens himself was a member of this fraternity. He had had a passion for the theatre since his childhood, when he had staged his own performances with puppets or cut-out figures, speaking all the parts and arranging elaborate sound effects. He carried this enthusiasm with him through adult life, getting up amateur dramatics with his children and friends as cast, as well as delivering readings of his novels that involved such histrionics they left him exhausted. A lifelong playgoer, he had a wide knowledge of the city's theatres and of those who performed in them. He had almost become a professional actor – illness had prevented him attending an audition at Covent Garden – and the theatrical giant William Macready was among his friends. He was also sensitive to the quality of acting because his own works were performed. In November 1838, only a month after its final instalment had been published, *Oliver Twist* was put on at the Surrey Theatre in Blackfriars Road. He attended a production of *Nicholas Nickleby* at the same theatre and, according to his friend and biographer, John Forster, it was:

So excruciatingly bad that in the middle of the first scene the agonised novelist lay down on the floor of his box and never rose until the curtain fell.

The English stage in Dickens' time was languishing between two of its many heydays. It had lost the afterglow of the great Georgian players: David Garrick, Mrs Siddons and John Kemble. The flood of creativity that would be unleashed by the ending of the patent theatres' monopoly was still in the future. To modern taste, acting was mannered, overelaborate and unnatural. It could be hilarious, moving and uplifting, but more commonly it was uninspired.

Nevertheless, revival had already begun. At the beginning of 1814 a young and impoverished actor called Edmund Kean arrived at Drury Lane and, after persistent lobbying, was engaged to play Shylock. The night he made his debut in this role was to be remembered as a theatrical milestone. Word of his skill and power travelled round the corner to Covent Garden, where some members of the audience, and even the cast, abandoned their play and crowded in to see his last act. He was to dominate the English stage for more than a decade.

A small and wizened man who became an alcoholic, Kean was driven by resentment of years spent in impecunious obscurity and used this tortured passion to good effect on the stage. Repudiating the mannered and formal acting technique of the time, he brought a naturalness, a seeming spontaneity, that breathed new life into ancient texts. He had a peculiarly strong stage presence. The power of his eyes, and his range of voice and expression, added an entire new dimension to roles that had long since jaded the public. His performances were uneven. Rather than being consistently strong, they contained high points – 'electrical shocks', as the critic William Hazlitt described them, a sort of repeated crescendo – that thrilled the audience. As well as Shylock he had immense successes with Hamlet, Othello and, greatest of all, Richard III. Samuel Taylor Coleridge remarked that 'to see him act is like reading Shakespeare by flashes of lightning'.

Always an unstable genius, Kean drank so heavily that his performances suffered and, having conquered the theatre, he gradually became a laughing-stock, slurring – or forgetting – his lines and falling around the stage. His last years were therefore tragic rather than triumphant, and his reign ended on stage at Covent Garden. In March 1833 he was playing Othello, with his son Charles taking the role of Iago. He suddenly collapsed into Charles's arms and gasped: 'Oh, God, I am dying ... speak to them for me.' Though this exit was appropriate to the Kean legend, the reality was less dramatic, as *The Times* reported the next day:

> Mr Kean appeared at this theatre last night as Othello. His performance, as far as it proceeded, was generally sound, and although it was marked by a tameness and want of that energy which used to characterize his personation of this character, the audience appeared disposed to think he was only husbanding his strength for those positions of the play which demand greater exertion. When, however, the trial came, his powers were unequal to it. In that speech in the third act, which those who have heard him deliver it in happier times can never forget,
>
> " – O now, for ever,
> Farewell the tranquil mind –"
>
> he completely broke down. It became evident that he was unable to conclude the speech, and he was led off the stage. The drop-scene fell, and Mr Bartley requested the indulgence of the audience, expressing a hope that Mr Kean would be able to resume the character after a short interval. At the end of a quarter of an hour Mr Bartley returned and announced that it was the opinion of Mr Kean's medical attendant that he would be unable to appear again in the course of the evening; that Mr Warde had been sent for, and had undertaken the part at a very short notice. The play then went on. Mr Warde acted the rest of the part of Othello as well as, under the circumstances, would have been expected. Mr Charles Kean, who sustained the character of Iago, played with care and discrimination, but without displaying any remarkable excellence. Miss F. Tree, as Desdemona, deserved more able coadjutors. The other parts were filled as usual. The audience bore the failure with great forebearance and good temper, and seemed to regret their disappointment less than the painful event, by which it had been occasioned.

In a sense, his son did indeed carry on his theatrical career, but Kean died shortly afterward, aged about 43.

The second actor to dominate the stage during this era was William Macready. He came from a thespian background, and he too had suffered hardship when his father's debts had forced him to take over the running of the family's theatre company at the age of 15, in 1808. Prior to that he had been intended for a career in law or the Church, and he never lost the desire to gain respectability. For him the theatre was simply a job, not a world of romance or excitement. He considered his fellow actors, as a species, 'miserable wretches' or 'beasts of Hell', and he regarded the audience as 'brutes'. Having arrived in the acting profession by accident, he set himself to reach the top of it, which he did by unremitting study, constant practice and unflagging determination. He was a good actor and manager and a shrewd businessman, but he retired (in 1851) as soon as he had made enough money to do so, remarking, as he finished his last performance as Macbeth at Drury Lane: 'I shall never have to do this again.' Because Macready was known among his casts for rough handling and violence on stage, they are likely to have shared his sense of relief.

In contrast to Kean, Macready was an actor of painstaking steadiness. He set himself standards of personal excellence and was highly self-critical when he failed to reach them, even if his audiences had been impressed. He expected the same devotion from those in his company and drove them relentlessly with terrifying scorn and abuse. He also set out to rediscover the original Shakespeare, long since encumbered with rewritings and reinterpretations. His careful nature made him seem dull, and his genius was not as apparent to some critics and audiences as that of the fiery Kean. Nevertheless, he enjoyed triumphs as Romeo, Othello, Macbeth, Hamlet and Julius Caesar. His professionalism and dignity also helped the theatrical profession on its way to social acceptance.

Samuel Phelps, a rival of Macready, made similar progress toward this end by taking over in 1844 the suburban playhouse at Sadler's Wells (which was already well known for its bourgeois clientele) and, banishing pantomime and all similar fripperies, began to offer the public nothing but serious drama. It was a significant development.

The theatre might have been gaining respectability, but those who worked in it had not: their social status was on a par with that of servants. It was a dreary enough existence. Most actors could not find sufficient work in London to remain there throughout the year and were obliged to go on lengthy provincial tours. When in the capital, working as a 'walking gentleman' (in walk-on parts) gave an income of only about a pound a week – admittedly a princely sum by the standards of the very poor – and many were typecast as minor stock characters. The contract signed by an actress at the Queen's Theatre in 1833, for this same salary, concludes with the words: 'My line of work [is] to be old women and utility'.

At least those who worked in the playhouses of central London stood a good chance of being paid. In the smaller establishments, the travelling companies and, at the lowest ebb of the profession, the 'penny gaffs', it was not unknown for actors to go hungry for days on end. On the other hand, they often had an undemanding life between performances: when Kean made his debut as Shylock at Drury Lane, the single rehearsal for the production had been on the morning of the opening night, and often there was none at all. Cast members would learn their lines at home and simply arrive when the play opened, to perform with people they might never have met. It was also common for actors to make their own interpretation of the text, ad libbing wherever the inadequacies of the script, or of their preparation, made it necessary.

Theatre on the Move

Travelling theatre companies had a relatively pleasant existence during the summer and could make an adequate living performing in towns and villages or at country fairs. The camaraderie of the profession could also create close-knit and supportive communities. The company led by the genial Mr and Mrs Crummles in *Nicholas Nickleby* was probably typical of the better sort of theatrical troupe. Its members are introduced:

> There were present a slim young gentleman with weak eyes, who played the low-spirited lovers and sang tenor songs, and who had come arm-in-arm with the comic-countryman – a man with a turned-up nose, large mouth, broad face, and staring eyes. Making himself very amiable to the infant phenomenon was an inebriated elderly gentleman in the last depths of shabbiness, who

played the calm and virtuous old men; and paying especial court to Mrs Crummles was another elderly gentleman, a shade more respectable, who played the irascible old men. Besides these, there was a roving-looking person in a rough great-coat, who strode up and down in front of the lamps, flourishing a dress cane ... He was not quite so young as he had been, and was rather running to seed; but there was an air of exaggerated gentility about him, which bespoke the hero of swaggering comedy. There was, also, a little group of three or four young men with lantern jaws and thick eyebrows, who were conversing in one corner; but they seemed to be of secondary importance, and laughed and talked together without attracting any attention.

The female members of the company were a similarly varied lot:

The ladies were gathered in a little knot by themselves round the rickety little table. There was Miss Snevellicci – who could do anything, from a medley dance to Lady Macbeth, and also always played some part in blue silk knee-smalls, glancing, from the depths of her coal-scuttle straw bonnet, at Nicholas, and affecting to be absorbed by the recital of a diverting story to her friend Miss Ledbrook ... There was Miss Belawney – who seldom aspired to speaking parts, and usually went on as a page in white silk hose. There was Miss Lenville, in a very limp bonnet and veil; there was Miss Gazingi, within an imitation ermine boa tied in a loose knot round her neck, flogging Mr Crummles, junior, at both ends, in fun. Lastly, there was Mrs Grudden in a brown cloth pelisse and a leather bonnet, who assisted Mrs Crummles in her domestic affairs, and took money at the doors, and dressed the ladies, and swept the house, and held the prompt book when everybody else was on for the last scene, and acted any kind of part in any emergency without ever learning it, and was put down in the bills under any name or names whatever, that occurred to Mr Crummles as looking well in print.

A veteran of a similar company explained to Henry Mayhew the structure of the profession:

What are called strolling actors are those who go about the
country and play at the various fairs and towns. As long as
they are acting in a booth they are called canvas actors; but
supposing they stop in a town a few days after a fair, or build up
in a town where there is no fair, that constitutes what is termed
private business. We call strolling actors 'mumming', and the
actors 'mummers'. All spouting is mumming. A strolling actor's
supposed to know something of everything. He doesn't always get
a part given to him to learn, but he's supposed to be able to find
words capable of illustrating the character; in fact, he has to 'gag',
that is, make up words.

Mumming at fairs is harder than private business, because you
have to perform so many times. The actor will have to dance
perhaps sixteen quadrilles in the course of the day, and act about
as often outside. The company generally work in shares, or if
they pay by the day, it's about four or five shillings a-day. When
you go to get engaged, the first question is, 'What can you do?'
and the next, 'Do you find your own properties, such as russet
boots, your dress, hat and feathers, &c.?' Of course they like
your dress the better if it's a showy one; and it don't matter much
about its corresponding with the piece. For instance, Henry the
Second in 'Fair Rosamond' always comes on with a cavalier's
dress, and nobody notices the difference of costume. In fact,
the same dresses are used over and over again for all the pieces.
The general dress for the ladies is a velvet skirt with a satin
stomacher, with a gold band round the waist and a pearl band on
the forehead. They, too, wear the same dresses for all the pieces,
for they only goes to the same places once in a year, and of course
their costumes ain't remembered.

Private business is a better sort of acting. There we do nearly
the entire piece, with only the difficult parts cut out. We only do
the outline of the story, and gag it up. We've done various plays of
Shakespeare in this way, such as 'Hamlet' or 'Othello', but only
on benefit occasions. Then we go as near as memory will let us,
but we must never appear to be stuck for words. Our prices for
admission in the country for private business is threepence and
sixpence, or sometimes sixpence or one shilling. But in London

it's oftener one penny and twopence. We only go to the outskirts
and act there, for they won't allow us in the streets. The principal
parts for pitching the booth for private business in London, is
about Lock's Fields, Walworth.

Penny Gaffs

At the bottom of the theatrical world were the 'penny gaffs' – theatres
that catered for a sensation-seeking and largely illiterate audience. These
provided basic performances that were more or less made up on the spot.
They had no pretence to artistic merit, though they often numbered
among their performers men and women who had once been well known
and highly regarded. They were a sufficiently important part of London's
culture that a number of foreign visitors and social commentators went
to see them and, like television today, they were blamed for several of
the ills of society: the idleness and corruption of youth, the glorification
of violence and crime, and the stealing that many young people went
in for in order to finance their addiction. James Grant described the
popularity of this form of theatre:

> Penny Theatres, or 'Gaffs' are places of juvenile resort. There
> exist no means for ascertaining satisfactorily either their number,
> or the number of young persons in the habit of attending them.
> There is not a single one of them in any respectable part of the
> town. They exist only in poor and populous neighbourhoods. At
> the east end of the town, they literally swarm as to numbers. One
> of them, in Paddington, is capable of containing two thousand
> persons, but the average attendance I should estimate at 150, but
> then a large proportion of these places have, in the winter season,
> from two to nine distinct audiences, or 'houses'. About three-
> quarters of an hour's worth of tragedy, or comedy, or farce, or
> very likely all three hashed up together, is all that is allowed for a
> penny. Each successive 'house' has its two pieces and a song, thus
> allowing about twenty minutes to each piece, and five minutes to
> the doggrel dignified with the name of song. Their great patrons
> are the children not only of poor parents, but of parents who pay

no attention to the morals of their offspring. Youths, from eight to sixteen years of age, are the great patrons of such places. There is always a tolerable sprinkling of girls at the Penny Theatres; but, usually, the boys considerably predominate.

With thousands, the desire to witness the representations at the Penny Theatres amounts to an absolute passion. They are present every night, and would at any time infinitely sooner go without a meal than be deprived of that gratification. The little rascals, when they have no other way of getting pence to pay for their admission, commence by stealing articles out of their parents' houses, which are forthwith put in pledge for whatever can be got for them; and the transition from theft committed on their parents to stealing from others is natural and easy. Plans for thieving, and robbing houses and shops, by way of joint-stock concerns, are to be formed and promptly executed, unless the little rogues be detected in the act. Then there are the pieces that are performed at these places, which are of the most injurious kind. The dextrous thief or villain of any kind is always the greatest hero, and the most popular personage, with these youths. I have not a doubt that a very large majority of those who find their way to the bar of the Old Bailey may trace the commencement of their career in crime to their attendance in Penny Theatres.

Grant then described one of the theatres:

Most of the penny establishments are a sort of out-door houses; before being set aside for histrionic purposes they were small stables, sheds, warehouses, &c. They are, with scarcely an exception, miserable-looking places. Judging from their appearance when lighted up, I suppose they must have a frightful aspect through the day. The naked bricks encounter the eye wherever the walls are seen; while in an upward direction you see the joist-work in the same naked state in which it proceeded from the hands of the carpenter. The distinctions of boxes, pit, and gallery are, with few exceptions, unknown. It is all gallery together. The seats consist of rough and unsightly forms. There is nothing beneath the feet of the audience; so that any incautious movement may precipitate them to the bottom. The ascent to the galleries is usually by a clumsy sort of ladder, of so very dangerous a construction that he who mounts it and descends without breaking his neck has abundant cause for gratitude. In many of these establishments, the only light is that emitted by some half-dozen candles, price one penny each. The stage and the lower seats in the gallery communicate with each other, so that should the actors or actresses chance to quarrel with the occupiers of the front row, in consequence of anything said or done by the latter – and such things do happen – they can adjust their differences by a fistical decision [fighting]. The stages in all the Penny Theatres are of very limited dimensions, it being desirable, in the estimation of the proprietors, that as much space as possible should be set apart for the accommodation of the audience. In some places, the stage is so small that the actors must be chary of their gesture, lest they break one another's heads. On the article of scenery, the expenditure of the proprietors of Penny Theatres is not extravagant. They have usually some three or four pieces of cloth, which are severally daubed over with certain clumsy figures or representations; and these are made to answer all purposes. The wardrobe of these gentry is, for the most part, equally limited in quantity, and moderate in expense. The same dresses serve for all pieces, no matter what their diversity of character. The 'lovely bride', about to be led to the altar, appears in the same apparel as the widow overwhelmed with grief at the death of her husband. The Ghost of Hamlet is to be seen in the same suit as Paul Pry.

Most of the Penny Theatres have their orchestra, if the term can be applied to a couple of fiddlers. In fine weather, the musicians usually stand at the door, because in such cases their 'divine strains' are found to answer a double purpose: they attract the attention of the passers-by to what is going on inside, and they at the same time administer to the love of sweet sounds which may be cherished by any of the audience. In cold or rainy weather, the fiddlers take their station nearer the gallery, though even then they do not venture farther than the top of the ladder. In many cases, the proprietors dispense with the music

altogether, by which means the sixpence usually paid to the
fiddler is saved; and that is, in most of these establishments,
a very important consideration.

The cast often included competent actors, but Grant explained that they
had little scope for their talents:

I have seen some pieces, both in tragedy and farce, represented
at these establishments with wonderful effect. Indeed, I am
convinced that the acting, as a whole, in the cases to which I
refer, would have been applauded at some of our more respectable
larger theatres. Many of those who are now subsisting on the
miserable pittance they receive for their performances at Penny
Theatres were once great favourites at the larger establishments.
It is really painful to think that one who had for many years
been a popular actor should now, in his old age, partly from the
infirmities of advanced years, and partly from the fickleness of
the public taste, be unable to obtain an engagement in any of the
larger houses, and consequently be driven as a last resort against
the workhouse to toil night after night at one of these miserable
places. These unfortunate men, having been in the habit of acting
well, now act well without effort. There are others again who
have a natural talent for the stage but who, having never been
fortunate enough to get an engagement in any larger house, are
obliged to vegetate in obscurity in these Penny Theatres; so that
between these two classes of actors, good acting, where sufficient
time is allowed by the proprietors, may often be witnessed at
them. In the generality, however, of these establishments, there is
no such thing as acting at all. The performers say what they like
and do as they like. Stabbing and thrusting in the tragic pieces,
and slapping one another's faces, and pulling one another's caps
over each other's eyes in the farces, are the principal kinds of
acting which are to be seen.

There was, understandably, no attempt to treat the audience with
respect. The proprietor's only concern, once a performance had finished,
was to replace them with a new crowd as quickly as possible:

It is amusing to contrast the respect which the speculators in Penny Theatres pay to their audiences when going in, with the rudeness they often show them when coming out. When a person is going into one of these establishments, he meets with every politeness from the proprietor. When coming out again, the audience are ordered to clear the way, just as if they were so many serfs at the beck of the proprietor or his servants. At some establishments, the audience are told, on going out, in most authoritative tones, to 'make haste out of the way, to let in my fresh audience'.

The material performed by the company was as idiosyncratic as everything else about the establishment:

The histrionic gentlemen and ladies who grace the boards of Penny Theatres are remarkably dextrous hands at mangling or, as they call it, abridging pieces. *Hamlet* is often performed in twenty minutes; and *Macbeth*, and *Richard the Third*, and the other tragedies of Shakespeare, are generally 'done' in much about the same time. Of all Shakespeare's plays, *Othello* is the greatest favourite with these establishments; very possibly because it is easier to assume the appearance of the Moor, than of any other of Shakespeare's heroes. A little soot smeared over the phiz [face] of the actor undertaking the part, is deemed a sufficient external qualification for the part; whereas in many other cases something in the shape of dress is supposed to be necessary. In the abridging of pieces there are no fixed rules. Time is the only counsellor to whose directions they will lend an ear. They will sometimes unwittingly devote perhaps ten minutes to the representation of some of the more interesting scenes in the first act, and then on being apprised that they have only ten minutes to finish the whole, they overleap the second, third and fourth acts, and very possibly land about the middle of the fifth. In the case of Othello, for example, when the time has expired, even though the performers should not have got beyond the first act, he says, 'The time is up – commit the murder, and down with the curtain.' Desdemona is then strangled in a moment, down goes the curtain, and out go the audience.

The range of productions was often prodigious:

> In several of these establishments, as many as from ten to twelve
> new pieces are sometimes produced in one week. In such cases,
> little pains are bestowed on the composition. Even suppose the
> writer, and there are seldom more than one or two writers for
> one establishment, had the talents requisite to the production
> of a tolerable piece, he can neither have the time or the scope
> to display those talents to any advantage. The authors, who are
> always performers in the establishment, often begin not only to
> write them without having made up their minds how they will
> end, but even cause the acting of the first part to commence
> before the latter part is finished. With regard to the players
> committing pieces to memory, that were altogether out of the
> question. They are told a few of the leading incidents, and are
> either allowed to look at the manuscript of the piece, and by that
> means endeavour to remember some of the phrases, or to express
> themselves in any words which occur to them.

The Performance

Max Schlesinger's account of a performance gives some idea of the type
of offering that was for many thousands of Dickensian Londoners the
only form of theatre they ever encountered:

> We pass through a low door, and enter a kind of ante-chamber,
> where we pay a penny each. A buffet with soda-water, lemonade,
> apples and cakes is surrounded by a crowd of thinly-clad factory-
> girls, and a youthful cavalier with a paper cap is shooting at a
> target with a cross-bow, and after each shot he throws a farthing
> on the buffet. Passing through the ante-chamber and a narrow
> corridor, we enter the pit of the penny-theatre, a place capable
> of holding fifty persons. There are also galleries – a dozen of
> wooden benches rise in amphitheatrical fashion up to the ceiling;
> and, strange to say, the gentlemen sit on one side and the ladies
> on the other. This separation of the sexes is owing to the great

refinement of feeling. The gentlemen, chiefly labourers and apprentices, luxuriate during the representation in the aroma of their 'pickwicks' [a type of cheap and rank cigar], a weed of which we can assure the reader that it is not to be found in the Havana; but they are gallant enough to keep the only window in the house wide open.

Just as we enter we see the director, a small curly-headed man, with a red punch face, ascending the stage by means of a ladder. He makes two low bows, one for the ladies and one for the gentlemen, and delivers himself of a grand oration, to excuse some small deficiencies in his institution. At every third word he is interrupted by the cheers and remarks of the audience.

'Ladies and Gentlemen,' says he, 'I am sorry I cannot produce a prima donna to-night. Jenny Lind has sent me a message by my own submarine telegraph, asking for an extension of her leave. You would not surely shorten the honeymoon of the nightingale. Madame Sontag tells me, quite in confidence, that she is falling off, and that, although her voice is good enough for Yankee ears, she wants the courage to make her appearance before the refined public of No 17, Broad-street, London. Mdde. Wagner was at my service, cheap as any stale mackerel; but could I insult you by producing her! Would not every note have reminded you of the fact, that she values nothing in England but its copper pence. Besides, the terms that exist between myself and Mr Lumley – there are considerations – I hope you'll understand me, ladies and gentlemen? The overture is about to commence!'

The speaker vanishes through a trap-door, through which two fellows presently ascend. One is dressed up to represent an Irishman, the other wears the characteristic habiliments of a Scotch Highlander. They play some national airs, and while thus engaged strip themselves of every particle of their outer clothing and appear as American planters. Some one from below hands up a couple of straw hats, which they clap on their heads, and the metamorphosis is complete. They then go to the back of the stage and return with an unfortunate 'African'. The part is acted by no less distinguished a person than the director himself. His face is blackened, he has a woolly wig on his head, and heavy chains on his wrists and ankles; and to prevent all misunderstandings, there is pinned to his waistcoat an enormous placard, with the magic words of 'UNCLE TOM'.

The planters produce meanwhile a couple of stout whips, which instruments of torture they use in a very unceremonious manner, in belabouring the back of the slave, when all of a sudden that illustrious Negro, exclaiming 'LIBER-R-R-TY! LIBER-R-R-TY!' breaks his fetters, and turning round with great deliberation, descends into the pit. Exeunt the two planters.

Transformation: – Three forms issue from the back door; a colossal female, with a trident and a diadem of gilt paper, bearing the legend of 'BRITANNIA'; after her, a pot-bellied old gentleman, with a red nose and a spoon in his right hand, while his left holds an enormous soup-plate, with a turtle painted on the back of it.

Britannia, heaving a deep sigh, sits down on a stool, adjusts a telescope, which is very long and very dirty, and looks out upon the ocean. The gentleman with the red nose, who, of course, represents the Lord Mayor of the good City of London, kneels down at her feet, and indulges in a fit of very significant howlings and gnashings of teeth. The third person is a sailor boy complete with a south-wester, blue jacket and wide trousers, who dances a hornpipe while Britannia sighs and the Lord Mayor howls.

Now comes the great scene of the evening! Somebody or something, diving up from the very midst of the pit, makes a rush against the stage. It is the Uncle Tom of the last scene; his face is as black and his hair as woolly as ever; but a cocked hat, a pair of red trousers and top boots, and an enormous sword, brings it home to even the dullest understanding, that this is a very dangerous person! Besides, on his back there is a placard with the inscription: 'Solouque – NAPOLEON – EMPEROR!!'

The monster bawls out 'INVASION!' while, to the great delight of the ladies and gentlemen, he bumps his head several times against the chalky cliffs of Britain, which, on the present emergency, are represented by the wooden planks of the stage. The very sailor-boy, still dancing his hornpipe, shows his contempt for so much ferocity and dullness. He greets the invader with a scornful – 'Parli-vow Frenchi?'

At this juncture, the conqueror becomes aware of the presence of the short ladder, and mounts it forthwith. The boy vents his feelings of horror and disgust in an expressive pantomime, the Lord Mayor howls louder than ever, and the gnashing of his teeth is awful to behold; but just as the invader has gained the edge of the stage, he is attacked by the sailor who, applying his foot to a part of the Frenchman's body which shall be nameless, kicks him back into the pit. The public cheer, Britannia and the Lord mayor dance a polka, and the sailor sings 'God Save the Queen'.

This type of drama gave to some performers a fleeting, spurious celebrity, for the notion of actors being recognized in the streets is nothing new. One man who, in a piece entitled *Groans from the Gallows* played Calcraft, the executioner at Newgate Prison and therefore a man of considerable fame in London, found himself noticed:

That piece was very successful, and run for three weeks. It drew in a deal of money. The boys used to run after me in the streets and call me Calcraft, so great was the hit I made in the part. On one occasion a woman was to be hung, and I was going along Newgate, past the prison, on the Sunday evening. There was a quantity of people congregated, and some of the lads then recognized me from seeing me act in the 'Groans from the Gallows', and they sung out 'Here comes Calcraft!' Every eye was turned towards me. Some said, 'No, no; that ain't him;' but the boys replied, 'Oh, yes it is; that's the man that played it at the gaff.' Of course, I mizzled for fear of a stone or two.

This was the theatre – more ebullient, full-blooded and philistine than it would be for more than a century – that shaped and inspired the creative outlook of Dickens. In a few decades, the music halls would draw away the rowdier, less intellectual audiences and leave the theatre the undisputed province of the bourgeoisie.

PLATE 18. Cremorne Gardens, 1864. Pleasure gardens, an invention of the Georgians, continued to flourish in the Victorian era. Usually busier at night than in daytime, they offered orchestras, dancing, supper in private 'boxes', fireworks, costume balls and balloon ascents. The platform shown here, beneath a pagoda in which an orchestra is playing, could accommodate 1,000 dancers at a time.

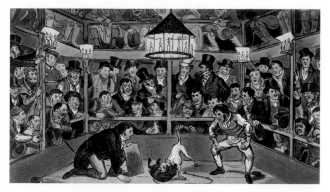

PLATE 19. A dog-fight. Spectacles of this kind, which encouraged huge wagers, symbolized a casual and unthinking cruelty that thankfully died out in the later 19th century. The gentler approach to leisure developed by the Victorians – who organized many of the sports we enjoy today – was one of their greatest achievements.

PLATE 20. The Xanthian Room of the British Museum, pictured just after its opening. The re-housing of this enormous national collection in purpose-built premises took a whole generation to complete (1828–47). The exhibits shown here are still on display. Until 1883 when the Natural History Museum opened in Kensington, these monuments shared their home with fossils and stuffed animals.

PLATE 21. Street-performers. Players of barrel-organs and hurdy-gurdies were almost invariably Italian, although many other nationalities were represented among the thousands of artistes – far more than are seen today – who entertained passers-by in exchange for coppers. They brought colour, skill and excitement to those who could not regularly afford the theatre or circus.

PLATE 22. This illustration from *Our Mutual Friend* shows the living conditions of the poor. Families would live and sleep in a single room without sanitation or running water. As a result, people did not have a level of cleanliness, or privacy, that we would consider desirable. Birth, death and all that lay between were invariably played out in such crowded conditions.

PLATE 23. Street urchins, rescued by Dr Barnardo in the decade after Dickens' death but typical of children he would have encountered. The boy – less emaciated than most – is probably wearing cut-down adult clothing while the girl, perhaps his sister, wears the cast-off and once-elegant frock of a wealthy child, as is evident from its bow and embellishment.

PLATE 24. Paupers, several of them elderly, await admission to a workhouse Casual Ward in this Gustave Doré painting. In theory it was not necessary for anyone to starve, for the parish authorities provided the poor with both shelter and assistance at home. Such was the shame attached to accepting charity, however, that only acute desperation drove many to do so.

PLATE 25. A 'Ragged School'. Before education became compulsory in 1870, street children had little access to learning. Ragged Schools, staffed by volunteers, set out to find and help the poorest. From this beginning developed a widespread movement to provide meals, accommodation, professional training and even annual holidays for them.

PLATE 26. A Watch House, or local police station. The young Dickens was taken to one of these when lost in 'Gone Astray.' This one is in Covent Garden. The Church at right still stands, as does the gateway into the churchyard. Nothing else remains. On either side of the arch there are now subterranean public lavatories!

PLATE 27. Fagin in the condemned cell at Newgate. As a journalist, Dickens had visited the prison and had been shown these cells. He retained a vivid memory of their grim and dispiriting nature, and was able to convey this in *Oliver Twist* and in *Great Expectations*. Newgate's 700-year existence ended in 1902. The prison's exercise yard is also shown in the illustration on page 234.

PLATE 28. An apprehended criminal, as seen by the *Punch* cartoonist John Tenniel. The Metropolitan Police underwent several changes in the first half-century of its existence, notably the replacement of the stovepipe hat, in 1864, with a more practical, military-style helmet. Officers were also equipped with the famous 'bullseye' lantern, as seen here.

PLATE 29. Clerkenwell House of Correction was a prison for less serious criminals. Despite its cheerless and functional architecture, it was one of the city's more modern prisons. Its precincts included gardens in which the inmates could work. This access to fresh air, together with regular food, meant that many prisoners left the institution healthier than they arrived.

PLATE 30. To us the dress, furniture and decorations of the Victorians seem fussy and impractical. They liked formality, and saw clothing as an important badge of status and respectability. In fact, men's formal dress was more colourful than it is today. Businessmen often wore coats of red, blue or green, and their trousers might have loud checks or a stripe down the side.

PLATE 31. Rotten Row, Hyde Park. The most fashionable place to be in the late afternoon was riding, driving or strolling along this track. At centre is Apsley House, home of the Duke of Wellington (and now a museum). To the right of it is the screen and gate at Hyde Park Corner. Far right is Wellington Arch, crowned by a monstrous statue of the Duke that was later removed and replaced by a quadriga. The track is now a Tarmac road, though similar ones exist elsewhere in the park for riding. Otherwise, the scene looks the same today.

Plate 32. In a First Class railway compartment, a naval officer enthrals a fellow passenger and his winsome daughter. If, as the artist implies, a friendship developed between the young people, they will have had few opportunities for time alone; Victorian courtship was highly circumscribed. Notice the gentleman's top hat stowed in a rack above him.

Plate 33. The Great Exhibition, a display of arts, technology and manufactures held in 1851, was a pivotal moment in the Victorian experience – an expression of Britain's wealth, influence and industrial might. The Crystal Palace, a temporary building created to house it, was perhaps the most remarkable structure of the age. This illustration shows the section devoted to India.

The POOR

Early morning belonged to the poor. In all seasons, hours before the clerks and shopmen were at their desks or behind their counters, and well before the rich had emerged from their homes, great masses of men and women were on the move, trudging to their places of work. Those who had no work would also be about, beginning the day's task of feeding themselves with whatever they could scavenge or beg. Henry Mayhew observed that:

> As the streets grow blue with the coming light, and the church spires and roof-tops stand out against the clear sky with a sharpness of outline that is seen only in London before its million chimneys cover the town with their smoke – then come sauntering forth the unwashed poor; some with greasy wallets on their backs to hunt over each dust-heap, and eke out life by seeking refuse bones, or stray rags and pieces of old iron; others, whilst on their way to their work, are gathered at the corner of some street round the early breakfast-stall, and blowing saucers of steaming coffee, drawn from tall tin cans that have the red-hot charcoal shining crimson through the holes in the fire-pan beneath them.

Dickens, who liked to experience the life of London at all hours of day and night, remarked on the daily procession, just after dawn, of shawl-clad figures along the south side of Piccadilly. Most were market women, on their way to Covent Garden. Men and boys who worked hauling meat, fish, or vegetables in the other London markets – Newgate, Clare, Hungerford, Oxford, Farringdon, Billingsgate – would similarly be on their way. The countrymen and gardeners who brought produce to these places would be streaming in through the turnpike gates at Notting Hill, Islington or Kennington with their beasts or their bundles, and many Londoners would be woken by the drumming of sheep's hooves on the cobbles, as a flock went by on its way to the pens of Smithfield. It must have been a comforting sound, symptomatic of that quiet part of the day before the streets were filled with noise and dirt. Max Schlesinger was similarly intrigued by this short period of comparative tranquillity:

Early in the morning, before the chimneys of the houses and factories, of the railway-engines and steamers, have had time to fill the air with smoke, London presents a peculiar spectacle. It looks clean. The houses have a pleasing appearance; the morning sun gilds the muddy pool of the Thames; the arches and pillars of the bridges look lighter and less awkward than in the daytime, and the public in the street, too, are very different from the passengers that crowd them at a later hour.

Slowly, and with a hollow, rumbling sound do the sweeping-machines travel down the street in files of twos and threes to take off every particle of dust and offal. The market-gardeners' carts and wagons come next; they proceed at a brisk trot to arrive in time for the early purchasers. After them, the coal-waggons and brewers' drays, which only at certain hours are permitted to unload in the principal streets of the city. At the same time, the light, two-wheeled carts of the butchers, fishmongers, and hotel-keepers, rattle along at a slapping pace; for their owners – sharp men of business – would be the first in the market to choose the best and purchase at a low price. Here and there a trap is opened in the pavement, and dirty men ascend from the regions below; they are workmen, to whose care is committed the city under-ground, which they build, repair, and keep in good order. Damaged gas and water-pipes, too, are being repaired, and the workmen make all haste to replace the paving-stones and leave the road in a passable condition. For the sun mounts in the sky and their time is up. They return to their lairs and go to sleep just as the rest of the town awakens to the labours of the day.

Besides this, there are a great many other classes whose avocations compel them to take to the street by break of day. At a very early hour they appear singly or in small knots, with long, white clay pipes in their mouths; as the day advances, they come in troops, marching to their work in docks and warehouses. Ill-tempered looking, sleepy-faced barmen take down the shutters of the gin-shops; cabs, loaded with portmanteaus and band-boxes, hasten to deposit their occupants at the various railway-stations; from minute to minute, there is an increase of life and activity. At length the shops, the windows and the doors of houses are opened; omnibuses come in from the suburbs and lend their living freight to the heart of the city; the pavements are crowded with busy people, crowded with vehicles of every description.

George Sala wrote of yet another straggling procession. Incongruously this one, which was made up entirely of women, passed along one of the most illustrious streets in London:

As eight o'clock chimes from the smoky-faced clock of the Horse Guards, the magnificent promenade of the Park [the Mall], on which look the stately mansions of the nobles, is pervaded by figures very mean, very poor and forlorn in appearance. Little troops of girls and young women are coming from the direction of Buckingham Palace and Birdcage Walk, but all converging on the Duke of York's Column; that beacon to the great shores of Vanity Fair. These are sempstresses and milliners' workwomen, and are bound for the great Dress Factories of the West End. Pinched faces, pale faces, sullen faces, peer from under the bonnets as they pass along and up the steps. There are faces with large mild eyes that seem to wonder at the world and its strange doings, and the necessity for Jane or Ellen to work twelve hours a day, nay, in the full London season, work at her needle not infrequently all night, in order that the Countess or the Marchioness may have her ball dress ready.

These women would see little of a bright summer's day. They usually worked in small back rooms off the fashionable streets of the West End. Before the advent of the sewing machine, the creation of a single dress would involve long hours of laborious stitching by several women. Some would piece together the garment while others, more experienced, would add ribbons, embroidery, buttons and bows. The meticulous nature of a seamstress's work was extremely tiring on the eyes, particularly in premises that were likely to be badly lit. Added to this would be the exhaustion of working days that were up to 16 hours long during the busiest periods of the year. They were most fully occupied during the London Season, from Easter until the end of August, but they were also very busy between December and February when there were a number of balls and receptions. Throughout these hectic weeks it would be common for women to continue sewing all night, either in their workshop or at home, to complete orders in time for specific occasions. This labour was without doubt a physical and mental strain and it was much commented upon at the time as a social evil (*Punch* cartoons depicted exhausted young women slumped over their sewing, or showed one appearing ghost-like in the mirror behind an aristocratic lady who was admiring herself in the finished dress). It is worth remembering, however, that this level of activity did not have to be kept up all the time, and that it was worse to have no work at all. If for any reason a social event was cancelled, the result could be (at least temporarily) destitution for many women. If, on the other hand, a prominent personage died, they would find themselves working in terrible haste to outfit ladies in mourning clothes.

Apprentice and Servant

Milliners' apprentices were girls, but virtually all others were boys. For young men of often minimal education the key to a secure future lay in being taken on by a merchant or craftsman as an unpaid assistant. To be 'put to a trade' at the age of about 13 and undergo training for five or six years meant a chance to join the ranks of the respectable, but it was not open to everyone. The master would provide what meals were necessary (just a midday repast if the apprentice lived at home) and, if the boy stayed in the master's home, a room, or at least a place to sleep. The boy's father had to clothe and support him, for he would not begin earning until he had 'served his time' and emerged as a qualified craftsman. The poor could often do this by judicious saving and by calling upon the generosity of other family members. For the very poor, whose children had to begin work at the age of five or six, this was not a possibility. On the other hand, the poorest children of all – the inmates of the workhouse – were often given training as tailors or shoemakers and might be apprenticed in these trades by the parish, which would pay £5 a head to their employer.

There were scores of trades in London from which to choose if a young man sought an apprenticeship. Most boys followed their fathers or brothers into an occupation, or were taken on by a family friend. Some personal connection, even a tenuous one, was the starting point of many careers. Pip, in *Great Expectations*, was intended from early childhood to work for his brother-in-law, the blacksmith Joe Gargery. Pip described how a boy without the possibility of schooling would occupy himself until he could begin life in earnest:

> When I was old enough, I was to be apprenticed to Joe, and until I could assume that dignity I was not to be what Mrs Joe called 'Pompeyed', or (as I render it) pampered. Therefore, I was not only odd-boy about the forge, but if any neighbour happened to want an extra boy to frighten birds, or pick up stones, or do any such job, I was favoured with the employment.

Even a blacksmith's apprentice would find the ability to read useful, and for most other apprentices it would be vital. Pip had a smattering of learning and was in this respect probably typical of many young men of the same sort:

> Mr Wopsle's great-aunt kept an evening school in the village; that is to say, she was a ridiculous old woman of limited means and unlimited infirmity, who used to go to sleep from six to seven every evening, in the society of youth who paid twopence per week each for the improving opportunity of seeing her do it ... Much of my unassisted self, and more by the help of Biddy [the school-mistress's grand-daughter] than of Mr Wopsle's great-aunt, I struggled through the alphabet as if it had been a bramble-bush; getting considerably worried and scratched by every letter. After that, I fell among those thieves, the nine figures, who seemed

every evening to do something new to disguise themselves and
baffle recognition. But, at last I began, in a purblind, groping way,
to read, write, and cipher, on the very smallest scale.

An indenture (the document that bound a boy to the master for the
prescribed period) was a legal commitment by both parties, but it does
not seem to have been especially unusual for an apprentice to leave his
employment, and he could in any case be dismissed. He would begin
as a general dogsbody and work his way up. Many young men were
delighted to be embarked on a career, finding the company of like-
minded workmates agreeable and relishing the technical ability they
were accumulating. If a boy was apprenticed, for instance, to a carriage-
maker, he might well be working in the heart of London, for the street
called Long Acre, which runs parallel with Covent Garden, was entirely
devoted to this trade (the name of a carriage-works can still be seen,
high up on one of the walls there). He would be working with boys of
his own age and background, in a close-knit world of professional pride,
defined status and technical jargon, with friendly rivalry between his
own firm and those around it.

When the apprentice's time was up and he had proved his ability
he would be free to seek proper employment. The finishing of an
apprenticeship was a moment of considerable ceremony and importance.
Frederick Willis was a skilled hat-maker in the West End and
remembered the ritual that accompanied the end of training:

When an apprentice had served his seven years (his
apprenticeship ceased at noon on the day the term expired)
the ceremony of 'Ringing Him Out' began. A hatter's shop is
full of metal instruments suitable for this purpose, and every
man prepared himself by securing a suitable tool. As the clock
struck twelve an enormous din was raised by clanging metal
against metal and the duration of the demonstration depended
upon the popularity of the apprentice. When the noise ceased
the constable of the shop (a man elected by his colleagues as
a temporary foreman) went to the master and formally asked,
'Shop a bodymaker to-day?' The master then asked, 'Who is it?'
although, of course, he knew well enough, having employed the

man for the last seven years. 'Jack Blench,' the constable would
reply. To this the master would answer: 'All right, I'll give him
a pad (i.e. a batch of work).' The constable then returned to the
shop and announced: 'A new shopmate, gentlemen!' 'Who is it!'
the men asked in unison. 'Jack Blench!' came the reply, which
was received with great applause. The ceremony was now over
and Jack Blench established as a journeyman-hatter. The rest
of the day was spent in celebration. A barrel of beer and glasses
were produced and the men sat around in a circle, drinking and
singing. Most of them had good voices and some fine effects were
obtained. 'Hearts of Oak', ''Twas in Trafalgar's Bay', 'Bay of
Biscay', and 'Tom Bowling' were the favourites.

Willis explained the value of this newly acquired position:

Skilled workers with seven years' apprenticeship to their credit
formed an aristocracy of labour. They were more assured and
confident than the unskilled worker, with good reason, for they
knew they had a fair chance of earning their living and maintaining
their standard of life, providing their health remained good. The
unskilled worker had no such confidence. If he lost his job the
whole fabric of his life might collapse before he was lucky enough
to get another, whereas the skilled worker was not tied to one firm
and would change from one to another as circumstances required.

Although this status was well worth having, much of the poorer
population managed to live in dry homes, have sufficient to eat and
enjoy a degree of security without any such skills. This was because they
were servants. The great wealth of the aristocracy and the new class of
industrialists meant that there was a huge demand for domestic staff,
and up to a third of London's population was employed in this way. It
was, in particular, by far the biggest source of employment for women.
Many of them were not Londoners, but girls and boys from the country,
whose parents were able to put them into lifelong employment at about
the age of 13. They would work either indoors as servants or outside in
the stables or as gardeners. They would start by doing odd jobs such as
washing dishes or cleaning boots, and ascend the hierarchy to become

maids and footmen. A woman could reach the upper echelons of the servant world by becoming a cook, a lady's-maid or a housekeeper; a man could become a butler. It was not uncommon for a man and woman in these corresponding positions of authority to marry and retire from service to run a public house.

The work could be extremely hard and the hours long. Servants had to be up very early to light fires, and would not go to bed until their multitude of tasks was finished. They might have one afternoon off a week, but they could often see nothing of London beyond the street in which they lived and might know no one apart from other servants and the tradesmen who delivered to the kitchen door – though their conditions varied enormously according to the nature of their employers. Even under hard circumstances, in terms of food and shelter they belonged to a privileged world.

William Tayler came from rural Oxfordshire. He was a footman in the home of a wealthy widow living in Marylebone, and he kept a journal for 1837. This provides a useful insight into the life of a Victorian servant and shows that, with a mistress who was not over-strict, life could be perfectly agreeable for a junior servant. He itemized his daily routine:

This day has been spent about the same as most of my others. The first thing I do in the morning is to get up at half past six, goes [for a walk], stays until eight, comes home, haves my breakfast, gets theirs ready at nine upstairs, then cleans the knives, fetches their breakfast down at ten, does a few other odd jobs, and then goes out for a walk a little before eleven, and comes home a little before one. Gets their lunch ready and haves my own dinner by two, rests myself until three, then goes for a ride with the ladies until four, comes home, haves my tea, gets their dinner things ready at five, waits on them at dinner, brings it down and clears my part of it away by half past six, takes a walk or sits down and reads until eight, goes for another walk for half an hour, then comes home and haves my supper. Goes to bed a little before eleven. In this way I go on every day and so I mean to continue. Very few servants go out as much as I do. Many have not an opertunity, some would rather stay at home and sleep, others would rather go to the publick house and get drunk.

He enumerated the advantages he enjoyed, though he saw his profession as less profitable than formerly:

> We are payed every quarter. I get ten pound, ten shillings a quarter. That is forty two pounds per year, my victuals and drink and lodgings in the bargain, besides all the perquisites I can make in such service as mine. These generally amount to about ten or fifteen pounds per year more or less, but it's more frequently less as service is getting very bad business.

He also described the meals that servants ate:

> They breakfast at eight in the kitchen on bread and butter and toast – or anything of the kind if they like to be at the trouble of making it – and tea. For my own part I care very little about breakfast at all, therefore I generally wait until the breakfast comes down from the parlour at ten o'clock and I can then git a cup of coco, which I am very fond of, and a rowl or something of the kind. Anyone that like to have lunch, here it is for them but, as I have breakfast so late, I want no lunch. This day we all had for dinner a piece of surloin of beef, roasted broccoli and potatoes and preserved damson pie. We all have tea together at four o'clock with bread and butter and sometimes a cake. At nine o'clock we have supper; this evening it's cold beef and damson pie. We keep plenty of very good table ale in the house and every one can have as much as they like.

Although he had a pleasant existence, many of his counterparts in other houses were not as fortunate. Many thousands of servants were needed to keep the households of London functioning, but there was no shortage of applicants for these positions. This meant that employers could be very selective and that servants could easily be dismissed. Tayler observed that:

> Servants are so plentifull that gentlefolk will only have those that are tall, upright, respectable looking young people and must bare the very best character, and mechanics are so very numerous that

most tradespeople sends their sons and daughters out to servise rather than put them to a trade. By that reason, London is over run with servants.

He expressed a sense of frustration at the constraints of life in service and indicated that what could sometimes be an easy form of existence was still likely to wear out those who were involved in it:

The life of a gentleman's servant is something like that of a bird shut up in a cage. The bird is well housed and well fed but is deprived of liberty, and liberty is the dearest object of all Englishmen. In London, men servants has to sleep down stairs underground, which is jenerally very damp. Many men loose their lives by it or otherwise end up with the rheumatics. One mite see fine blooming young men come from the country to take services, but after they have been in London one year, all the bloom is lost and a pale yellow sickley complexion in its stead. There is money to be made in service, but the person must be luckey enough to get in good places and begin service when very young. I was very much to old when I began service, therefore I shall never be worth a jot.

However, he concluded:

If a person wish to see life, I would advise them to be a gentleman's servant. They will see high and low life, above stairs as well as life below. They will see and know more than any other class of people in the world.

Any kind of scandal would finish a servant's career. Tayler recalled an incident in his native county that illustrates this danger:

I knew a footman and a housemaid that was living together in a family. They were married and left their places and went to keep a publick house just by, and the family they had been living with were very kind to them and assisted them by giving them many things. The young woman proved in the family way and all the ladies set too and made a great many things that mite be wanted

at such a time, but unfortunately, the poor girl was brought to
bed about six weeks or two months before the time she aut from
the time she was married. For this shocking offence, as these old
witches chose to call it, everything was kept from her and gave
to someone elce and this unfortunate young couple got in sad
disgrace and these hags took good care to cry this matter from one
end of Oxfordshire to the other. And if a servant girl happen to
be in the famley way, her character is rueind at once, and no lady
will take them after and would think it quite shocking to have
such a person in their house.

Henry Mayhew examined the servant class when investigating London's
'fallen women' and found that the temptation toward misbehaviour, and
the consequent risk of disgrace and destitution, was immense:

> Maid-servants live well, have no care or anxiety, no character
> worth speaking about to lose, for the origin of most of them
> is obscure, are fond of dress, and under these circumstances it
> cannot be wondered that they are as a body immoral and unchaste.
> They seldom have a chance of marrying, unless placed with a good
> family, where, after putting by a little money by pinching and
> careful saving, the housemaid may become an object of interest to
> the footman, who is looking out for a public house, or when the
> housekeeper allies herself to the butler, and together they set up
> in business. In small families, the servants often give themselves
> up to the sons, or to the policemen on the beat, or to soldiers in
> the parks; or else to shopmen, whom they may meet in the streets.
> Female servants are far from being a virtuous class. They are badly
> educated and are not well looked after by their mistresses as a rule,
> although every dereliction from the paths of propriety by them
> will be visited with the heaviest displeasure, and most frequently
> be followed by dismissal of the most summary description, without
> the usual month's warning, to which so much importance is
> usually attached by both employer and employed.

After a fall from grace of this sort, most young women would have no
choice but to join the throng in the Haymarket.

Labourers and Peddlers

Life was understandably difficult for those without secure employment. While hundreds of thousands of Londoners had skilled or semi-skilled jobs, providing the city with carpenters, glaziers, plasterers, sign-painters, upholsterers, drivers, watermen, grooms, lamplighters and myriad other services, there were many whose only ability was to wield a pick or spade. These men could work as labourers on the numerous building projects of an expanding city. They could expect periodic employment at a rate of about a pound a week, but in winter this workforce faced weeks of inactivity and starvation (in the severe winter of 1860–1, workhouse casual wards were filled with men like these and their families).

Even in normal circumstances, labouring was an unstable occupation. The construction of the railways, probably the biggest building project since the Egyptian pyramids, involved a workforce of 20,000 labourers, and there was considerable anxiety in the Government and press as to what would become of them once the work was finished. In the event, this moment more or less coincided with the start of two other large projects in the city: the sewerage system and the Metropolitan Railway. Thousands of men worked in the various London docks, loading and unloading ships, but this was badly paid (threepence a day, or the equivalent in coupons to purchase necessities) and there was no security of employment. Men had to wait at the dock gates every morning to see if they would be chosen for a day's labour.

Women also worked, though there were far fewer opportunities for them. They could 'take in washing' or act as 'baby farmers' (today called childminders), looking after the children of other women who had to go out to work. This practice suited older women and many of them advertised their services in the press. The arrangement was frequently that the children stayed with them more or less permanently, and it was open to abuse because they could take money to care for children whom they then deliberately neglected or, in the worst cases, murdered. Women could also find work as cooks and barmaids or, if they were sufficiently presentable, as shop assistants. They could work on market stalls and sell flowers, or indeed any other commodity, in the streets.

There were crowds of street peddlers. They might have their own 'pitch' so that regular customers could find them (they had to stand

in the gutter rather than on the pavement so that they did not cause
an obstruction), or walk a beat that brought them through particular
districts. Mayhew made a practice of talking to these men and women,
and as a result a great deal is known about them. He interviewed an
elderly and infirm woman who sold 'small ware'. Her situation was
characteristic of many:

I used to go out washing, and walking in my pattens I fell down.
My hip is out of the socket. I am obliged to walk with a stick.
After I put my hip out, I couldn't get my living as I'd been used
to do. I couldn't stand all day. I must sit down. So I got a little
stall, and sat at the end of the alley here with a few laces and
tapes and things. I've done so for this nine year past. My husband
used to sell small articles in the streets – black lead and furniture
paste, and blacking. We got a sort of a living by this, the two of
us together. I think I could safely state that for the last nine years
me and my husband has earned together 5 shillings a week, and
out of that the two of us has to pay 1s 9d a week.

Another instance was a man who sold stationery. Like many in his
situation, he carried his wares on a tray that was supported by a strap
round his neck. A helpful, personable man, he supplemented his sales by
offering to write letters for customers who could not do so themselves:

The times have changed since I was first in business. There
wasn't no 'velops [envelopes] then, and no note-paper. I sell to
ladies and gentlemen, and to servant–maids, and mechanics, and
their wives. I was two years with a saddler [as apprentice], and
was set to work to make girths and horse-clothes. My master
died, and all went wrong, and I had to turn out, with nobody to
help me – for I had no parents living; but I was a strong young
fellow of sixteen. I first tried to sell a few girths, but I was next to
starving. I got into stationery at last, and it's respectable.
    [Reading and writing] has been, and is still, a few pence to me.
I write notes and letters for some as buys paper of me. I've often
got extra pennies for directing and doing up valentines in nice
'velops. Why, I spoke to a servant girl the other day, and says

I, 'Any nice paper today, to answer your young man's last love-letter?' That's the way to get them to listen, sir. Well, I finds that she can't write, and so I offers to do it for a pint of beer, and she to pay the paper of course. And then there was so many orders what to say. Her love to no end of aunts, and all sorts of messages and inquiries about all sorts of things. I writes them when I get a bite of dinner. I write perhaps forty in a year. I charge 1d or 2d. I take more for note and 'velops than for anything else. Perhaps I make 2s a day, take it all round. Some days I get as much as 3s 6d; at others, 'specially wet days, not 1s. But I call mine a tidy round, and better than average. I've only myself, and pays 1s 9d a week for a tidy room, with a few of my own sticks in it.

This man had been fortunate. Starting with a loan of a shilling to purchase stock, he had built up a business. It was necessary to have money to buy materials to sell and therefore many could not even begin as street traders. One London character who succeeded against the odds was Jacobus Parker. After working for two decades at the Treasury as a vellum-binder and spending his evenings as an actor, he lost the sight of an eye, and his job, and ended up in Lambeth workhouse. He claimed that he was rescued by a gift of £10 from William Gladstone (Liberal MP and later Prime Minister). With this he was able to set up as a shoe black – a job usually done by small boys – and a seller of sweets and matches. He, too, was fortunate. Elderly and middle-aged people, whose physical resources were in decline, often gave up the struggle. Many committed suicide in autumn to avoid having to survive the winter, and this was commonplace until the introduction of the old-age pension in the early 20th century.

In Pawn

If people possessed anything of value they could gain some income from it without having to part with it forever. A pawnbroker would give them money for it, and keep it as security until they could afford to reclaim it, but the item could be bought from the pawnshop by anyone else who wanted it. Pawnbrokers still exist and the symbol of their trade, three golden balls, can be seen all over London, though today they are comparatively rare; one might see two or three in the course of a day's walk. In the 19th century there were hundreds and a single street in a poor area might have a dozen of them. Today pawnbrokers are often attached to jewellers' shops and deal only in precious objects – gold, silver, jewellery, watches. In Dickens' time they took virtually any usable commodity. Their windows were filled with furniture, candlesticks, pictures and clothes. Until well into the 20th century, it was not uncommon for people to pawn their best clothes during the week, reclaim them on Saturday when they had been paid, wear them on Sunday and pawn them again on Monday.

While the very poor would not care about any 'disgrace' attached to visiting one of these shops, those who valued their respectability would have found it humiliating. For that reason, pawnshops often enabled transactions to be carried out in secrecy. In *Martin Chuzzlewit*, Dickens illustrated how this was possible:

[Martin] passed more Golden Balls than all the jugglers in Europe have juggled with in the course of their united performances, before he could determine in favour of any particular shop. In the end he came back to the first he had seen, and entering by a side-door in a court, where the three balls, with the legend 'Money Lent' were repeated, passed into one of a series of little closets, or private boxes, erected for the accommodation of the more bashful and uninitiated customers. He bolted himself in; pulled out his watch, and laid it on the counter.

'Upon my life and soul!' said a low voice in the next box to the shopman who was in treaty with him, 'you must make it a trifle more, you must indeed! Make it two-and-six.'

'You're always full of your chaff,' said the shopman, rolling up the article (which looked like a shirt) quite as a matter of course.

'You are making it two-and-six, I think,' said Mr Tigg.

'I'm making it,' returned the shopman, 'what it always has been – two shillings. Same name as usual, I suppose?'

'Here! Please to give me the most you can for this,' said Martin, handing over the watch to the shopman. 'I want money sorely.'

'I can lend you three pounds on this, if you like,' said the

shopman to Martin, confidentially. 'It is very old-fashioned.
I couldn't say more.'

Martin, who had no resource but to take what was offered him,
signified his acquiescence by a nod of his head, and presently
came out with the cash in his pocket.

After the initial embarrassment had been overcome, a visit to the
pawnshop quickly became a routine errand, as it was for many thousands
in the city:

It was very strange, even to himself, to find how he lost his
delicacy and self-respect, and gradually came to do that as a matter
of course, without the least compunction, which but a few short
days before had galled him to the quick. The first time, he felt on
his way there as if every person whom he passed suspected whither
he was going, and on the way back again, as if the whole human
tide he stemmed, knew well where he had come from. What did
he care to think of their discernment now! Now, in his comings-
out and goings-in he did not mind to lounge about the door, or
to stand sunning himself in careless thought beside the wooden
stem, studded from head to heel with pegs, on which the beer-pots
dangled like so many boughs upon a pewter-tree. And yet it took
but five weeks to reach the lowest round of this tall ladder.

Living Hand to Mouth

Below the level of street traders, there were thousands of casual workers
who picked up whatever unskilled and hand-to-mouth jobs they could
find – working as porters, carrying advertising signs or, as one of them
put it when interviewed by Mayhew, 'helping at funerals' (carrying
and lowering coffins, or helping to dig graves). This casual workforce
included boys who would begin work as young as five, earning what
coppers they could by running errands or holding the bridles of horses
while the owners were engaged elsewhere.

Men and women who couldn't work at all lived by begging and
scavenging. They might explore dust heaps and sell whatever they

could find that was of value. Dealers in 'dust' bought the right to create these mountains (a big one would cost over £10,000) by having refuse delivered to specified locations and then having it sifted. They gained the value of whatever was salvaged and the people who sorted the rubbish were paid for doing so. The father of John Harmon, the 'Mutual Friend' in the novel of that name, made his fortune from ownership of dust heaps. Though they brought him wealth, they did not confer social standing. At a gathering in the home of the snobbish Veneerings, one guest says to another:

The man whose name is Harmon, was only son of a tremendous old rascal who made his living by Dust. By which means, or by others, he grew rich as a Dust-Contractor, and lived in a hollow in a hilly country entirely composed of Dust. On his own small estate the growling old vagabond threw up his own mountain range, like an old volcano, and its geological formation was Dust. Coal-dust, vegetable-dust, bone-dust, crockery-dust, rough-dust and sifted dust – all manner of Dust.

Those who did not live by this form of scavenging could lift horse dung from the streets to sell as fertilizer, and human waste was also saleable in this way. Dog turds could be sold at a rate of eightpence a bucket to the tanneries at Bermondsey for use in the dyeing of leather. For those who could endure the conditions, the city's sewerage system, both before and after its rebuilding, proved a source of moderate wealth: men, usually working in pairs or groups, roamed the underground passages at night with lanterns, searching the effluent for dropped coins, rings or other objects of value.

For scavengers, the river was a major hunting ground. At low tide the viscous mud on both banks of the Thames swarmed with people, many of them children, known as 'mudlarks.' London's great waterway yielded a huge and continuous harvest of multifarious objects that could be pocketed, used, repaired or resold: bottles and jars, cans of food, hats, umbrellas, wooden crates, items of furniture, coins and watches, rope, timber from boats or wharves – anything, in other words, that could have been dropped or thrown from a boat, a bridge or the bank. The Thames also saw a constant procession of unfortunates who drowned

in its waters, whether by accident or intent. These too could be useful
to the living, who could take their clothes and the contents of their
pockets, and who might also claim a reward for a body, or pretend to
have tried to save the person in order to gain a reward from the Royal
Humane Society. Dickens examined this murky subspecies of the
scavenger breed in *Our Mutual Friend*:

> A boat of dirty and disreputable appearance, with two figures in
> it, floated on the Thames, as an autumn evening was closing in.
> The figures in the boat were those of a strong man with a sun-
> browned face, and a dark girl of nineteen or twenty, sufficiently
> like him to be recognizable as his daughter. The girl rowed,
> pulling a pair of sculls very easily, the man kept an eager look-out.
> The tide, which had turned an hour before, was running down,
> and his eyes watched every little race and eddy in its broad sweep.
> Trusting to the girl's skill and making no use of the rudder, he
> eyed the coming tide with an absorbed attention. Wheresoever
> the strong tide met with an impediment, his gaze paused for an
> instant. At every mooring-chain and rope, at every stationary
> barge that split the current into a broad arrowhead, at the offsets
> from the piers of Southwark Bridge, at the paddles of the river
> steamboats as they beat the filthy water, at the floating logs of
> timber lashed together lying off certain wharves, his shining eyes
> darted a hungry look.
> Presently the boat swung round, quivered as from a sudden
> jerk, and the upper half of the man was stretched over the stern.
> [When] the upper half of the man came back into the boat, his
> arms were wet and dirty, and he washed them over the side. In his
> right hand he held something, and he washed that in the river too.
> It was money. He chinked it once, and he blew upon it once, and
> he spat upon it once – 'for luck,' he hoarsely said – before he put
> it in his pocket.

Gaffer Hexham and his daughter Lizzie prowled the Thames in search
of corpses. Though she had to assist her father, she hated this 'line of
business' and could not get used to the proximity of the dead. Her father
chided her:

'It's my belief you hate the sight of the very river.'

'I–I do not like it, father.'

At these latter words the girl shivered again, and for a moment paused in her rowing, seeming to turn deadly faint. It escaped his attention, for he was glancing over the stern at something the boat had in tow.

Gaffer's response to Lizzie's unease expressed the view of hundreds of near-destitute Londoners who looked to the Thames for a living:

'How can you be so thankless to your best friend, Lizzie? The very fire that warmed you when you were a babby, was picked out of the river alongside the coal barges. The very basket that you slept in, the tide washed ashore. The very rockers that I put upon it to make a cradle of it, I cut out of a piece of wood that drifted from some ship or another.'

Many people also relied on scavenging to feed themselves, by haunting the markets at closing time to pick up discarded food. This was especially true at Billingsgate, where fish not sold in the course of a day was of no further use. It was also commonplace at Covent Garden, where the reformer James Greenwood saw small boys, 'street arabs', gorging on rotten fruit, and observed:

Being goaded to desperation by the thoughts of the plentiful feed of cast-out plums and oranges to be picked up in 'Common Garden' at this 'dead ripe' season of the year, they have hit on this ingenious expedient.

It may be mentioned as a contribution towards solving the riddle, 'How do these hundred thousand street prowlers contrive to exist?' that they draw a considerable amount of their sustenance from the markets. And really it would seem that by some miraculous dispensation of Providence, garbage was for their sake robbed of its poisonous properties, and endowed with virtues such as wholesome food possesses. Did the reader ever see the young market hunters at such a 'feed,' say in the month of August or September? They will gather about a muck heap and gobble up plums, a sweltering mass of decay, and oranges and apples that have quite lost their original shape and colour, with the avidity of ducks or pigs. I speak according to my knowledge, for I have seen them at it. I have seen one of these gaunt wolfish little children with his tattered cap full of plums ... There must have been cholera enough to have slain a dozen strong men in that little ragamuffin's cap, and yet he munched on till that frowzy receptacle was emptied, finally licking his fingers with relish. It was not for me to forcibly dispossess the boy of a prize that made him the envy of his plumless companions, but I spoke to the market beadle about it, asking him if it would not be possible, knowing the propensities of these poor little wretches, so to dispose of the poisonous offal that they could not get at it; but he replied that it was nothing to do with him what they ate so long as they kept their hands from picking and stealing; furthermore he politely intimated that 'unless I had nothing better to do' there was no call for me to trouble about the 'little varmint', whom nothing would hurt. He confided to me his private belief that they were 'made inside such that farrier's nails wouldn't come amiss to 'em if they could only get 'em down'. Perhaps it is too much to assume that the poor little beings whom hunger prompts to feed off garbage do so with impunity. It is not impossible that, in many cases, they slink home to die in their holes as poisoned rats do. That they are never missed from the market is no proof of the contrary. Their identification is next to impossible, for they are like each other as apples in a sieve, or peas in one pod. To tell their number is out of the question.

The Perils of Poverty

The poorest Londoners lived in the centre of the city, jammed into tenements in slum districts called, in the language of the time, rookeries. London's poverty and crime were greatly exacerbated by immense overcrowding. At the beginning of the century, the city had had a population of 1 million. By mid-century it was over twice that, and by 1900 it was to be 4½ million. Periodic agricultural depression meant

large-scale migration from the countryside, and the potato famine
brought many thousands from Ireland in 1845–6. Upheavals in Europe –
revolutions in France, Italy, Germany, Poland and the Habsburg Empire
– meant a significant growth in the number of immigrants from abroad.
A constantly increasing number of people were therefore competing for
London's resources, whether for dwellings, water supplies, jobs, or even
burial plots.

The result was, predictably, continuous disease. Typhus and diphtheria
were ever-present, as were scurvy and smallpox. Most terrible of all was
cholera, of which there were four outbreaks during the 1840s and 1850s.
They were caused by polluted water, though the medical profession
was slow to recognize this. The vital connection was made by Dr John
Snow (1813–58) during the 1854 epidemic. In the space of just over two
weeks during the late summer, 616 inhabitants of Soho perished from
the disease. Snow traced these fatalities to a street water-pump in Broad
Street. He further noticed that men who worked in a nearby brewery,
and therefore drank beer instead of water, had not become infected.
He had the water-pump handle removed by the parish authorities. The
result was a sharp and immediate drop in the rate of infection, and
a breakthrough in control of the disease. Broad Street is now called
Broadwick Street, but a replica pump there commemorates one of the
19th century's great medical discoveries.

Mortality was, nevertheless, appalling in the city's sunless courts and
alleys. The life expectancy of Londoners was only 27 years, and many
could not expect to live even that long. Children were constantly dying
from a host of causes and made up half the deaths that were registered
in the city.

The Battle of Life

For all children, but especially for the poor, death was often present
at their cradles and would be a constant companion throughout
childhood. Dickens' description of the birth of Oliver Twist has about
it a touch of authenticity. Many young women, to avoid the shame that
went with illegitimacy, left their homes to give birth in areas where
they were not known:

As Oliver gave his first proof of the free and proper action of his lungs, the patchwork coverlet, which was carelessly flung over the bedstead, rustled; the pale face of a young woman was raised feebly from the pillow; and a faint voice imperfectly articulated the words, 'Let me see the child and die.'

The surgeon had been sitting with his face turned towards the fire. As the young woman spoke, he rose, and said, with more kindness than might have been expected of him –

'Oh, you must not talk about dying yet.'

'Lor bless her dear heart, no!' interposed the nurse, 'when she has lived as long as I have, sir, and had thirteen children of her own, and all on 'em dead except two, and them in the workus with me, she'll know better than to take on in that way, bless her dear heart!'

Apparently this conciliatory perspective of a mother's prospects failed in producing its due effect. The patient shook her head, and stretched out her hand towards the child. The surgeon deposited it in her arms. She imprinted her cold white lips passionately on its forehead; passed her hands over her face; gazed wildly round; shuddered; fell back – and died. They chafed her breast, hands, and temples; but the blood had stopped for ever.

'It's all over, Mrs Thingummy!' said the surgeon at last.

He put on his hat, and, pausing by the bedside on his way to the door, added, 'She was a good-looking girl, too; where did she come from?'

'She was brought here last night,' replied the old woman, 'by the overseer's order. She was found lying in the street. She had walked some distance, for her shoes were worn to pieces; but where she came from, or where she was going to, nobody knows.'

The surgeon leaned over the body, and raised the left hand; 'no wedding-ring, I see. Ah! Goodnight!'

Her son had joined the millions who belonged to the underclass:

He was badged and ticketed, and fell into his place at once – a parish child – the orphan of a workhouse – the humble, half-starved drudge – to be cuffed and buffeted through the world – despised by all and pitied by none.

The next phase of his life, from infancy until he could be put to some form of work, was taken care of by the workhouse authorities:

> The parish magnanimously and humanely resolved, that Oliver should be 'farmed', or, in other words, that he should be dispatched to a branch-workhouse some three miles off, where twenty or thirty juvenile offenders against the poor-laws rolled about the floor all day, without the inconvenience of too much clothing, under the parental superintendence of an elderly female, who received the culprits at and for the consideration of sevenpence-halfpenny's worth per small head per week. Sevenpence-halfpenny's worth per week is a good round diet for a child; a great deal may be got for sevenpence-halfpenny: quite enough to overload its stomach, and make it uncomfortable. The elderly female was a woman of wisdom and experience; she knew what was good for children: and she had a very accurate perception of what was good for herself. So, she appropriated the greater part of the weekly stipend to her own use, and consigned the rising parochial generation to even a shorter allowance than was originally provided for them.

Large families were normal in the 19th century and poorer people produced numerous children on the assumption that many of them would not survive to adulthood. Lack of hygiene, lack of adequate care, unnoticed symptoms of illness or lack of money for medicines might carry them off at any time. Mr Toodle in *Dombey and Son* is sanguine in admitting to the death of one of his children, the implication being that replacements are always arriving:

> 'We're doin' pretty well, sir,' said Toodle, turning his oilskin cap round and round, 'we haven't no cause to complain in the worldly way, sir. We've had four more since then, sir, but we rubs on. We lost one babby,' observed Tootle,' there's no denyin'.'
>
> 'Lately,' added Mr Dombey, looking at the cap.
>
> 'No, sir, up'ard of three years ago, but all the rest is hearty.'

However tragic would have been the loss of a child through illness (and despite the much higher rate of child mortality the Victorians were just as capable of feeling grief in these circumstances as modern parents are), a large family of children could also be a burden. As soon as they were old enough, the sons and daughters of the poor would be obliged to begin working for a living. James Greenwood explained the practice:

Anyone who has any acquaintance with the habits and customs of the labouring classes, must be aware that the 'family' system is for the younger branches, as they grow up, to elbow those just above them in age out into the world; not only to make room at the dinner-table, but to assist in its substantial adornment. The poorer the family, the earlier the boys are turned out, 'to cut their own grass', as the saying is. Take a case – one in ten thousand – to be met with to-morrow in the city of London. Tom is a little lad – one of seven or eight – his father is a labourer, earning, say, a guinea a week; and from the age of seven Tom has been sent to a penny-a-week school; partly for the sake of what learning he may chance to pick up, but chiefly to keep him 'out of the streets'. And to effect a simultaneous saving of his morals and his shoe-leather.

It is Tom's father's pride to relate how he was 'turned out' at eight, and had to trudge through the snow to work at six o'clock of winter mornings; and, that though on account of coughs and chilblains and other frivolous and childish ailments, he thought it very hard at the time, he rejoices that he was put to it, since he has no doubt that it tended to harden him and make him the man he is.

Accordingly, when Tom has reached the ripe age of ten, it is accounted high time that he 'got a place', as his father did before him; and, as there are a hundred ways in London in which a sharp little boy of ten can be made useful, very little difficulty is experienced in Tom's launching. He becomes an 'errand boy', a newspaper or a printing boy. The reader may, any morning at six or seven o'clock witness the hurried trudging to work of as many Toms as the pavement of our great highways will conveniently accommodate, each with his small bundle of food in a little bag, to last him the day through.

The same account gives some notion of an important 'rite of passage'. Insignificant though it may seem to be given a packed lunch for the first time in one's life, this simple gesture underlined the fact that, in this world, a ten-year-old boy was now an adult:

> When he first goes to work, his pride and glory is the parcel of food his mother makes up for the day's consumption. There he has it – breakfast, dinner, tea! Possibly he might get as much, or very nearly, in the ordinary course of events at home, but in a piece-meal and ignoble way. He never in his life possessed such a wealth of food, all his own, to do as he pleases with. Eight – ten slices of bread and butter, and may be – especially if it happen to be Monday – a slice of meat and a lump of cold pudding, relics of that dinner of dinners, Sunday's dinner!

The next milestone in his life might well be marriage. Cohabitation was far more common in Victorian times than we perhaps believe, and of all the social classes it was the poor who were least likely to be willing to spend money on rings (theirs would be brass, not gold) or ceremonies. Indeed, in many slum districts, to have been married in church was seen as a snobbish attempt to be better than one's neighbours. Nevertheless Greenwood discovered that there was a 'fashion' for matrimony among some members of this class:

> At fifteen the London factory-bred girl in her vulgar way has the worldly knowledge of the ordinary female of eighteen or twenty. She has her 'young man', and accompanies him of evenings to 'sing-songs' and raffles, and on high days and holidays to Hampton by the shilling van, or to Greenwich by the sixpenny boat. At sixteen she wearies of the frivolities of sweethearting, and the young man being agreeable the pair embark in housekeeping, and 'settle down'.
>
> Perhaps they marry, and be it distinctly understood, the estate of matrimony amongst her class is not lightly esteemed. On the contrary, it is a contract in which so much pride is taken that the certificate attesting its due performance is not uncommonly displayed on the wall of the living-room as a choice print or

picture might be. When questioned on this subject the common answer was, 'They say that it's lucky.'

For a large number, however, this option was not seriously considered. Apart from the question of cost, they just preferred a loose arrangement:

> The instinct that incites people to herd like cattle in a lair also induces them to blend their fortunes and live 'for better, for worse' till the end of their life. It requires no depth of affection on the man's part to lead him to take up with a woman who, in consideration of board and lodging and masculine protection will create some semblance of a home for him. ... If the pair have children already, the woman will be only too anxious to secure to herself legal protection in addition to that that is already secured to her through her mate's acquired regard for her.

A couple, whether or not they were married, would find lodgings wherever they could. They might obtain a room of their own, or a share in one, or they might go on living with the family of one or the other through lack of any alternative.Overcrowding was taken for granted among the poor. An entire family would live in a single room. If it contained a bed, several would sleep in this, while the others lay on the floor. As well as immediate family members, there might be others occupying the room – relatives, friends, strangers. There was considerable risk of infection where people were packed together in this way, but the danger from inadequate sanitation was worse.

The dwellings of the poor did not have plumbing, and the privies, usually communal, led into cesspits that simply stagnated underneath the houses, or into ancient sewers that led into the Thames – which provided drinking water. Many people simply used a convenient corner, or a hole in the floorboards, and excrement lay around in hallways and rooms and on stairways. The stench in these buildings was unbearable to those not used to it. In addition, there were the nuisances that inevitably go with lack of cleanliness: rats and mice were everywhere, as were cockroaches. Mayhew noted that water left standing overnight in poor homes often had insects floating in it the next morning, many having fallen from the ceiling owing to the tread of people overhead.

Without sufficient water to wash their bodies, their clothes, their bedding or their homes, people crawled with lice and fleas; anyone looking closely at an urchin would probably notice movement in his hair or on his clothing. It was often believed by those who were infested that to have a few such parasites brought good luck. Most poor people's beds consisted of straw or rags, which were a breeding-ground for vermin. Dr Lethaby, the author of a report to the Commissioners for Sewers, provided a picture of these conditions:

I have been at much pains to ascertain the precise conditions of the dwellings, the habits, and the diseases of the poor. In this way 2,238 rooms have been most circumstantially inspected, and the general result is that nearly all of them are filthy or overcrowded or imperfectly drained, or badly ventilated, or out of repair. In 1,989 of these rooms, there are 5,791 inmates, belonging to 1,576 families; and to say nothing of the too frequent occurrence of necessitous overcrowding, where the husband, the wife, and young family of four or five children are cramped into a miserably small and ill-conditioned room, there are numerous instances where adults of both sexes, belonging to different families, are lodged in the same room, regardless of all the common decencies of life, and where from three to five adults, men and women, besides a train or two of children, are accustomed to herd together like brute beasts or savages. I have seen grown persons of both sexes sleeping in common with their parents, brothers and sisters, and cousins, and even the casual acquaintance of a day's tramp, occupying the same bed of filthy rags or straw; a woman suffering in travail, in the midst of males and females of different families; where birth and death go hand in hand; where the child but newly born, the patient cast down with fever, and the corpse waiting for interment, have no separation from each other, or from the rest of the inmates.

I visited the back room on the ground floor of No 5. I found it occupied by one man, two women, and two children; and in it was the dead body of a poor girl who had died in childbirth a few days before. The body was stretched out on the bare floor, without shroud or coffin. There it lay in the midst of the living,

and we may well ask how it can be otherwise than that the human
heart should be dead to all the gentler feelings in our nature,
when such sights as these are of common occurrence.

The doctor concluded:

So close and unwholesome is the atmosphere of some of these
rooms that I have endeavoured to ascertain, by chemical
means, whether it does not contain some peculiar product of
decomposition that gives to it its foul odour and its rare powers
of engendering disease. I find it not only deficient in the due
proportion of oxygen, but it contains three times the usual
amount of carbonic acid, besides a quantity of aqueous vapour
charged with alkaline matter that stinks abominably. This is
doubtless the product of putrefaction, and of the various foetid
and stagnant exhalations that pollute the air of the place.

Many people who had no family or friends with whom they could live
dwelt in lodging-houses. There were thousands of these establishments
all over the poorer parts of London. They were effectively dormitories
– houses in which every room was filled with as many beds as could be
fitted in. They offered no privacy and no facilities, and they were the
normal accommodation for poor single Londoners. Some landlords
had converted whole streets into lodging-houses, for they represented
a good investment: a room containing ten beds would bring that many
shillings in rent every week. The insalubrious nature of lodging-houses
and tenements explains why so much of Victorian life was lived in the
streets. Mayhew examined these establishments:

In order to find these houses it is necessary to journey eastwards.
Whitechapel, Wapping, Ratciff Highway and analogous
districts are prolific in the production of these infamies. St
George's-in-the-East abounds with them, kept, for the most
part, by disreputable Jews. There are numbers in Lambeth;
in the Waterloo Road and contiguous streets; in small streets
between Covent Garden and the Strand, some in one or two
streets running out of Oxford Street. There is a class of women

technically known as 'bunters', who take lodgings, and after staying some time run away without paying the rent. A 'bunter', known about town this ever so long as Swindling Sal, said she never paid any rent, and never meant to. They was mostly Christ-killers, and chousing a Jew was no sin.

The animosity was mutual between landlords and this type of tenant, of either sex. Mayhew continued:

The people who keep the low lodging-houses where these women live are rapacious, mean, low and often dishonest. They charge enormously for their rooms in order to guarantee themselves against loss in the event of their harbouring a 'bunter' by mistake, so that the money paid by their honest lodger covers the default made by those who are fraudulent.

The diet of the poor was not altogether unwholesome, for they had access to fruit, fish, vegetables and some forms of meat. Despite the wealth of markets and the fresh produce supplied by the gardens beyond the city, little of this reached them except, as we have seen, in the form of scavenged goods. In their homes there were no kitchens or cooking facilities, with the result that any hot food they consumed had to be bought from a street vendor.

Some of the things that they ate would be familiar to us. Instead of chips (which were not a feature of British life until they arrived from Belgium, via Dundee, in the 1850s) people ate roast or baked potatoes, which were sold for a halfpenny by men who prepared them in portable stoves. The baked potato was a form of commercial 'fast food' that died out almost entirely in Britain until it was reintroduced in Scotland in the 1970s.

Pies were also popular and the itinerant pieman was one of the staple London characters. As well as fruit fillings, his pies might contain such things as veal and eel. Extremely common in the 19th century was the mutton pie, a pillbox-shaped affair with a crisp pastry covering. Though this has become virtually extinct in England it survives and continues to flourish in Scotland. Many such pies were jokingly suspected of containing 'bow-wow mutton' (dog-meat).

The saveloy, a highly seasoned form of pork sausage that was sold by street vendors, can still be found in chip shops, as of course can fried fish. Roast chestnuts were sold (as they still are) from barrows in the streets but another commonplace, the oyster, has vanished as a convenience food. In Dickens' time they were brought from Whitstable and numerous other places on the Kent and Essex coasts. They cost a penny a dozen, and the gutters of London were filled with their shells.

Londoners were much given to drinking and beer was the national beverage. Since time immemorial, it had been drunk by millions, because water was not considered safe. Beer was cheap, about twopence a pint, and workmen were encouraged to consume it because it was thought to make them strong. The other drink of the poor was gin. This was so common that there were shops that sold nothing else. It was as cheap as beer and was regarded as a cure-all, often used to keep babies quiet. It was frequently diluted, as was the more expensive brandy (Dickens' novels contain countless references to gin-and-water or brandy-and-water). Entire families virtually lived on gin. Whisky was not widespread; it was drunk almost entirely by expatriate Scots and members of the large Irish community in London.

There were no licensing hours until the end of the 1830s, and there was no age limit on the selling of alcohol until the 20th century, so children could get as drunk as their parents. Inebriation was a colossal scourge. Alcohol was the only form of comfort that many could afford, and the temptation to purchase this form of amnesia was everywhere.

The World of the Workhouse

For those who sank to the very bottom of society, there was the workhouse. We perhaps imagine that the Dickensian world was one in which no 'safety-net' existed for unfortunates, but in fact there was a system, albeit usually haphazard, for providing them with assistance. Dickens wrote of it. He visualized a man fallen on hard times:

His goods are distrained, his children are crying with cold and hunger, and the very bed on which his sick wife is lying, is dragged from beneath her. What can he do? To whom is he to apply for relief? To private charity? To benevolent individuals? Certainly not – there is the parish. There are the parish vestry, the parish infirmary, the parish surgeon, the parish officers, the parish beadle.

The woman dies – she is buried by the parish. The children have no protector – they are taken care of by the parish. The man first neglects, and then afterwards cannot obtain, work – he is relieved by the parish; and when distress and drunkenness have done their work upon him, he is maintained, a harmless, babbling idiot in the parish asylum.

This system had been in place since 1608. Although today many Londoners have no idea to what parish they belong, all 19th-century paupers knew exactly the name of their local church, for this dictated where and in what form they could obtain help.

Workhouses offered accommodation for paupers, who were admitted if they could prove themselves unable to work. Men and women lived in separate wards and were fed and housed at parish expense. They were expected to carry out work such as breaking stones or picking oakum (unravelling old rope for recycling), but could at least expect to be fed. Others, more fortunate, received 'outdoor relief': they were given a sum of money and went on living in their own homes. Both practices ran concurrently, though in the 1830s the law was made stricter and outdoor relief was in theory discontinued.

The difficulty was that, for even the poorest people, the workhouse was regarded with unmitigated dread as a source of shame. Such was the work ethic of the 19th-century that no one with a shred of self-respect wanted to end up there. For others, who could not afford self-respect, the workhouse, like prison, could be preferable to a life spent shivering in the streets, and in any case one was not necessarily confined to it for life. There were many whose residence was temporary – a few weeks or months – to see them through the winter.

James Grant, in his research on the London poor in the 1830s, made a study of these institutions, particularly the important one at Marylebone. He indicated that, though there was a good deal of ill-treatment, there were also kindness, sensitivity and intelligent organization. Dickens, after all, wrote *Oliver Twist* as propaganda: his workhouse was a caricature, and conditions in many were not as bad. Not all those who entered them were the congenitally poor:

In the workhouses are always to be found people of every clime: they are refuges for the destitute and the indolent of all nations. As regards their past history, the inmates of the metropolitan workhouses are as promiscuous an assemblage as it were possible to get together. Those who were born in the splendid mansion are there reduced to the same level as those who first drew their breath in the most wretched hovel. He who rolled in wealth and luxury, is there on a footing of perfect equality with the poor wretch who had all his life long to struggle with the demon of poverty in its most repulsive aspect; it lays the axe at the root of all the conventional differences which exist in society.

Grant chose the most conspicuous example for his investigation:

The parish of Marylebone is the largest and, in every respect, the most important workhouse in London. It is a building of very great size: it is not only the largest in the metropolis, but the largest in the United Kingdom ... Of course, the number of inmates varies according to circumstances. Want of trade, a bad harvest, the high price of provisions, a long continuance of inclement weather, and other causes, compel paupers to seek refuge in the workhouse, who, but for those causes, would have struggled on with the ills of poverty out of doors. The average number of inmates in Marylebone workhouse, for some months past, has been 1200. The number of adults in the workhouse, at the close of last year, was 808; of whom 272 were men; the remaining 536 were women. The number of children was 410 ... Each pauper costs the parish 3s 6d per week: this applies to those who are in health. In the infirmary, each pauper costs within a fraction of 6s 6d per week, including wine and other expensive medicines. The entire weekly expenses of the workhouse exceed £1000 ... But it must be borne in mind that the entire expenses of the establishment are not confined to within doors. The parish, not being under the jurisdiction of the New Poor

Law Commissioners, give a great deal of out-door relief. On an average, the number of persons receiving out-door relief is about 2000. In times of great pressure, whether from the inclemency of the season, the want of employment, or bad harvests, the number greatly increases: some years ago it was as high as 8000. So large a number of persons are never, however, likely to be again dependent on the compulsory support of the rate-payers.

Like the benefits system of today, parish relief was open to abuse:

When an enquiry was instituted into the circumstances of the out-door pensioners on the parish bounty, a very large majority of them had no claim whatever to parochial relief, being all in the way of earning, or having it in their power to earn, a competent subsistence for themselves. One woman was found to have had four laundresses in her employ for several years, during which she had been regularly receiving a weekly allowance from the parish.

The great defect of the old system was the encouragement it held out to idleness and fraud. A clever rogue, of indolent disposition, could always contrive to make a very comfortable living of it. A case was mentioned to me in which a woman was in the habit of receiving four shillings per week from the parish of St Paul, Covent Garden, while carrying on business on a rather extensive scale, and renting an excellent shop, as a bonnet-maker, in the Mile-end-road. In another case, a person was dextrous enough in the arts of deception to impose on no fewer than four parishes at one time, in each of which she professed to have a right of settlement, and from all of which she continued for some years to receive three or four shillings, beside a certain quantity of bread, per week.

The Poor Law guardians of the parish of Marylebone have appointed a number of inspectors to institute a careful enquiry into the circumstances of all who apply for parochial relief. The consequence is that persons having no claims on parish aid are refused such aid; while those who really are proper objects for parochial assistance at once receive it. The same enlightened

caution is observed in the administration of the Poor laws
in the parish of St Pancras; and the result has been that in both
these parishes the poor-rates have been reduced much more
than one-half – nearly, I believe, two-thirds – without in the
slightest degree entrenching on the legitimate claims of the
pauper population.

Grant's analysis suggests that conditions, at least in terms of feeding,
were by no means harsh:

The amount of out-door relief varies, according to the
circumstances of the parties, from one shilling and a loaf per
week to three shillings and sixpence. As might be expected, there
is a vast consumption of bread in the workhouse. The average
quantity is six hundredweight per day. The paupers are allowed
three meat dinners a week. The average quantity of butchers'
meat consumed per week is about 240 stones, or 3840 pounds.

He explained the organization:

The establishment is divided into two departments. The healthy
department is called the workhouse: the department for the sick
is called the infirmary. The lunatic paupers are not kept in the
workhouse, but are farmed out.
    Some of the parishes in the City, and in Southwark, 'farm out'
their paupers at so much per head per week. They are taken into
the keeping of persons in the neighbourhood, who speculate in
them just as some individuals do in providing black cattle and
horses with 'keep' for whatever period may be agreed on. The
parties who engage to provide these paupers with food, clothing
and lodging, at the small sum – generally about four shillings
per head a week – agreed on, make, as a matter of course, the
most they can of them, by causing those of them who can work,
to do whatever they are most adapted for. Some of them make
the workhouse clothes for the men and boys; others make and
mend shoes; others, again, prepare hair for upholstery articles;
while the cooking, washing, cleaning &c. of the workhouse,

are all performed by paupers chosen for the purpose. The
same principle of making all work who can, is adopted at all
metropolitan workhouses.

In Marylebone workhouse, the principle is practically carried
into effect in a manner which is pleasing to witness. Of all
the workhouses which I have seen, the arrangements in that
of Marylebone seem to be better than in any other. While the
strictest economy is practised, the utmost attention is paid to the
comforts of the inmates. They appear to me, taken altogether,
to be the happiest inmates I have ever seen in a workhouse.
Under any circumstances the workhouse is a place of misery to a
sensitive and high-principled mind; but the horrors of the place
can be very materially lessened by kind and humane treatment.

Grant also discussed the widespread fear of the workhouse that was to
characterize the British poor right up until the founding of the Welfare
State after World War II:

The horror with which a sensitive mind regards a workhouse
is not confined to those who have been at one time in affluent
or easy circumstances; though, as might be expected, it is most
generally felt by them. It is gratifying to be able to state that it
obtains to a very considerable extent among the working classes;
and that it causes them to submit to the greatest privations
rather than submit themselves to the degradation of crossing the
threshold of a workhouse. From circumstances which have come
under my own personal observation, I am convinced that there
are hundreds of our mechanics and working men who perish
every year of absolute want, from their extreme horror of the
workhouse. The feeling is one which reflects the highest honour
on the artisans of the metropolis, though it is to be regretted that
it should be pushed to such an extent as this.

There are many who, in being compelled to seek an asylum
in one of these places, resign themselves to utter despair. They
regard themselves as entirely out of the world, and as placed
beyond the pale of society, as well as beyond the reach of
sympathy. They see and hear their fellows in adversity, but they

never bestow a thought on them. They are as much wrapped up in their own thoughts as if they were in the midst of the greatest solitude to be found on the face of the earth. Others again, act on the principle of making a virtue of necessity: they labour to discipline their minds into submission to a fate which they cannot avert. They speak to those around them, and eagerly grasp at anything which is likely to divert their minds from unavailing regrets at their unhappy destiny.

He did not know that Dickens was soon to write about the subject when he made this very pertinent observation:

The workhouses of London abound with the romance of real life. I have often wondered that none of our novel-writers have thought of singling out their heroes or heroines from among their inmates. There are persons of both sexes there, whose lives would afford incidents of the most striking nature for a work of fiction, and which, skilfully managed, could not fail to make one of the most attractive works of the kind, of modern times.

It was, of course, in *Oliver Twist* that Dickens dealt with the subject of workhouses, though in *A Christmas Carol* the character Scrooge makes a comment typical of those whose only interest in the function of these places was that they got the destitute off the streets:

'Are there no prisons? And the Union Workhouses, are they still in operation? The treadmill and the Poor Law are in full vigour, then? I was afraid, from what you said, that something had occurred to stop them in their useful course. I pay to support the establishments I have mentioned: they cost enough: and those who are badly off must go there.'
'Many can't go there; and many would rather die.'
'If they would rather die, they had better do it, and decrease the surplus population.'

Some paupers did prefer death to accepting institutional charity. A woman interviewed by Mayhew said of her sick and aged husband:

What shocked him most was that I was obligated in his old age
to go and ask for relief of the parish. You see, he was always a
spiritful man, and it hurted him sorely that he should come to
this at last, and for the first time in his lifetime. The only parish
money that ever we had was this, and it *does* hurt him every day
to think that he must be buried by the parish after all. He was
always proud, you see.

Outdoor relief enabled paupers to receive help without needing to live
within the workhouse walls. James Grant showed that this was not
always much helpto the destitute:

The guardians of the poor, in most of the workhouses, have
a fixed day, once a week, for the purpose of granting out-door
relief. The scene on such occasions is usually one of a grotesque
nature. Ragged mothers, with children in their arms, and children
at their feet, are seen congregated together in vast numbers at the
place of distribution ... There is not only their ragged appearance,
but their starved looks: you see, from their faces, that few and
far between are their ample meals, even of the plain and homely
fare to which they are accustomed. The scenes, however, of this
kind which possess the greatest interest are exhibited at those
workhouses which are under the operation of the New Poor
Law Act, and where, consequently, the applicants are uncertain
whether they are to be successful in their applications for bread
or not. A few weeks since, I witnessed a scene of this kind, of a
very touching nature. It was at the house of a small parish, and
the number of applicants who had besieged the office, whence the
loaves are distributed, was under one hundred. A more miserable
group of human beings I have never seen. When one succeeded
in getting a loaf, every eye was directed to it in a moment, with
an eagerness and intensity of gaze which told much more forcibly
than words could, the hunger which the poor creatures were
enduring. The eyes of the children looked with an especially
expressive gaze at the article of food. But what was most eloquent
and affecting of all, as showing the agony which the poor young
creatures were suffering from want of food, was the almost

ferocious-like manner in which they seized the loaf, the moment their mothers got one, and the ravenous voracity with which they began to eat it.

Yet Grant was impressed by the institution itself:

It is a fact which is worthy of mention, that the best-regulated workhouses are conducive to health rather than otherwise. I ascribe this, in great measure, to the circumstances of the rules of these establishments being of such a nature as to ensure greater regularity of habits than the inmates were previously accustomed to. They are there regular in going to bed, regular in rising, and regular in their meals; and everyone knows how great an influence regularity in such matters has on the health of mankind. A guardian in one of the workhouses in the centre of the metropolis, lately mentioned to me some singular cases of paupers having entered those establishments in a very bad state of health, brought on by irregularity of living, and of their complete restoration to health after being a short time there. A female, when she applied for admission, was labouring under illness, brought on by irregularity, to such an extent that no one who saw her supposed she would survive a month. The medical gentleman who had attended her pronounced her case to be hopeless, and yet the regularity of habits enforced by the rules of the workhouse restored her in a few months to perfect health.

Precious Education

The suffering of the poor was not cavalierly ignored by the wealthy and the comfortable, not least because they feared revolution if a large, violent underclass developed. There was a great deal of genuine concern for the unfortunate and by the middle of the century there were over 500 private societies devoted to combating social ills. One of the most significant was the movement for teaching children to read and write. Education was seen, rightly, as the most precious benefit that could be bestowed by the wealthy on the poor.

The level of knowledge of a more or less typical street boy, aged about 13, was discovered by Mayhew in a conversation that he summarized thus:

> [He] had heer'd of the Duke of Wellington; he was Old Nosey; didn't think he ever seed him. Hadn't heer'd of the Battle of Waterloo, nor who it was atween. Thought he had heer'd of Bonaparte; didn't know what he was; thought he'd heer'd of Shakespeare, but didn't know if he was alive or dead, and didn't care. Had seen the Queen, but didn't recollec' her name just at the minute; oh! Yes, Wictoria and Albert. Had no notion what the Queen had to do. Should think she hadn't much power (he had first to ask me what 'power' was) as the Lord Mayor, or as Mr Norton as was the Lambeth beak [magistrate], and perhaps is still. Was never once before a beak and didn't want to.

Children with a living to earn had little opportunity for education, and whatever learning they could acquire had to be fitted in around their daily work. The first opportunity that many of them had came through the Sunday Schools. Begun in Gloucester in 1780 and developing into a national movement, the gift of literacy that these bestowed cannot be overestimated. By 1800 there was one in the London area, where a man called Thomas Cranfield began teaching children in Camberwell. In 1808 and 1811 two other movements, the British and Foreign Schools Society and the National Schools Society, were founded and these too provided education for the poor at a time when the state made no effort to do so. These schools charged a fee of a penny and were thus beyond the reach of the destitute.

The 'Ragged Schools' had no definite beginning but derived from the notion that starving children were too preoccupied to learn, and that they must therefore be fed as well as taught. From this developed an emphasis on character training and then on the teaching of useful trades. This concentration on 'life skills' rather than academic learning meant that the schools were looked down upon by educationalists and government officials alike. Yet 19 such schools were able to form the 'Ragged School Union' by 1844 and, as a national body, began to acquire political influence.

They derived their name from the rough-and-ready nature of both their facilities and their pupils. For some time after their beginnings none had permanent premises and classes were conducted in sheds, outhouses or underneath arches. The pupils did not have to be clean (infested children were not welcome at some of the other schools) and they needed no money, since teaching was entirely free. The pioneers of this movement, such as the well-born Quentin Hogg, sought to educate the 'untouchables.' A fellow enthusiast, William Locke, described the type of child whom they wanted to reach:

Those who go with barrows about the streets; they are the children of brick-makers; of pig-feeders; the children of rag-dealers and Spitalfields weavers out of employment, and many others of uncertain occupations, who are in a dreadful state during the winter months. Sometimes the children of labourers, who are out of work in bad weather, or are thrown out of work at the docks frequently by ships not arriving; the children of knackers and cat's-meat men; of slop-tailors, who earn a bare subsistence, and who yet will not condescend to accept parochial relief; the children of washer women who go out to work in the daytime, neglecting their children; the children of crossing-sweepers and street-musicians, and persons who get their living by theft; the children of hawkers, pigeon-dealers, dog-fanciers, and other men of that class. A great proportion of the children are those of worthless and drunken parents who, from their poverty, are too poor to pay even a penny a week for schooling.

This type of pupil was not usually inclined to sit quietly and absorb learning, and the schools were often rowdy. Nevertheless, they did invaluable work. By 1861 there were 176 of them affiliated to the RSU, representing almost 26,000 children. The schools had begun by teaching on Sunday evenings. They expanded their outreach to include weekdays too. The curriculum included reading and writing, history and geography, with tailoring and shoemaking for the boys (skills for which the demand would never cease) and sewing for the girls. In 1857 the founding of yet another movement, the Industrial Schools, developed this notion of vocational training. Since the pupils often had no access to wholesome food, the schools began to provide meals. Because they often had nowhere to go once lessons ended, basic accommodation began to be provided. In 1850 a scheme was initiated to organize pupils for part-time work that could run parallel with their education. They were equipped and trained as shoe-blacks and divided into 'brigades', each of which worked in a different part of London. The boys' earnings were divided in three: a third was paid to them, a third was banked for them, and the remainder was put toward expenses. Another initiative, beginning in 1869, was the sending of children on annual holidays to the country.

Much of the movement's thunder was stolen when, in 1870, elementary education was made compulsory and the state took over the task of teaching the young. The social work in which it was involved carried on, though it was an uphill task, for the numbers suffering from want and destitution in the world's largest city were simply too great. As another pioneer, Mary Carpenter, put it:

Until there is a very great change in the social conditions of our country, there is and must be a large proportion of the population who are, from whatever cause, barely above starvation, and whose precarious means scarcely suffice for their daily bread, without the power of providing decent clothing or other necessaries; also that the low moral, intellectual, and often physical condition of this class necessarily perpetuates the same state of things, unless a helping hand is held out to the children to aid them to rise to a higher and better life.

CRIME and
Punishment

D avid Copperfield described a walk through London with his aunt,
Betsey Trotwood:

> My aunt, who had this general opinion in reference to London,
> that every man she saw was a pickpocket, gave me her purse to
> carry for her, which had ten guineas in it and some silver. We
> were crossing to [St Paul's Churchyard] when I noticed that
> my aunt quietly accelerated her speed and looked frightened. I
> observed at the same time that a lowering, ill-dressed man, who
> had stopped and stared at us in passing, a little before, was coming
> so close as to brush against her.

Miss Trotwood was right to be concerned, for London was an extremely
dangerous place. With a level of poverty, and therefore desperation,
that is scarcely imaginable today, thieves and swindlers preyed on
the vulnerable, the careless and the credulous as an urgent matter of
survival. Anything that could be used, consumed or sold on would
be hunted by some species of criminal. The whole infrastructure of
surveillance and protection that Londoners now take for granted
(telecommunications, CCTV, police patrols) did not of course exist.
The most that a victim could usually hope for was the help of passers-by.

As well as purse-snatching there was also 'clouting': the stealing
of handkerchiefs by pickpockets, typified by the Artful Dodger, who
specialized in this field. 'Reader merchants' was the slang term for
thieves who stole the pocketbooks of people as they left the Bank of

England. (On the swallow-tailed cutaway coats worn by men in the
Regency and early Victorian period, the pockets were at the back,
making it relatively easy for pickpockets to empty them). 'Onion
hunters' targeted the seals and fobs on gentlemen's watch-chains, while
'silk-snatchers' made a grab at the fashionable hoods or hats of passing
pedestrians. Those involved in the 'noisy dog racket' stole brass knockers
from front doors. There were criminals who cut the saddle-bags from
horses or the trunks from coaches, or stole pewter tankards from public
houses, or snatched washing that had been hung out to dry ('nabbing the
snow'). There were 'curtails' who literally cut the tails off women's gowns
or snipped pieces of cloth hanging in shop windows. And there were
thieves who would break a single pane in a shop window and abscond
with whatever they could gather up. Others had a more subtle means
of stealing from shops. Francis Grose's *Classical Dictionary of the Vulgar
Tongue* defines a ploy known as the 'fan lay' as:

> **Going into a goldsmith's shop, under pretence of buying a
> wedding-ring, and palming one or two, by daubing the hand with
> some viscous matter.**

Among the most villainous subspecies were those who stole dogs in
order to claim the reward (if none were offered, they would kill the
animal and sell its skin) and those who would lure children off the
streets and strip them of their clothes.

Thieves often worked in pairs. Grose defined a 'bulk and file' as:

> **Two pickpockets. The bulk jostles the party to be robbed, and the
> file does the business.**

If the streets were dangerous, any public event carried even greater risk,
for within the tight crush of people groups of thugs could intimidate and
rob the public with virtual immunity. Grose provides an example:

> **STALL UP. To stall a person up, (a term used by pickpockets),
> is to surround him in a crowd, or violent pressure, and even
> sometimes in the open street, while walking along, and by
> violence force his arms up, and keep them in that position while**

others of the gang rifle his pockets at pleasure, the [victim] being
unable to help or defend himself; this is what the newspapers
denominate hustling, and is universally practised at the doors
of public theatres, at boxing matches, ship launches, and other
places where the general anxiety of all ranks, either to forward,
or to obtain a view of the scene before them, forms a pretext for
jostling, and every other advantage which the strength or numbers
of one party gives them over a weaker one, or a single person.

In addition to those who took from others by violence, there were armies
of swindlers and confidence-tricksters who waylaid passers-by on a host
of pretexts. Some pretended to be soldiers or sailors wounded in famous
battles; others posed as victims of crime or misfortune. Even indoors the
public was not safe. In churches, where men would hang up their hats
in the lobby, thieves would attend for the purpose of stealing the best
quality headgear and leaving shabby replacements.

Those who rented out rooms had to beware a ruse known as the
'lodging slum': criminals renting furnished lodgings and immediately
making off with all the furniture, crockery and linen. There were also
tricksters who, according to Grose, practised:

A mode of stealing in houses that let lodgings, by rogues
pretending to be postmen, who send up sham letters to the
lodgers and, while waiting in the entry for the postage [before the
invention of the stamp, the cost of postage was paid on delivery
by the recipient] go into the first room they see open, and rob it.

Children and young men were among the most likely victims. Grose
describes one common type of deceit:

Rogues who make it their business to defraud young apprentices,
or errand-boys, of goods committed to their charge, by prevailing
on them to execute some trifling message, pretending to take care
of their parcels till they come back. Even porters and other grown
persons are sometimes defrauded of their load by this artifice. To
kid a person out of any thing is to obtain it from him by means of
a false pretence.

Equally, children and young girls were often criminals themselves. Henry Mayhew, in his 1862 survey of London's underworld, described how juvenile thieves might steal goods from outside shops:

The coat [displayed outside a secondhand clothes shop] is stolen from the dummy in this way: One boy is posted on the opposite side of the street to see if a police-officer is in sight, or a policeman in plain clothes, who might detect the depredation. Another stands two or three yards from the shop. The third comes up to the dummy, and pretends to look at the quality of the coat to throw off the suspicion of any bystander or passer-by. He then unfastens the button, and if the shopkeeper or any of the assistants come out, he walks away. If he finds that he is not seen by the people in the shop, he takes the coat off the dummy and runs away.

If seen, he will not return at that time, but watches some other convenient opportunity. When the young thief is chased by the shopkeeper, his two associates run and jostle him, to try and trip him up, so as to give their companion an opportunity of escaping. This is generally done at dusk, in the winter time, when thieving is most prevalent.

In stealing a piece of bacon from the shop-doors or windows, they wait till the shopman turns his back, when they take a piece of cheese in the same way. This is commonly done by two or three boys in company. Handkerchiefs at shop-doors are generally stolen by one of the boys and passed to another who runs off with it. When hotly chased, they drop the handkerchief and run away.

These young thieves are ragged boys, varying from 9 to 14 years of age, without shoes or stockings. Their parents are of the lowest order of Irish cockneys, or they live in low lodging-houses, where they get a bed for 2d or 3d a night, with crowds of others as destitute as themselves.

There are numbers of young women of 18 years of age and upwards, Irish cockneys, belonging to the same class, who steal from shop-doors. They are poorly dressed, and live in some of the lowest streets in Surrey and Middlesex, but chiefly in the Borough and the East End. Some of them are dressed in a clean cotton dress, shabby bonnet and faded shawl, and are accompanied by

one or more men, costermongers in appearance. They steal rolls
of printed cotton from the outside of linen-drapers' shops, rolls
of flannel, and of coarse calico, hearthrugs and rolls of oilskin
and table-covers: and from brokers' shops they carry off rolls
of carpet, fenders, fire-irons, and other articles, exposed in and
around the shop-door. The thefts of these women are of greater
value than those committed by the boys. They belong to the
felon-class and are generally expert thieves.

The mode by which they commit these thefts is by taking
advantage of the absence of the person in charge of the shop, or
when his back is turned. It is done very quickly and dexterously,
and they are often successful in carrying away articles such as
those named without anyone observing them.

In spite of the often vicious lawlessness that characterized the city in
Dickens' youth, London was gradually becoming less perilous than it had
been in the 18th century. Highwaymen, once the scourge of travellers on
the outskirts of the city, had been effectively suppressed by the 'Rollers'
– the armed horse patrol that roamed the suburbs at night. The Thames
too was patrolled by law enforcement officers.

The Constabulary

London boasted a police force of sorts: a disparate collection of thief-
takers and constables, including the 'Bow Street Runners', which had
replaced the elderly night-watchmen or 'Charleys' of past generations.
This system was swept away within seven years of Dickens' arrival in
London, when the Home Secretary, Sir Robert Peel, established the
Metropolitan Police. A decade later James Grant, remarked in his
Sketches in London on the vast improvement that this brought:

The constabulary system which now exists is only, as most of
my readers are aware, of recent origin. It was introduced by Sir
Robert Peel in 1829. Previous to that time, the police of the
metropolis was in a most defective and inefficient state. It was the
subject of loud and general complaint. And no wonder, for the

number of felonies, and other offences of every kind, which were weekly committed without the parties being detected or brought to justice, was almost incredible.

In the first place, no attention was paid to the character of the persons chosen to the office of constables. They were, almost without exception, Irishmen of the very worst class in point of moral character; and, in addition to this, the smallness of their wages – from 13s 6d to 17s per week – necessarily rendered them more liable to be bribed than if they had been better paid. They might, in the majority of cases, be bribed at the instance of any private gentleman who 'did the handsome' by 'tipping' them half a sovereign ...

They were not inspired with the spirit of their office. They had no pleasure in taking offenders into custody. They did not, as the new police do, engage in the duties of thief-catching with gusto. They preferred being suffered to crawl about as if there had been no such animal as a thief in the metropolis, or to doze away their time in a comfortable sleep, with their heads resting on their arms, in their little comfortable boxes. Their cowardice, as a body, was proverbial.

Peel's recruits to the new force, on the other hand, meant that:

One very rarely hears of any one attacking them. They are a body of men of great physical vigour and activity; and in the great majority of cases, are men of spirit and courage. A more feeble and inefficient set of men than the old police could scarcely have been got together. But, in addition to the mental and physical incompetency of the old constabulary, the want of intercourse with each other greatly impaired their efficiency. They were chosen by the various parishes, and all the police in a particular parish were entirely under the control of the authorities of that parish. The consequence was, that there was nothing like concert among them. Responsibility did not rest anywhere. The authorities in one parish had their constant quarrels and bickerings with the authorities of other parishes, which was the direct way to prevent any general understanding among them in regard to the best means of repressing crime.

Grant concluded that the effect on the crime rate was not encouraging:

> The amount of crime committed in the metropolis under this
> defective system of police was, as might have been expected, very
> great. No man's property was safe; and the difficulty which was
> then experienced in bringing the offender to justice, had the effect
> of preventing many of the parties robbed from engaging in the
> pursuit. Crimes were committed under this system in open day.

Officers of the Metropolitan Police dressed in distinctive dark blue
coats (they were nicknamed 'bluebottles') and black stovepipe hats.
They quickly became a conspicuous presence on the streets and
added significantly to the safety of the city, but they did not prove
as incorruptible and effective as Grant had imagined: between 1866
and 1870 nearly a quarter of uniformed officers would be dismissed
for misconduct. They kept the main thoroughfares relatively safe but
there were, and remained throughout Dickens' lifetime, parts of central
London that pedestrians were wise to avoid even in daytime, let alone
after dark. The area north of the Strand between Drury Lane and St
Martin's Lane consisted largely of rookeries – dark streets and alleys
through which no stranger could expect to find his way, and in which
ambush could wait around every corner. Captain Shaw, an otherwise
unknown author who wrote a reminiscence describing the London of
his youth from the perspective of the Edwardian era, illustrated the risks
that were run by visitors or theatregoers in the neighbourhood of Covent
Garden at night:

> The approaches to Evans's after dark were by no means free
> of danger in the long-ago sixties. The market porters, who
> for the most part were cut-purses and pugilists, were apt to
> waylay solitary foot-passengers whilst awaiting the arrival of
> the vegetable vans, and I recollect an Uxbridge farmer named
> Hillyard entering the hotel one night with a broken wrist after
> being waylaid and robbed in Russell Street.
> The old Olympic, hard by, was another nasty place to leave after
> the performance, except in a cab. Within fifty yards the alleys
> bristled with footpads, and any foolhardy pedestrian traversing

the dimly-lighted Drury Lane or Newcastle Street was pretty sure
not to reach civilisation without a very rough experience from the
denizens of Vinegar Yard and Betterton Street.

Most notorious of all was the district known as the Seven Dials, near the
church of St Giles-in-the-Fields. Dickens was to say of it: 'What wild
visions of prodigies of wickedness, want and beggary, arose in my mind
out of that place!' Captain Shaw stated that 'the half-dozen constables
within view would no more have thought of entering it than they would
the cage of a cobra', and recalled that:

The walk through the Dials after dark was an act none but
a lunatic would have attempted, and the betting that he ever
emerged with his shirt was 1,000 to 60. A swaggering ass named
Corrigan, whose personal bravery was not as highly assessed by
the public, once undertook for a wager to walk the entire length
of Great Andrew Street at midnight, and if molested to annihilate
his assailants.
    The half-dozen doubters who awaited his advent in the Broadway
were surprised about 1 a.m. to see him running as fast as he could
put legs to the ground, with only the remnant of a shirt on him ...

Within a district like this there would have been innumerable thieves'
dens in which stolen property could be hidden, dismantled, melted
down or divided up – places similar to the one in which Oliver Twist
encountered Fagin and his gang of juvenile pickpockets:

The walls and ceiling were perfectly black with age and dirt.
There was a deal table before the fire, upon which were a candle,
stuck in a ginger-beer bottle, two or three pewter pots, a loaf and
butter, and a plate. In a frying-pan, which was secured to the
mantel-shelf by a string, some sausages were cooking. [There
was also] a clothes-horse, over which a good number of silk
handkerchiefs were hanging. Several rough beds, made of old
sacks, were huddled side by side on the floor; and seated round
the table were four or five boys, smoking long clay pipes, and
drinking spirits with the air of middle-aged men.

Dickens gave the lie to Shaw's notion that even the police would not venture into Seven Dials at night, and suggested the difference that well-trained officers were making to the criminal underworld. While writing an article for *Household Words*, he visited the area in the company of Inspector Field of the Metropolitan Police, who knew the names and histories of many of those whom they met:

> Saint Giles' church strikes half-past ten. We stoop low, and creep down a precipitous flight of steps into a dark close cellar. There is a fire. There is a long deal table. There are benches. The cellar is full of company, chiefly very young men in various conditions of dirt and raggedness. Some are eating supper. There are no girls or women present. Welcome to Rats' Castle, gentlemen, and to this company of noted thieves!
>
> 'Well, my lads! How are you, my lads? What have you been doing today? Here's some company to see you, my lads!' Inspector Field is the bustling speaker. Inspector Field's eye is the roving eye that searches every corner of the cellar as he talks. Inspector Field's hand is the well-known hand that has collared half the people here, and motioned their brothers, sisters, fathers, mothers, male and female friends, inexorably to New South Wales [i.e. they have been sentenced to transportation]. Yet Inspector Field stands in this den, the Sultan of the place. Every thief here cowers before him, like a schoolboy before his schoolmaster. All watch him, all answer when addressed, all laugh at his jokes, all seek to propitiate him. This cellar company alone – to say nothing of the crowd surrounding the entrance from the street above, and making the steps shine with eyes – is strong enough to murder us all, and willing enough to do it; but let Inspector Field have a mind to pick out one thief here, and take him; let him produce that ghostly truncheon from his pocket, and say, with his business-air, 'My lad, I want you!' and all Rats' Castle shall be stricken with paralysis, and not a finger move against him, as he fits the handcuffs on!

Even outside the confines of inner-city rookeries, fear of violent crime was a major preoccupation for Londoners. In the 1850s there was an increase in knife attacks (these were thought to be the work of foreigners, since home-grown thugs were expected to use the traditional British cudgel). In the following years, particularly 1862, there was a rash of what would nowadays be called 'muggings' in the suburbs. However a number of these incidents involved strangulation, or 'garotting', from behind and this new dimension of horror also struck contemporaries as entirely un-British – something more suited to Sicilian *banditti* than to the footpads and cut-purses of London. The result was widespread hysteria. The attacks were purportedly made by gangs of three, two of whom kept watch or helped to apprehend the quarry while the third, known as the 'nasty man', carried out the attack. As *Cornhill Magazine* reported in 1863:

> The third ruffian, coming swiftly up, flings his right arm around the victim, striking him smartly on the forehead. Instinctively he throws his head back, and in that moment loses every chance of escape. His throat is fully offered to his assailant, who instantly embraces it with his left arm, the bone just above the wrist being pressed against the 'apple' of the throat. At the same moment the garrotter, dropping his right hand, seizes the other's wrist: and thus supplied with a powerful lever, draws his back upon his breast and there holds him. The 'nasty man's' part is done. His burden is helpless from the first moment, and speedily becomes insensible.

Satirical cartoons depicted middle-class citizens going out to tea, or coming home from the office, in large groups for mutual protection, armed to the teeth and wearing homemade body-armour. The 'mid-Victorian calm' of Dickens' mature years did not seem very serene to many of those who lived through it.

Arrest and Charge

Those on the other side of the equation – the criminals – had problems of their own. Whether they were guilty of murder or mere drunkenness, if caught they could expect little sympathy or comfort. Following arrest, their first port of call was usually the local Police Office. James Grant described what awaited them:

[They are] for the most part ill-ventilated, confined, sombre-looking places. They are not at all worthy of a great city like London, and the important space they fill in the public eye. There is a great want of room in them, considering the amount of the business which has to be transacted. They are often crowded to suffocation, to the great annoyance of every one who has occasion to be present. The cells in the station-houses, in which prisoners are locked up over the night, are the most uncomfortable places: they are narrow, damp, dark and cold. In some of the station-houses they are on a level with the streets; in others, they are under ground. In either case they are the most miserable receptacles into which a human being could be put, short of burying him alive. When the number of prisoners is few, each one has often a cell for himself. When an 'apartment' cannot be spared to each, two, in some cases three, four or five are shut up together in the same cell.

Here they would be dealt with by magistrates and, after sentencing, taken elsewhere for imprisonment. As a reporter, Dickens himself once watched a group of felons being escorted out of Bow Street Police Office, a scene that he described in an article entitled 'The Prisoners' Van':

The covered vehicle, in which prisoners are conveyed from the police offices to the different prisons, was coming along at full speed. The van drew up at the office door, and the people thronged around the steps. After a few minutes' delay, the first prisoners appeared. They were a couple of girls, of whom the elder could not be more than sixteen, and the younger of whom had certainly not attained her fourteenth year. They were both gaudily dressed, the younger one especially, and, although there was a strong similarity between them in both respects, which was rendered the more obvious by their being handcuffed together, it is impossible to conceive a greater contrast than the demeanour of the two presented. The younger girl was weeping bitterly – not for display, or in the hope of producing effect, but for very shame. 'How long are you for, Emily?' screamed a red-faced woman in the crowd. 'Six weeks and labour,' replied the elder girl with a flaunting laugh, 'and that's better than the stone jug [Newgate] anyhow.'

'Come! In with you,' interrupted the driver. 'Don't you be in a hurry, coachman,' replied the girl, 'and recollect I want to be set down in Cold Bath Fields [Coldbath Prison in Clerkenwell] – large house with a high garden-wall in front; you can't mistake it.' ...

There were other prisoners – boys of ten, as hardened in vice as men of fifty – a houseless vagrant, going joyfully to prison as a place of food and shelter, handcuffed to a man whose prospects were ruined, character lost, and family rendered destitute, by his first offence.

Some prisons were agreeable enough and represented a noticeable improvement for those whose lives had been lived in dank alleyways and back-courts. Coldbath Fields, the 'house of correction' in Clerkenwell to which these prisoners were being sent, was something of a model institution and the girl's description of it was not at all inaccurate. *London as it is Today* explained that:

Within the walls, to the right of the entrance, is the governor's house, which occupies a fine piece of ground; along and under the wall is a flower garden in the finest possible order. This is cultivated entirely by the prisoners. Outdoor employment, ample space, the full supply of light and air afforded to the prisoners, and the general system of the prison, causes Coldbath Fields to be one of the healthiest places of confinement in the metropolis.

Prison Life

There were multitudes who every year fell foul of the law without belonging to the 'criminal classes'. Those who lost their precarious footing on the ladder of respectability by being declared bankrupt or arrested for debt (and in 1837, a typical year, there were over 30,000 of them) forfeited freedom as well as good name, for they would be sentenced to one of London's debtors' prisons to languish for what might be years or even decades.

Dickens knew this situation well, for it was the fate that befell his own father. John Dickens was apprehended in February 1824 for failure to pay a £40 debt to a local baker and was sent to the Marshalsea Prison. His son Charles, who was then 12 years old, was already working at Warren's blacking factory. He moved into lodgings, but almost every day he walked across London Bridge and through the Borough to visit the prison. The experience of his family's incarceration profoundly affected him and provided impressions that he used in *Little Dorrit*, *David Copperfield* and *Pickwick Papers*. James Grant, in his *Sketches in London*, described the establishment:

> The Debtors' Prisons in London are five in number. They are, the King's Bench, the Fleet [nicknamed 'the Navy Office'], the Marshalsea, White Cross-Street, and Horsemonger Lane prisons. The Marshalsea Prison is situated in Southwark. The number of persons confined in this prison is always much smaller than in any of the other prisons in the metropolis. The reason of this is, that it is restricted to the reception of two classes of men; first, officers and privates of the Royal Navy under sentence of naval courts-martial for mutiny, desertion &c., and secondly, persons committed for debt or contempt, by the Palace Court, whose jurisdiction extends to the distance of twelve miles round the Palace at Westminster. It has no rules like the Fleet; once consigned to it there is no getting out again, until you are liberated altogether. The prisoners in this place are obliged to find themselves in their own bedding, furniture, fuel and every thing else. Their number does not average more than 130.

Once the initial humiliation was over – the arrival of the bailiffs, the eviction, the valuation of goods – it was possible to live pleasantly enough within a community in which everyone had something in common. Dickens described, in what was probably a reference to his father's experience, how:

> At last Mr Micawber's difficulties came to a crisis, and he was arrested early one morning, and carried over to the King's Bench Prison in the Borough. He told me, as he went out of

the house, that the God of day had gone down upon him – and I really thought his heart was broken, and mine too. But I heard, afterward, that he was seen to play a game of skittles before noon.

The prisons were crowded not only with the debtors themselves but with their families who, often by definition homeless, moved in with them, filling the scruffy rooms, stairs and doorways with the chatter of wives, the squeals of children and the comings and goings of servants. All these were free to enter and leave as they wished (at least until the gates were shut at ten o'clock each night) and would constantly pass through them to go shopping, deliver messages or go to work. Only the debtors themselves were confined within the walls. Though they suffered no serious privation, the inmates were felons and measures were taken to prevent their escape. The experience of Samuel Pickwick provides a useful glimpse of how each prisoner's appearance was recorded before the advent of the camera and the police 'mug shot'. John Dickens would have been subjected to the same process. Arriving in prison, Pickwick was told to wait in a room, where he:

... was appraised that he would remain, until he had undergone the ceremony known to the initiated as 'sitting for your portrait'. 'Sitting for my portrait!' said Mr Pickwick. 'Having your likeness taken, sir,' replied the stout turnkey. 'We're capital hands at likenesses here. Take 'em in no time and always exact' ... Mr Weller, who stationed himself at the back of the chair, whispered that the sitting was merely another term for undergoing an inspection by the different turnkeys in order that they might know prisoners from visitors ...

The stout turnkey having been relieved from the lock [come off duty], sat down, and looked at him carelessly, from time to time, while a long thin man who had relieved him, thrust his hands beneath his coat-tails, and planting himself opposite, took a good long view of him. A third rather surly-looking gentleman, who had apparently been disturbed at his tea, for he was disposing of the last remains of a crust and butter when he came in, stationed himself close to Mr Pickwick, and resting his hands on his hips, inspected him narrowly; while two others mixed with the group,

and studied his features with most intent and thoughtful faces. Mr
Pickwick winced a good deal under the operation, and appeared to
sit uneasily in his chair; but he made no remark to anybody while
it was being performed ... At length the likeness was completed,
and Mr Pickwick was informed that he might now proceed into
the prison.

The prisons were like small self-contained towns. Shielded by high walls
from the world beyond, and united by a sense of grievance or misfortune,
the inhabitants might develop strong friendships and find in their
irresponsible existence a greater happiness than they had known outside.
Even here not everyone was on the same level, for some inmates had not
lost all their financial resources, and could afford to pay for comparative
privacy. The term 'chummage', according to Grose's dictionary, meant:

Money paid by the richer sort of prisoners in the Fleet and King's
Bench, to the poorer, for their share of a room. When prisons are
very full, which is too often the case, particularly on the eve of an
insolvent act, two or three persons are obliged to sleep in a room.
A prisoner who can pay for being alone, chuses [sic] two poor
chums, who, for a stipulated price, called chummage, give up their
share of the room, and sleep on the stairs, or, as the term is, ruff it.

To fit into the community it was necessary to be cheerful and sociable.
Those who felt sorry for themselves risked becoming outcasts, as another
of Dickens' characters, Arthur Clennam, the object of Little Dorrit's
admiration, discovered:

The opinion of the community outside the prison gates bore hard
on Clennam as time went on, and he made no friends among
the community within. Too depressed to associate with the herd
in the yard, who got together to forget their cares; too retiring
and too unhappy to join the poor socialites of the tavern; he
kept his own room, and was held in distrust. Some said he was
proud; some objected that he was sullen and reserved; some were
contemptuous of him, for that he was a poor-spirited dog who
pined under his debts. The whole population were shy of him

on these various accounts of indictment, but especially the last,
which involved a species of domestic treason; and he soon became
so confirmed in his seclusion, that his only time for walking up
and down was when the evening Club were assembled at their
songs and sentiments, and when the yard was nearly left to the
women and children.

This suggests that Clennam was an exception to the general rule. Prince
Pückler-Muskau, who visited the King's Bench Prison as a tourist, was
struck by the contentment of some of the inmates. He found the prison:

A perfectly isolated world in miniature; – like a not insignificant
town, only surrounded by walls thirty feet high. Cookshops,
circulating libraries, coffee houses, dealers, and artisans of
all kinds, dwellings of different degrees, even a market-place
– nothing is wanting. When I went in, a very noisy game at ball
was going on. A man who has money lives as well and agreeably
as possible within these walls. Even very 'good society', male
and female, is sometimes to be found in this little commune of
a thousand persons, but he who has little fares ill enough. Lord
Cochrane passed some time in the King's Bench, for spreading
false intelligence with a view to lower the funds; and the rich,
highly respected, and popular Sir Francis Burdett was also
imprisoned here some time for a libel he wrote. The prisoner who
conducted me about had been an inhabitant of the place twenty
years, and declared in the best possible humour, that he had no
hope of ever coming out again. An old Frenchwoman of very
good air and manners said the same; and declared that she did not
intend ever to acquaint her relations with her situation, for she
lived very comfortably here.

Yet a debtors' prison, for all its tavern and skittles and card games,
could break spirits and leave mental scars on a large number of its
inmates. Most of those who were released through the sale of their
assets or rescue by their friends would swiftly try to forget their prison
acquaintances and avoid speaking of their experiences. James Grant
comments that debtors:

... are the only persons who feel their incarceration to be a punishment, for they did everything which human exertion made in an honest and honourable way could do to meet the demands of their creditors, and consequently escape imprisonment: they are the victims of adversity brought about by an agency not their own. One would think that this reflection would tranquillise their minds, and reconcile them to that which no exertions of theirs could have shielded them against. Such, however, is not the fact: they are degraded persons in their own estimation, and neither the dictates of reason nor the representations of friends can remove the erroneous impression.

That this shame was felt equally by their families is proved by Charles Dickens' own experience. He later told how, while at Warren's factory, he had avoided telling his workmates anything about his family circumstances. When one of them, Bob Fagin, wanted to keep him company on the walk home one evening, Dickens tried hard to put him off. As they went along, he announced that a house they passed was his home. He remembered that, to assist with the deception as his friend moved out of sight:

I knocked at the door, and asked, when the woman opened it, if that was Mr Robert Fagin's house.

The Dreaded Hulks

However difficult it might have been to endure the loss of face in a debtors' prison, conditions were infinitely worse for those who had committed criminal offences. Many prisons were brutal, insanitary and overcrowded. As a result of this overcrowding, thousands of convicted felons were housed offshore aboard prison hulks. These were superannuated warships, dismasted and with their decks roofed over, that lay at anchor in the Thames estuary off the north coast of Kent. Contemporary pictures capture the nature of these vessels: the rotting wooden bulkheads, the immense timber stakes holding the ships in place, the fluttering lines of washing and the chimney smoke emerging from below decks. Prisoners did not spend all of their time confined aboard, for they were sent ashore to work as labourers by day. Grose defines the term 'barrow man' as:

> **Alluding to the convicts at Woolwich, who are principally employed in wheeling barrows full of brick or dirt; a man under sentence of transportation.**

Hulks had the advantage that it was considerably more difficult to escape from them. A convict who succeeded in getting overboard would have to swim or wade to shore, and then find his way through the treacherous creeks of the estuary marshes. Since a cannon would be fired as soon as his absence was discovered, the whole countryside would be warned to look out for him, and with the large garrison of soldiers and sailors at nearby Chatham there would be plenty of armed men who could be sent to hunt him down. Such an incident occurs at the beginning of *Great Expectations*. The novel's narrator Pip, then a small boy, asks his sister and brother-in-law the reason for the commotion:

> 'Hark!' said I, when I was taking a final warm in the chimney-corner before being sent up to bed; 'was that great guns, Joe?'
>
> 'Ah!' said Joe. 'There's another convict off.'
>
> 'What does that mean, Joe?'
>
> Mrs Joe, who always took explanations upon herself, said snappishly, 'Escaped, Escaped.'
>
> While Mrs Joe sat with her head bending over her needlework, I put my mouth into the forms of saying to Joe, 'What's a convict?'
>
> 'There was a convict off last night,' said Joe aloud, 'after sunset-gun. And they fired warning after him. And now it appears they're firing warning of another.'
>
> 'Who's firing?' said I.
>
> 'Drat that boy,' interposed my sister, frowning at me over her work, 'what a questioner he is. Ask no questions, and you'll be told no lies.'
>
> 'Mrs Joe,' said I, as a last resort, 'I should like to know – if you wouldn't much mind – where the firing comes from?'
>
> 'Lord bless the boy!' exclaimed my sister, 'From the Hulks!'

'And please what's Hulks?' said I.

'That's the way with this boy!' exclaimed my sister, pointing me out with her needle and thread, and shaking her head at me. 'Answer him one question, and he'll ask you a dozen directly. Hulks are prison-ships, right 'cross th' meshes.' We always used that name for marshes in our country.

'I wonder who's put into prison-ships, and why they're put there?' said I, in a general way, and with quiet desperation.

It was too much for Mrs Joe, who immediately rose. 'I tell you what, young fellow,' said she, 'I didn't bring you up by hand to badger people's lives out. It would be blame to me, and not praise, if I had. People are put in the Hulks because they do murder, and because they rob, and forge, and do all sorts of bad; and they always begin by asking questions. Now, you get along to bed!'

The Hulks were not necessarily a destination in themselves; many of those aboard them were awaiting 'transportation'. For a number of crimes that did not warrant the death penalty, the punishment for those who survived the journey was exile to the other side of the world, and years of hard labour in New South Wales. The prisoners, known as 'lags', were sent to Australia either for seven years or for life. (This practice, which had begun in 1788 when convicts could no longer be sent to America, continued until 1867.) Any convict returning without authority to do so was liable to face execution, and this was the fate that befell Magwitch, Pip's benefactor in *Great Expectations*. Having reappeared in England and been betrayed by an informer, he attempted, with the help of Pip and others, to flee down the Thames in a boat at night. His vessel was overhauled by Government officers, one of whom shouted: 'You have a returned Transport there. His name is Abel Magwitch. I apprehend that man, and call upon him to surrender, and you to assist.' As Magwitch is later told during his trial: 'The appointed punishment for his return to the land which had cast him out, being Death, he must prepare himself to Die.'

As the 19th century progressed, notions of penal reform began to make headway. This was largely due to the work of Elizabeth Fry (1780–1845), a Quaker who made visits to prisons and, as a result of what she saw, agitated for improvements in conditions. Though the old prisons remained, more modern 'penitentiaries' were built, as at Millbank (on the site later occupied by the Tate Gallery, now Tate Britain). This represented a fresh approach to the treatment of felons. Previously, the proximity of inmates had meant that both illness ('gaol fever') and criminal knowledge had been able to spread rapidly (even today prisons are described as 'universities of crime'). In the new establishments prisoners were kept separate (in the event Millbank proved as wretched and unhealthy as other prisons, and was closed), lived in sound, dry cells and were given wholesome and regular meals. Dickens, usually such a champion of the unfortunate, poked fun at this relative luxury and at the naivety of those who believed that soft living would turn villains into good citizens, while describing David Copperfield's visit to one of them:

On the appointed day, Traddles and I repaired to the prison where Mr Creakle was powerful. It was an immense building, erected at vast expense. I could not help thinking, as we approached the gate, what an uproar would have been made in the country, if any deluded man had proposed to spend one half the money it had cost on the erection of an industrial school for the young, or a house of refuge for the deserving old.

In an office that might have been on the ground floor of the Tower of Babel, it was so massively constructed, we were presented to our old schoolmaster, who was one of a group, composed of two or three of the busier sort of magistrates, and some visitors they had brought. After some conversation with these gentlemen, from which I might have supposed that there was nothing in the world to be legitimately taken into account but the supreme comfort of prisoners, at any expense, and nothing on the wide earth to be done outside prison doors, we began our inspection. It being then just dinner-time, we went first, into the great kitchen, where every prisoner's dinner was in course of being set out separately (to be handed to him in his cell), with the regularity and precision of clockwork. I said aside, to Traddles, that I wondered whether it occurred to anybody that there was a striking contrast between these plentiful repasts of choice quality and the dinners, not to say of paupers, but of soldiers, sailors, labourers, the great bulk of the honest, working community; of whom not one man in five hundred ever dined half so well. But I learned that 'the system' required high living ...

As we were going through some of the magnificent passages, I inquired of Mr Creakle and his friends what were supposed to be the main advantages of this all-governing and universally over-riding system? I found them to be the perfect isolation of prisoners – so that no one man in confinement there knew anything about another; and the reduction of prisoners to a wholesome state of mind, leading to sincere contrition and repentance.

The traditional prisons remained. The most famous, and conspicuous, was Newgate, whose fortress-like grey stone bulk dominated the area west of St Paul's Cathedral. Known to London's criminals as the 'Stone Jug' or 'College', it was the most notorious jail in Britain and held a central place in the national consciousness, its name being synonymous, for Englishmen, with misery and evil. Trials took place in the Sessions House, the courtrooms next door, and those sentenced to death were executed on the 'New Drop', a public gallows erected one storey above ground level on the prison's street frontage.

In 1836, Dickens and a colleague made a visit to Newgate. By his day there had been a prison on the site for over 600 years. As a reporter, he was immensely curious to see it, and the experience fulfilled his expectations and fired his imagination. He recorded his impressions in detail in *Sketches by Boz* and, because the building is long gone (it was demolished in 1902 and replaced by the Central Criminal Court – the 'Old Bailey'), his account brings back to life a place as well as a way of life that has utterly vanished. His writings, like those of others dealing with Newgate, mentioned St Sepulchre's church, which still stands near the scene of the hangings. The tolling of its bell would have been clearly audible to those in the condemned cells, and on the morning of an execution its clock would have announced the moment at which the victims emerged on to the scaffold. Dickens began his description with the prison's entrance, almost with the sense of being in a museum:

Following our conductor, we arrived in a small room [in which were] casts of the heads and faces of the two notorious murderers, Bishop and Williams. Leaving this by an opposite

door, we found ourselves in the lodge which opens on the Old
Bailey; one side of this is plentifully garnished with a choice
collection of heavy sets of irons, including those worn by the
redoubtable Jack Sheppard [an 18th-century criminal who
escaped from prison several times] – genuine; and those *said* to
have been graced by the sturdy limbs of the no less celebrated
[highwayman] Dick Turpin – doubtful.

From this lodge a heavy oaken gate, bound with iron, studded
with nails of the same material, and guarded by another turnkey,
opens on a few steps ... which terminate in a narrow and dismal
stone passage running parallel with the Old Bailey and leading to
the different yards, through a number of tortuous and intricate
windings, guarded in their turn by huge gates and gratings, whose
appearance is sufficient to dispel at once the slightest hope of
escape that any new-comer may have entertained.

Newgate was divided in half, with male and female felons occupying
separate but identical wards, or large rooms, and exercise yards. The
visitors were shown one of the women's wards, which surprised them by
its cleanliness:

It was a spacious, bare, whitewashed apartment, lighted, of
course, by windows looking into the interior of the prison, but far
more light and airy than one could reasonably expect to find in
such a situation. There was a large fire with a deal table before it,
round which ten or a dozen women were seated on wooden forms
at dinner. Along both sides of the room ran a shelf; below it, at
regular intervals, a row of large hooks were fixed in the wall, on
each of which was hung the sleeping mat of a prisoner: her rug
and blanket being folded up, and placed on the shelf above. At
night, these mats are placed on the floor, each beneath the hook
on which it hangs during the day; and the ward is thus made to
answer the purposes both of a day-room and sleeping apartment.
Over the fireplace was a large sheet of pasteboard, on which
were displayed a variety of texts from Scripture, which were also
scattered about the room in scraps about the size and shape of the
copy-slips which are used in schools. On the table was a sufficient

provision of a kind of stewed beef and brown bread, in pewter dishes, which are kept perfectly bright, and displayed on shelves in great order and regularity when they are not in use.

As for the room's inhabitants, they too were more tidy and well-ordered than perhaps had been expected:

> The women rose hastily, on our entrance, and retired in a hurried manner to either side of the fireplace. They were all cleanly – many of them decently – attired, and there was nothing peculiar, either in their appearance or demeanour. One or two resumed the needlework which they had probably laid aside at the commencement of their meal; others gazed at the visitors with listless curiosity. Some old Irish women, to whom the thing was no novelty, appeared perfectly indifferent to our presence ...

They visited one of the men's wards, where the difference that struck them was the 'utter absence of any employment'. A near-contemporary sightseer, and one whose curiosity was as great as Dickens', was Prince Pückler-Muskau. He was struck by the same characteristics:

> The treatment, even here, is very mild, and a most exemplary cleanliness reigns throughout. The Government allows each criminal a pint of thick gruel in a morning, and a half a pound of meat or a mess of broth alternately for dinner, with a pound of good bread daily. Besides this, they are permitted to buy other articles of food, and half a bottle of wine a day. They employ themselves as they please; there are separate courts belonging to a certain number of rooms or cells; for those who like to work there are work-rooms; but many smoke and play from morning till night. At nine o'clock they must all attend divine service. Seven or eight generally inhabit one room. They are allowed a mattress and two blankets for sleeping, and coals for cooking, and, in winter, for warming the cells. Those condemned to death are put in separate less convenient cells, where two or three sleep together, but even these have a courtyard for recreation, and a separate eating-room.

Dickens and his party passed on to Newgate's chapel, which was the most sombre and thought-provoking place in the prison. The guidebook describes it:

> The chapel is neat and plain, with galleries for the male
> and female prisoners; and below, in the centre, is a chair,
> conspicuously placed, and set apart for the use of the condemned
> shedder of blood, in which he sits on the day previous to his
> execution, in presence of his fellow-criminals, and listens for the
> last time to the sound of solemn exhortation.

Dickens recorded his own comments:

> The meanness of its appointments – the bare and scanty pulpit,
> with the paltry painted pillars on either side – the women's gallery
> with its great heavy curtain – the men's with its unpainted benches
> and dingy front – the tottering little table at the altar, with the
> commandments on the wall above it, scarcely legible through lack
> of paint, and dust and damp. There is one object, too, which rivets
> the attention and fascinates the gaze, and from which we may turn
> horror-stricken in vain, for the recollection of it will haunt us for
> a long time afterwards. Immediately below the reading-desk, on
> the floor of the chapel, and forming the most conspicuous object in
> the little area, is the condemned pew; a huge black pen, in which
> the wretched people who are singled out for death are placed on
> the Sunday preceding their execution, in sight of all their fellow
> prisoners, to hear prayers for their own souls, to join in the
> responses of their own burial service, and to listen to an address,
> warning their recent companions to take example by their fate, and
> urging themselves, while there is yet time – nearly four-and-twenty
> hours – to 'turn, and flee from the wrath to come!' At one time
> – and at no distant period either – the coffins of the men about to
> be executed were placed in that pew, upon the seat by their side,
> during the whole service. It may seem incredible, but it is true.
> Let us hope that the spirit of civilization and humanity which
> abolished this frightful and degrading custom may extend itself to
> other usages equally barbarous.

Pückler-Muskau encountered some of the condemned:

> I saw six boys, the eldest of whom was not more than fourteen, all under sentence of death, smoking and playing merrily. The sentence was not yet confirmed, however, and they were still with the other prisoners. It was thought it would be commuted for transportation to Botany Bay. Four of a maturer age, in the same predicament – only that the enormity of their crimes left them no hope of a pardon – took their fate still more gaily. Three of them were noisily playing whist with Dummy, amid jokes and laughter, but the fourth sat in a window-seat busily engaged in studying a French grammar.

Lastly, Dickens was shown the condemned cells:

> The entrance is by a narrow and obscure staircase leading to a dark passage. From the left-hand side of this, the massive door of every cell on the storey opens. There are three of these ranges of cells; but in size, furniture and appearance, they are all precisely alike. All the prisoners under sentence of death are removed from the day-room at five o'clock in the afternoon, and locked up in these cells, where they are allowed a candle until ten o'clock; and here they remain until seven next morning. When the warrant for a prisoner's execution arrives, he is removed to the cells and confined in one of them until he leaves for the scaffold.
>
> We entered the first cell. It was a stone dungeon, eight feet long by six wide, with a bench at the upper end, under which were a common rug, a bible, and a prayer-book. An iron candlestick was fixed into the wall at the side; and a small high window in the back admitted as much air and light as could struggle in between a double row of heavy, crossed iron bars. It contained no other furniture of any description.

Dickens put these impressions to good use by incorporating them into one of his most vivid fictional scenes: the night on which Fagin awaits execution in the finale of *Oliver Twist*. The hanging itself is not described, for he was able adequately to convey a feeling of dread without it, and the sense of mounting tension is remarkable. For all Fagin's undoubted guilt, and lack of remorse, the author (and the reader) are forced to feel sympathy for him as he languishes in such oppressive and horrifying surroundings:

As it came on very dark, he began to think of all the men he had known who had died upon the scaffold, some of them through his means. They rose up in such quick succession that he could hardly count them. He had seen some of them die, and had joked, too, because they died with prayers on their lips. With what a rattling noise the drop went down, and how suddenly they changed, from strong and vigorous men to dangling heaps of clothes!

Some of them might have inhabited that very cell – sat upon that very spot. It was very dark: why didn't they bring a light? The cell had been built for many years. Scores of men must have passed their last hours there. It was like sitting in a vault strewn with dead bodies – the cap, the noose, the pinioned arms, the faces that he knew, even beneath the hideous veil. Light, light!

Other watchers are glad to hear the church clock strike, for they tell of life and coming day. To [Fagin] they brought only despair. The boom of every iron bell came laden with the one, deep hollow sound – Death!

The space before the prison was cleared, and a few strong barriers, painted black, had already been thrown across the road to break the pressure of the crowd. Day was dawning when [Oliver and Mr Brownlow] emerged [from the prison]. A great multitude had already assembled; the windows were filled with people, smoking and playing cards to beguile the time; the crowd were pushing, quarrelling and joking. Everything told of life and animation but one dark cluster of objects in the very centre of all – the black stage, the cross-beam, the rope, and all the hideous apparatus of death.

Captain Shaw, in his memoir of London, described a public hanging. Little had changed between the 1830s, when *Oliver Twist* was written, and the occasion witnessed by Shaw three decades later:

The scene on the night preceding a public execution afforded a study of the dark side of nature not to be obtained under any other circumstances. Here was to be seen the lowest scum of London densely packed together as far as the eye could see, and estimated by *The Times* at not less than 20,000. Across the entire front of Newgate heavy barricades of stout timber traversed the streets in every direction, erected as a precaution against the pressure of the crowd, but which answered a purpose not wholly anticipated by the authorities. As the crowd increased, so wholesale highway robberies were of more frequent occurrence; and victims in the hands of some two or three desperate ruffians were as far from help as though divided by a continent from the battalions of police surrounding the scaffold.

The scene that met one's view on pulling up the windows [wealthy people paid large sums to rent upstairs-windows from which to view the event; they, like the crowd in the street below, had to be in their places the night before in order to make sure of seeing anything] and looking out on the black night and its blacker accompaniments baffles description. A surging mass, with here and there a flickering torch, rolled and roared before one; above this weird scene arose the voices of men and women shouting, singing, blaspheming, and, as the night advanced and the liquid gained firmer mastery, it seemed as if hell had delivered up its victims.

After a wait of several hours, preparations began in earnest:

The first step towards the morning's work was the appearance of workmen about 4 a.m.; this was immediately followed by a rumbling sound, and one realised that the scaffold was being dragged round. A grim, square, box-like apparatus was now distinctly visible, as it slowly backed against the 'debtors' door' [the door through which the condemned appeared was one storey above the pavement]. Lights now flickered about the scaffold – the workmen fixing the cross-beams and uprights. Every stroke of the hammer must have vibrated through the condemned cells, and warned the wakeful occupants that their time was nearly come.

Meanwhile, a little unpretending door was gently opened; this was the 'debtor's door', and led directly through the kitchen on to the scaffold. The kitchen on these occasions was turned into a temporary mausoleum and draped with tawdry black hangings, which concealed the pots and pans, and produced an effect supposed to be more in keeping with the solemn occasion. Presently an old and decrepit man made his appearance, and cautiously 'tested' the drop. This was Calcraft, the hangman.

The tolling of St Sepulchre's bell about 7.30 a.m. announced the approach of the hour of execution; meanwhile a steady rain was falling, though without diminishing the ever-increasing crowd. As far as the eye could reach was a sea of human faces. Roofs, windows, church-rails, and empty vans – all were pressed into service, and tightly packed with human beings. The rain had made the drop slippery, and necessitated precautions on behalf of the living if not of those appointed to die, so sand was thrown over a portion. The sand was for the benefit of the 'ordinary', the minister of religion, who was to offer the dying consolation at 8 a.m., and breakfast at 9.

At last the victims emerged on to the scaffold. On this occasion there were seven of them:

The procession now appeared, winding its way through the kitchen, and in the centre of the group walked a sickly, cadaverous mob securely pinioned, and literally as white as marble. As they reached the platform a halt was necessary as each was placed one by one immediately under the hanging chains. At the end of these chains were hooks which were eventually attached to the hemp round the neck of each wretch. The concluding ceremonies did not take long, considering how feeble the aged hangman was. A white cap was first placed over every face, then the ankles were strapped together, and finally the fatal noose was put around every neck, and the end attached to the hooks.

The silence was now awful. One felt one's heart literally in one's mouth, and found oneself involuntarily saying, 'They could be saved yet – yet – yet,' and then a thud that vibrated

through the street announced that the [felons] were launched
into eternity. One's eyes were glued to the spot and, fascinated
by the awful sight, not a detail escaped one. Calcraft, meanwhile,
apparently not satisfied with his handiwork, seized hold of one
poor wretch's feet, and pressing on them for some seconds with all
his weight, passed from one to another with hideous composure.
Meanwhile, the white caps were getting tighter and tighter, until
they looked ready to burst, and a faint blue speck that had almost
immediately appeared on the carotid artery gradually became
more livid, till it assumed the appearance of a huge black bruise.
Death, I should say, must have been instantaneous, for hardly a
vibration occurred, and the only movement that was visible was
that from the gradually-stretching ropes as the bodies kept slowly
swinging round and round. The hanging of a body for an hour
constituted part of the sentence, an interval that was not lost
on the multitude below. The drunken again took up their ribald
songs, conspicuous amongst which was one that had done duty
pretty well through the night, and ended with 'Calcraft, Calcraft,
he's the man.'

This execution, which took place in 1864, was in fact one of the last
occasions on which such a thing was seen in London. Public opinion
increasingly felt that these sights were too barbaric for a civilized capital
city and, from 1868 until the closure of Newgate, hangings were carried
out inside the prison. The abolition of public executions was a major
step in the progress of London from the rambunctious, emotional and
savage place of Dickens' youth to the more dignified and orderly city
that it would have become by the end of Queen Victoria's reign in 1901.

A. Dorè

The RESPECTABLE

The wish of persons in the humbler classes of life to ape the manners and customs of those whom fortune has placed above them is often the subject of remark, and not infrequently of complaint. The inclination may, and no doubt does, exist to a great extent, among the small gentility – the would-be aristocrats – of the middle classes. Tradesmen and clerks, with fashionable novel-reading families, and circulating-library-subscribing daughters, get up small assemblies in humble imitation of Almack's, and promenade the dingy 'large room' of some second-rate hotel with as much complacency as the enviable few who are privileged to exhibit their magnificence in that exclusive haunt of fashion and foolery.

So Dickens summed up, in *Sketches by Boz*, the aspirations of London's 'respectable', those stationed in society above the struggling millions of the destitute, the desperate and the simply poor. The respectable divided into many social strata, but included everyone from the most lowly clerk to the grandest marquess. Those on the lower rungs of this social ladder were often content with their lot, for the world they inhabited was a comfortable one. Their ambitions were usually modest: a rented house (most people did not own, or think of owning, their homes), domestic help in the form of a servant (probably a girl of 12 or 13, recruited from the local workhouse); neat Sunday clothes and a seat on the parochial church council; an occasional trip to the seaside; a place for their son and daughter at one of the umpteen private schools that flourished in the suburbs, followed by a position for the boy in the firm where his father worked and marriage for the girl to one of her brother's colleagues.

There were many things to which the respectable could not aspire. Though they might have a small dog-cart or donkey-cart, they could not dream of owning a carriage. Not only would the vehicle itself have to be paid for, it would also be necessary to buy and maintain a pair of horses and to have a coachman, a groom and a coach house. Instead, the middle class went by omnibus (a distinctly bourgeois conveyance at that time) and travelled second class on the railways. They did not aspire to go abroad – at least not until Mr Thomas Cook made mass tourism possible in the 1840s – and would instead spend their holidays at Ramsgate or Broadstairs, or at one of the English spas such as Malvern. They could not expect to attend Society balls or have any part in the London Season, but they found fulfilment in staging their own small-scale versions of these events. In the process, they were creating a distinct middle class culture that would become increasingly significant as the century went on. It was to be these people who made the Great Exhibition a success by attending it in such numbers, who enrolled their sons in the new University of London, and whose suburban lecture societies developed popular interest in science and literature.

Dickens himself came from the lower middle class, and he began his career as a novelist by writing about this particular world, in the series of articles collected and published in 1836 as *Sketches by Boz*. The stories struck an immediate chord with the public, who recognized the lives they and their acquaintances led. As often happens, those who are the target of satire, even if woundingly unkind, are delighted by the accuracy with which they are depicted. The stories were, after all, written by one of their own. The young author's unerring eye for detail gave his observations impact. He described an elderly couple who might have been anyone's next-door neighbours:

He and his wife – who is as clean and compact a little body as himself – have occupied the same house ever since he retired from business twenty years ago. They have no family. They once had a son, who died at about five years old. The child's portrait hangs over the mantelpiece in the best sitting-room, and a little cart he used to draw about is carefully preserved as a relic.

In fine weather the old gentleman is almost constantly in the garden; and when it is too wet to go into it, he will look out of

the window at it, by the hour together. The perseverance with
which he lugs a great watering-pot about is perfectly astonishing.
The only other recreation he has is the newspaper, which he
peruses every day, from beginning to end, generally reading the
most interesting pieces of information to his wife during breakfast.
The old lady is very fond of flowers, as the hyacinth-glasses in the
parlour-window, and geranium-pots in the little front court, testify.

On a summer's evening, when the large watering-pot has been
filled and emptied some fourteen times, and the old couple have
quite exhausted themselves by trotting about, you will see them
sitting happily together in the little summer-house. These are
their only recreations, and they require no more. They have
within themselves the materials of comfort and content; and the
only anxiety of each is to die before the other.

The English passion for gardening was already noticeable in the 19th-
century London suburbs, and again the young author was able to depict
this with an accuracy born of personal observation. Several notches
higher up the social scale, a man with a comfortable income (clearly
one of the 'carriage folk') and several outdoor servants has a mania for a
garden which he himself never actually touches:

If the regular City man, who leaves Lloyd's at five o'clock, and
drives home to Hackney, Clapton, Stamford Hill, or elsewhere,
can be said to have any daily recreation beyond his dinner, it is
his garden. He never does anything to it with his own hands; but
he takes great pride in it notwithstanding ... He always takes a
walk round it, before he starts for town in the morning, and is
particularly anxious that the fish-pond should be kept specially
neat. If you call on him on Sunday in summertime, about an hour
before dinner, you will find him sitting in an arm-chair, on the
lawn behind the house, with a straw hat on, reading a Sunday
paper ... ten to one the two eldest girls are loitering in one of the
side walks accompanied by a couple of young gentlemen, who are
holding parasols over them – of course only to keep the sun off
– while the younger children, with the under nursery-maid, are
strolling listlessly about in the shade. Beyond these occasions, his

delight in his garden appears to arise more from the consciousness of possession than actual enjoyment of it. When he drives you down to dinner on a week-day, he is rather fatigued with the occupations of the morning, and tolerably cross into the bargain; but when the cloth is removed and he has drunk three or four glasses of his favourite port, he orders the French windows of his dining-room (which of course look into the garden) to be opened, and throwing a silk handkerchief over his head, and leaning back in his armchair, descants at considerable length upon its beauty, and the cost of maintaining it. This is to impress you – who are a young friend of the family – with a due sense of the excellence of the garden, and the wealth of its owner; and when he has exhausted the subject, he goes to sleep.

Much of the middle class was moving out of town to escape the smoke, the crush and the proximity of disease by building or renting villas on the healthier slopes of hills both north and south of the river – Hampstead and Highgate, Nunhead and Norwood – or by settling west of London in Richmond, Kew, Chiswick or Putney. Their residence in these places was largely made possible by the development of a public transport system, and with it arrived that archetypal experience of the professional classes: the commute. Others preferred to remain amid the streets and squares of the city centre, inhabiting the large town houses that had originally been built for the aristocracy. As more squares were built (such as the Grosvenor Estate, developed during the 1820s on the marshes behind Buckingham Palace), fashion shifted westward to the white-fronted 'stucco canyons' of Belgravia; and formerly respectable quarters, such as the brown-brick squares of Bloomsbury, became the province of less socially exalted tenants. Nevertheless, these houses were still impressive. Max Schlesinger visited one, the dwelling of a knight and Member of Parliament who, though unquestionably respectable, was not 'top drawer'. Schlesinger's description of the premises gives us an idea of how these homes – virtually all long since converted to offices or divided into flats – were organized and run:

The small space between the street-door and the stairs, hardly sufficient in length and breadth to deserve the pompous name of a 'hall', is usually furnished with a couple of mahogany chairs or, in the wealthier houses, with flower-pots, statuettes, and now and then a sixth or seventh-rate picture. The floor is covered with oil-cloth, and this again is covered with a breadth of carpet. The English houses are like chimneys turned inside-out; on the outside all is soot and dirt, in the inside everything is clean and bright.

From the hall we make our way to the parlour – the refectory of the house. The parlour is the common sitting-room of the family, the centre-point of the domestic state. It is here that many eat their dinners, and some say their prayers; and in this room does the lady of the house arrange her household affairs and issue her commands ... Large folding doors, which occupy nearly the whole breadth of the back wall, separate the front from the back parlour, and when opened, the two form one large room. The number and the circumstances of the family devote this back parlour either to the purposes of a library for the master, the son, or the daughters of the house, or convert it into a boudoir, office, or breakfast-room. Frequently, it serves no purpose in particular, and all in turn. These two rooms occupy the whole depth of the house. All the other apartments are above, so that there are from two to four rooms in each storey. Hence each storey has its particular destination in the family geographical dictionary. In the first floor are the reception-rooms; in the second the bed-rooms, with their large four-posters and marble-topped wash-stands; in the third storey are the nurseries and servants' rooms; and in the fourth, if a fourth there be, you find a couple of low garrets, for the occasional accommodation of some bachelor friend of the family.

In an age in which labour was cheap and housework had to be done without the aid of modern appliances, a home of this sort would have required more than half-a-dozen indoor servants: a butler and a cook, several maids, a footman and one or two junior domestics. Unlike the workhouse girl of the barely respectable families, these would have been trained staff who were expected to spend years in the service of the family. The butler and footman would have to be literate, since they had to be able to scrutinize mail and the visiting-cards of callers, but illiterate maids might have been chosen so that they could not read their mistress's letters. Schlesinger, showing more curiosity than his English host would have considered polite, went down to the basement – the realm of the servants – to examine the arrangements:

> Descending a good many more stairs than we ascended, we find our way to the haunts of those who, in England, live underground – to the kitchen. In the place of the carpets which cover the floors of the upper rooms, we walk here on strong, solid oilcloths which, swept and washed, look like marble. Add to this, bright dish-covers of gigantic dimensions fixed to the wall, plated dishes, and sundry other utensils of queer shapes and silvery aspect, interspersed with copper saucepans and pots and china, the windows neatly curtained, with a couple of flower-pots on the sill, and a branch of evergreens growing on the wall around them – such is the English kitchen in its modest glory. A large fire is always kept burning; and its ruddy glow heightens the homeliness and comfort of the scene.
>
> Several doors in the kitchen open into sundry other subterraneous compartments. There is a back-kitchen, whither the servants of the house retire for the most important part of their daily labours – the talking of scandal apropos the whole neighbourhood. There is also a small room for the washing-up of plates and dishes, the cleaning of knives and forks, of clothes and shoes. Other compartments are devoted to stores of provisions, of coals, and wine and beer. All these are strictly separate.

As for the upstairs inhabitants, George Sala portrayed the sort of family that would have lived in a house of this kind. They are seen at breakfast:

> Hungry London breakfasts, at nine o'clock in the morning. In quietly grim squares, in the semi-aristocratic North-West End – I don't mean Russell and Bloomsbury, but Gordon, Tavistock, Queen, and Camden, on the one side, and Manchester and Portman on the other – the nine o'clock breakfast takes place in the vast comfortless dining-room, with the shining side-board (purchased at the sale of Sir Hector Ajacks, the great Indian general's, effects), and the portrait of the master of the house (Debenham Storr, R.A.,

pinxit), crimson curtain and column in foreground, dessert plate, cut orange, and silver bell in front. This is the sort of room where there is a Turkey carpet that has been purchased at the East India Company's sale rooms, and which went cheap because there was a hole in one corner, carefully darned subsequently by the mistress of the house. The master comes down stairs gravely, with a bald head – the thin, grey hair carefully brushed over the temples, and a duffel dressing-gown. He spends five minutes in his 'study' behind the breakfast dining-room; not, goodness knows, to consult the uncut books on the shelves, but to break the seals of the letters ranged for him on the leather-covered table – he reads his correspondence at breakfast, and to catch up and snuggle beneath his arm the copy of the 'Times' newspaper, erst dumped, but since aired at the kitchen fire, which the newsvendor's boy dropped an hour since down the area …

The mistress of the house comes down to nine o'clock breakfast, jingling the keys in her little basket, and with anxious pre-occupation, for those fatal crimson housekeeping books are to be audited this morning, and she is nervous. The girls come down in brown-holland jackets and smartly dowdy skirts, dubious as to the state of their back-hair; the eldest daughter frowning after her last night's course of theology (intermingled with the latest novel from Mr Mudie's [subscription library]). As a rule, the young ladies are very ill-tempered; and, equally as a rule, there is always one luckless young maiden in a family of grown-up daughters who comes down to breakfast with her stockings down at heel, and is sternly reprimanded during breakfast because one of her shoes comes off under the table; he who denounces her being her younger brother, the lout in the jacket, with the surreptitious peg-top in his pocket, who attends the day-school of the London University, and cribs his sisters' Berlin-wool canvas to mend his Serpentine yacht-sails with. The children too old to breakfast in the nursery come down gawky, awkward, tumbling, and discontented, for they are considered as yet too young to partake of the frizzled bits of bacon which are curling themselves in scorched agony before the grate, the muffins, which lie sodden in yellow butter-pools in the Minton plates, or the dry toast in the rack.

The servants come in, not to morning breakfast, but to morning prayers. The master of the house reads prayers in a harsh, grating voice, and Miss Charlotte, aged thirteen, is sent to her bed-room, with prospects of additional punishment, for eating her curl-papers during matins. The first organ-grinder arrives during breakfast; and the master of the house grimly reproves the children who are beginning to execute involuntary polkas on their chairs, and glowers at the governess, who manifests symptoms of beating her sad head to the music. How happy, at least how relieved, everybody is when the master exchanges his duffel dressing-gown for a blue body-coat, takes his umbrella, and drives off in his brougham to the city or Somerset House! The children are glad to go to their lessons; Miss Meek, the governess, is glad to install herself in her school-room till the children's dinner-hour, at one o'clock. The mistress finds consolation, too, in going downstairs and quarrelling with the cook, and then going upstairs and being quarrelled with by the nurse. Besides, there will be plenty of time for shopping before Mr. M. comes home. The girls are delighted that cross papa is away. Papa always wants to know what the letters are which they write at the little walnut-tree tables with the twisted legs. Papa calls novel-reading and pianoforte practice 'stuff', with a very naughty adjective prefixed thereunto.

This is the sort of house that is neatly, solidly furnished from head to toe, with every modern convenience and improvement: with bath-rooms, conservatories, ice-cellars; with patent door-handles, dish-lifts, asbestos stoves, gas cooking ranges, and excruciatingly complicated ventilatory contrivances; and this is also the sort of house where, with all the conveniences mentioned, every living soul who inhabits it is uncomfortable.

Farther west, at the opposite end of Piccadilly, the regions of Mayfair and Belgravia were indisputably upper class, as was the new residential quarter that was built on the south side of the road to Kensington in the years before and after the Great Exhibition. Bayswater too had its stucco ramparts and elegant terraces, though this north side of Hyde Park was never to enjoy quite the same prestige. In these areas, as in private housing developments today, the inhabitants were protected from the

vulgar world by railings, gates and uniformed gatekeepers. Many of
the grand streets off Westbourne or Gloucester Terraces, for example,
began as private thoroughfares. Only two of this species remain: Ely
Place in Holborn and Kensington Palace Gardens, the latter retaining
its secluded nature because it is the home of several foreign embassies.
Schlesinger noted the character of these tranquil enclaves:

> These fashionable quarters are as quiet as provincial towns.
> They have no shops; no omnibuses are allowed to pass through
> them, and few costermongers or sellers of fruit, onions, oysters
> and fish find their way into these regions, for the cheapness of
> the wares has no attractions for the inhabitants of these streets.
> These streets, too, are macadamised expressly for the horses and
> carriages of the aristocracy; such roads are more comfortable for
> all parties concerned, that is to say, for horses, horsemen, and
> drivers, and the carriages are, moreover, too light to do much
> harm to the road. In these streets, too, there are neither counting-
> houses nor public-houses to disturb the neighbourhood by their
> daily traffic and nightly reveries. Comfort reigns supreme in the
> streets and in the interior of the houses.
>
> The roadway is lined with pavements of large beautiful white
> flagstones, which skirt the railings; it is covered with gravel, and
> carefully watered, exactly as the broad paths of public gardens,
> to keep down the dust and deaden the rumbling of the carriages
> and the step of the horses. The horses, too, are of a superior kind,
> and as different from their poorer brethren, the brewer's, coal-
> merchant's, and omnibus horses, as the part of town in which
> they eat is different from that in which the latter work.

He concluded by referring to the existence of the 'mews', the street of
little coach-houses that was tucked out of sight behind the grand houses
and in which the horses and carriages lived side by side, while the
grooms and coachmen (and often their families) slept in rooms above:

> A wealthy merchant who passes his days in a narrow city
> street, in a dingy office and at a plain desk, would think it very
> 'ungenteel' if he or his family were to live in a street where

there are shops. And there are many streets shut up with iron gates, which gatekeepers open for the carriages and horses of the residents or their visitors. These gates exclude anything like noise and intrusion. For no house, not even the largest, has a carriage-gate, and what we, in Germany, shelter under our roofs – our horses, grooms, and all the odours of the stable, appears to the English strange and mysterious.

Among these could be found families with well-rehearsed pretensions to gentility. Such were the Barnacles, whom Arthur Clennam encountered in *Little Dorrit*. Their home made a striking impression:

Arthur Clennam came to a squeezed house, with a ramshackle bowed front, little dingy windows, and a little dark area like a damp waistcoat pocket, which he found to be Number Twenty-four, Mews Street, Grosvenor Square. To the sense of smell the house like a sort of bottle filled with a strong distillation of mews; and when the footman opened the door, he seemed to take the stopper out.

'Be so good as to give that card to Mr Tite Barnacle, and to say that I have just now seen the younger Mr Barnacle, who recommended me to call here.'

The footman (who had as many large buttons, with the Barnacle crest upon them, on the flaps of his pockets as if he were the family strong-box, and carried the plate and jewels about him buttoned up) pondered over the card a little; then said, 'Walk in.' It required some judgement to do it without butting the inner hall-door open, and in the consequent mental confusion and physical darkness slipping down the kitchen stairs. The visitor, however, brought himself up safely on the doormat.

Still the footman said 'Walk in,' so the visitor followed him. At the inner hall-door another bottle seemed to be presented, and another stopper taken out. This second vial appeared to be filled with concentrated provisions, and extract of Sink from the pantry. After a skirmish in the narrow passage, occasioned by the footman's opening the door of the dismal dining-room with confidence, finding someone there with consternation, and

The aristocracy, however, did like to display their skill in horsemanship, and its young female members, especially, found in 'the Row' an opportunity for energy and high spirits that had no other outlet apart from the ballroom. It was these young women, trotting, cantering and galloping to and fro, whom the sauntering, overdressed men principally came to admire. Sala witnessed the daily procession:

> I am glad to say that I am by no means alone as I lean over the rails. Whether it is that they can't or won't ride, I know not; but I find myself surrounded by groups of exquisites, who, to judge by their outward appearance, must be the greatest dandies in London. Such peg-top trousers! Such astounding waistcoat patterns! Such lofty heels to the varnished boots! Such Brobdignagian moustaches and whiskers! Such ponderous watch-chains! Such breezy neckties and alarming scarves! Ladies, too – real ladies – promenade in an amplitude of crinoline difficult to imagine and impossible to describe; some of them with stalwart footmen following. Little foot-pages; swells walking three, sometimes four, abreast; gambolling children; severe duennas; wicked old bucks, splendidly attired, leering furtively under the bonnets – what a scene of more than 'Arabian Nights' delight and gaiety!
>
> The Danaes! The Amazons! The lady cavaliers! The horsewomen! Can any scene in the world equal Rotten Row at four in the afternoon, and in the full tide of the season? Rotten Row is a very Peri's Garden for beautiful women on horseback. I count the male riders absolutely for nothing, though there may be marquises among them.

Schools and Schooling

The sons of the aristocracy were sent to school at Westminster, Harrow or Eton (to which Dickens sent his own son, Charles junior – proof that social barriers were not absolute) while their daughters were largely educated at home. Although careers were not open to girls, there were numerous accomplishments that they had to possess. Apart from the duties of running a household, it was desirable that they be able to

backing on the visitor with disorder, the visitor was shut up, pending his announcement, in a close back-parlour.

The wealthiest aristocracy lived not even in these rarefied districts but in their own town mansions. Most of these have since been demolished and virtually none are still owned by the original family, but two survivors – Spencer House in St James's and Hertford House, which now houses the Wallace Collection – give some notion of their size and grandeur. Many had their frontages hidden from the street by a high wall, so that the public could see only the rooftops. Northumberland House, where the young Dickens had admired the lion atop the façade, was among the most ostentatious. Many of the homes of the nobility were Georgian or Regency buildings, but Northumberland House was considerably older: it had been completed in 1610 before the West End existed, so it was situated not in a fashionable district but amid the bustle of the Strand, with shops and taverns jammed against it on both sides. It was, however, huge. When it opened to the public for a short time during the Great Exhibition, a guidebook offered this description:

> The front is 160 feet in length, and the court is 81 feet square. The garden between the house and the river consists of a fine lawn, surrounded by a gravel walk. This house came into the family of the Percies [sic] by the marriage of a nephew of the Earl of Northumberland with a daughter of the Earl of Suffolk. The lion on the central parapet is a copy of the celebrated one by Michael Angelo, and is the crest of the Percies.

The Jacobean exterior concealed splendid interiors of more recent design. Arranged around a courtyard, they included a drawing-room entirely walled with mirrors and coloured glass, a picture gallery more than 30m/100ft in length, and a huge marble staircase that was considered 'without exception the most splendid feature of the building.' As the area around Charing Cross began to change its character, it became increasingly extraordinary that what was effectively a country house, with a large formal garden running down to the Thames, should survive within a few feet of Trafalgar Square. Cut off by new development and openly coveted by railway builders, the house only just survived Dickens' lifetime, despite valiant attempts to save it. Its site was covered by other buildings but the famous lion was rescued and can be seen today on the roof of Syon Park, a country house to the west of London that is still owned by the Dukes of Northumberland.

A mansion that fared better, but was much newer, was Apsley House, the home of the Duke of Wellington. The same guidebook described the house but was equally interested in its owner:

> The situation is one of the finest in the metropolis, standing at the very beginning of the town. The principal front, next Piccadilly, consists of a centre with two wings, having a portico of the Corinthian order, raised upon a rusticated arcade of three apertures, leading to the entrance hall. The front is enclosed by a rich bronzed palisade, corresponding with the gates to the grand entrance to the Park. The ball room, extending the whole length of the mansion, and the picture gallery, are superb. The banqueting room is splendidly decorated, being of dead white, richly gilt.

The 'Iron Duke' himself was often to be seen on horseback, travelling down Piccadilly to visit Hatchard's bookshop, the United Services Club or the House of Lords. His military exploits had made him a hero (indeed a monstrous statue of him was to be placed on an arch opposite his house in 1846, several years before his death), but his subsequent political career had made him unpopular with radicals and his home had been attacked.

The French Revolution had demonstrated the danger of an angry mob whose energies were directed against the aristocracy. There had been no equivalent upheaval in Britain, but the passing of the Great Reform Bill in 1832, which had widened the franchise and effectively ended aristocratic dominance of Parliament, had seemed almost as bad. The Duke and his peers no longer had things all their own way. Schlesinger noticed the effect of this state of affairs on Wellington's home:

> It has rarely been the lot of a man so frequently to witness his own apotheosis as the Duke of Wellington; and yet how gloomy looks Apsley House on the fresh green borders of the park. The windows, shut up from year's end to year's end, and protected by bullet-proof shutters of massive iron – the very railings in front the house boarded up, to exclude the curiosity of the passers-by – all owing to the riots which preceded the passing of the Reform bill – riots in which the castles of the Tories were burnt down in the provinces, while in the metropolis the populace threatened the life of the greatest Englishman of the age.

The Park

Only a few yards from Apsley House, the aristocracy, and indeed the whole of London's *beau monde*, was on display in the afternoons. Rotten Row, the track for riders and carriages that runs from east to west through Hyde Park, was an essential place of resort for those who wished to be seen. To drive or ride there in the late afternoon, or at the least to lean on the wooden rails and watch those passing, was an essential social ritual for anyone who aspired to beauty and fashion. While the dandies who lined the rails might be extravagant in their dress, Schlesinger realized that the comparative drabness of the aristocrats was symptomatic both of their confidence and their fear of arousing envy. His observation was a useful summing-up of the attitude of Society toward the display of wealth:

> Those who have seen the Prater [a pleasure garden] of Vienna will be rather disappointed with the aspect of the drive in Hyde Park, where the upper classes of London congregate in the evening between five and seven o'clock, partly to take the air, and partly because it is considered fashionable. Extravagant turn-outs and liveries, such as the Viennese produce with great ostentation, are not to be found in London. The English aristocracy like to make an impression by the simplicity and solidity of their appearance; and the metropolis is the last of all places where they would wish to excite attention by a dashing and extravagant exterior. They have not the least desire either to dazzle or to awe the trades-people or to make them envious. They are too sure of their position to be tempted to advertise it; whoever wants this assurance cannot pretend to belong to the aristocracy.

dance, play some instrument (the piano or harp) and negotiate the other social rituals that were involved in gaining a husband. Lower down the social scale, education was more widely available to girls. School-teaching was not yet a respectable profession, but giving tuition in 'academies' and 'seminaries' for young ladies and gentlemen of the middle class was a worthy and even lucrative occupation for educated and well-bred women. Many of these establishments were situated in ordinary town houses on the streets of passably genteel districts such as Walworth and Brixton. Typical of them were these two, advertised in *The Times* in January 1829:

> Miss H. Rae, the only surviving daughter of the late Mr Andrew Rae, of Islington, will be happy to receive YOUNG LADIES at her Establishment, 5, Queen's Row, Walworth, upon terms that will suit the views of parents who wish to unite domestic comfort with mental improvement. Miss Rae having for many years devoted herself to the task of tuition with much success, can with confidence refer to many respectable persons whose children she has had the pleasure of educating.

> At Mrs and Miss FINCH'S ESTABLISHMENT, 37 Southampton Street, Camberwell, a limited number of YOUNG LADIES are educated in the English and French languages, geography, history, and every branch of useful and ornamental needlework. There are at present TWO VACANCIES. Parents may rely on every attention being paid to the health, happiness, and improvement of their daughters, and that they will uniformly experience the most liberal treatment. Respectable references given and required.

Schools like these educated thousands of children of both sexes throughout the 19th century. Though most were adequately run, Dickens several times attacked them in his writings. There was nothing to prevent anyone setting themselves up as a schoolteacher and taking classes in their home. They could create their own curriculum, feed their boarders as much or as little as they cared to and administer thrashings whenever they felt it necessary. Many would have begun life as private tutors in wealthy families and all they would need to commence business would be a flurry of references, genuine or spurious. Doctor Blimber's establishment, to which the young and sickly Paul Dombey was sent, was a school that boasted of its results. These were achieved at the cost of relentless discipline, unimaginative teaching and misery for the pupils. The curriculum:

> ... comprised a little English, and a deal of Latin – names of things, declensions of articles and substantives, exercises thereon, and preliminary rules – a trifle of orthography, a glance at ancient history, a wink or two at modern ditto, a few tables, two or three weights and measures, and a little general information.

Salem House, the school attended by David Copperfield, provides another example of the cheerless pursuit of learning. It was based on Dickens' own memories of Wellington House Academy in Camden:

> I gazed upon the schoolroom into which he took me, as the most forlorn and desolate place I had ever seen. I see it now. A long room, with three long rows of desks, and six of forms, and bristling all round with pegs for hats and slates. Scraps of old copy-books and exercises litter the dirty floor. Some silkworms' houses, made of the same materials, are scattered over the desks. Two miserable little white mice, left behind by their owner, are running up and down a fusty castle made of pasteboard and wire, looking in all the corners with their red eyes for anything to eat. A bird, in a cage, very little bigger than himself, makes a mournful rattle now and then in hopping on his perch, but neither sings nor chirps. There is a strange unwholesome smell upon the room, like mildewed corduroys, sweet apples wanting air, and rotten books. There could not well be more ink splashed about it, if it had been roofless from its first construction, and the skies had rained, snowed, hailed, and blown ink through the varying seasons of the year.

While this sounds grim, it was no worse than a classroom at one of the great public schools, and the fact that the pupils were allowed to keep pets suggests that they had some pleasure to balance the drudgery of

learning and the fear of punishment. Copperfield's old schoolfellow
Traddles, recalling their experiences years afterward, exclaimed:

> 'Dear me, there was a lot of fun going on. Do you remember
> the nights in the bedroom? When we used to have the suppers?
> And when you used to tell the stories? Ha, ha, ha! And do you
> remember when I got caned for crying about Mr Mell?'

Pupils of this type of school were not always without opportunities,
either. Another of Copperfield's schoolmates, Steerforth, went on to
Oxford. The majority of boys who passed through this education would,
however, have gone into clerical employment, very much of the sort that
Dickens himself encountered when he joined a legal firm. They would
have maintained, just as old boys of the public schools did, a network of
acquaintance and mutual assistance that might well have lasted the rest
of their lives – marrying members of each other's families, standing as
godfathers to each other's children and finding positions, or husbands,
for those same children when the time came.

Bachelor Life

For young women of good family, somewhat higher up the social scale
than Traddles, the interlude between school and matrimony was likely
to be short, for they would commonly marry in their teens and might
have several children by their mid-twenties. Prior to that, and with
the necessary 'accomplishments' duly attained, they might well have
nothing to do except enjoy a range of social pleasures. Sala summed
these up when observing girls of this sort in the Pantheon Bazaar:

> The world for them is yet a place for flirting, and shopping, and
> dancing, and making themselves as fair to view as they and the
> looking-glass and the milliner can manage. The world is yet a
> delightful Pantheon, full of flowers – real, wax and artificial, and
> all pleasant – sandal-wood fans, petticoats with worked edges, silk
> stockings, satin shoes, white kid gloves, varnished broughams,
> pet dogs, vanilla ices, boxes at the opera, tickets for the Crystal

Palace, tortoise-shell card-cases, enamelled visiting-cards, and
scented pink invitation-notes, with 'On dansera' in the left-hand
bottom corners, muslin slips, bandoline [gum for stiffening the
hair], perfumes, ballads and polkas with chromo-lithographed
frontispieces, and the dear delightful new novels from Mudie's
with uncut leaves, and mother-o'-pearl paper knives with coral
spring handles to cut them withal. They have kind mammas and
indulgent port-wine papas, who bring them home such nice things
from the city. They sit under such darling clergymen, with curls
in the centre of their dear white foreheads; they have soft beds,
succulent dinners, and softly-pacing hacks, on which to ride in
coquettish-looking habits and cavalier hats. John the footman
is always anxious to run errands for them; and their additional
male acquaintance is composed of charming creatures with
white neckcloths, patent leather boots, irreproachable whiskers,
and mellow tenor voices. Oh! The delightful world; sure, it is
the *meilleur des mondes possible*, as Voltaire's Doctor Pangloss
maintained. It is true that they were at school once, and suffered
all the tyranny of the 'calisthenic exercises' and the French mark,
or were, at home, mewed up under the supervision of a stern
governess, who set them excruciating tasks; but, oh! That was
such a long time ago. You silly little creatures! It was only the day
before yesterday, and the day after tomorrow ... But 'gather ye
rosebuds while ye may,' and regard not old Time as he is a-flying.
For my part, I will mingle no drop of cynicism in the jewelled
cup of your young enjoyment; and I hope that the day after tomorrow, with unkind husbands and ungrateful children, with
physic-bottles and aches and pains, and debts and duns, may never
come to you, and that your pretty shadows may never be less.

The men whom these girls would marry, whether young or older, would
have been living in 'rooms', or bachelor quarters. They would not know
how to cook, or to perform any other domestic task; even the moderately
wealthy had a manservant to dress them and provide their meals and a
laundress to take care of their linen. The most famous haunt of bachelors
(which still survives) was Albany, the set of gentlemen's apartments
off Piccadilly, whose inmates have included Lord Byron and William

Gladstone. Another famous resident, though a fictitious one, was Fascination Fledgeby in *Our Mutual Friend* and Dickens set one of the novel's most memorable scenes there. The historian Thomas Babington Macaulay occupied rooms in Albany from 1841, and he pictured his domestic arrangements in a letter to his friend Thomas Flower Ellis:

> I have taken a very comfortable suite of chambers in Albany, and I hope to lead, during some years, a sort of life peculiarly suited to my taste – college life at the West End of London. I have an entrance hall, two sitting-rooms, a bedroom, a kitchen, cellars and two rooms for servants – all for ninety guineas a year; and this in a situation which no younger son of a Duke need be ashamed to put on his card. We shall have, I hope, some very pleasant breakfasts there, to say nothing of dinners. My own housekeeper will do very well for a few plain dishes, and the Clarendon is within a hundred yards.'

Though Macaulay mentioned a kitchen, this would not have been in his apartment. The apartments had neither kitchens, bathrooms or lavatories. Food would have been prepared by his servant in the basement and carried upstairs. Ablutions were carried out in a tin bath that was brought into the bedroom from elsewhere and filled by a servant, from jugs of hot water. As for the delicate matter of calls of nature, the solution would, like so much else about Dickens' time, surprise modern sensitivities. Many bachelors setting up home would buy, or be given, a type of bureau called a 'night table'. Though these varied in design, they usually comprised a desk with a drop-front for writing. Below this there would be drawers used for keeping bills and letters, or for storing clothing. The bottom drawer was a commode and had folding legs to support the weight of someone sitting on it. This drawer would be shut once business had been concluded and the contents subsequently removed by a servant, for whom 'emptying slops' was an entirely routine part of his duties.

Though bachelor apartments provided a comfortable setting for the basics of living, the gentlemen's club was an essential part of a sociable young man's existence. Max Schlesinger explained the function of this very English institution:

A younger son of an old house, with an income of, say, from two to four hundred pounds [a year], cannot live and do as others do, within the limits of that income. He can neither take and furnish a house, nor can he keep a retinue of servants or give dinners to his friends. The club is his home, and stands him in the place of an establishment. At the club, spacious and splendidly furnished saloons are at his disposal; there is a library, a reading-room, baths, and dressing-rooms. At the club, he finds all the last new works and periodicals; a crowd of servants attend upon him; and the cooking is irreproachable. The expenses of the establishment are defrayed by the annual contributions and the entrance fees … Members dine at the clubs: indeed, the providing of dinners is among the leading objects of these establishments, and the dinners are good and cheap, compared to the extortionate prices of the London hotels. The club provides everything, and gives it at cost price; a member of a good club pays five shillings for a dinner, which in an hotel would be charged, at least, four times that sum.

Courtship and Marriage

The surroundings in which young men and women might meet were usually circumscribed and would not, among the genteel, involve being alone together. David Copperfield's first sight of Dora, the daughter of his employer, while visiting the latter's home, was a circumstance with which the novel's readers could have identified, including the fact that the young woman had a professional companion from whom it was nigh-impossible to part her:

We went into the house, which was cheerfully lighted up, and into a hall where there were all sorts of hats, caps, great-coats, plaids, gloves, whips, and walking-sticks. 'Where is Miss Dora?' said Mr Spenlow to the servant. 'Dora!' I thought, 'what a beautiful name!'
    We turned into a room near at hand, and I heard a voice say, 'Mr Copperfield, my daughter Dora, and my daughter Dora's confidential friend!' It was, no doubt, Mr Spenlow's voice, but I

didn't know it, and I didn't care whose it was. All was over in a
moment. I had fulfilled my destiny. I was a captive and a slave. I
loved Dora Spenlow to distraction!

Another courtship was described in *A Christmas Carol*, at the party
given by Scrooge's nephew, Fred. Christmas was, of course, an important
annual ritual. It received an exotic touch in the 1840s with the
introduction of the Christmas tree, allegedly by Prince Albert, but
homes were in any case decorated in seasonal manner with holly-boughs.
There was an exchange of presents, and perhaps even the giving of
Christmas cards; the first one known dates from 1843, the year in which
Dickens' best-known Christmas story was written:

> After a while they played at forfeits; for it is good to be children
> sometimes, and never better than at Christmas ... There was first
> a game of blind-man's buff. Of course there was! And I no more
> believe that Topper was blind than I believe he had eyes in his
> boots. The way he went after the plump sister in the lace tucker,
> was an outrage on the credulity of human nature. Knocking
> down fire-irons, tumbling over chairs, bumping up against the
> piano, smothering himself among the curtains, wherever she
> went, there went he. He always knew where the plump sister
> was. He wouldn't catch anyone else. She often cried out that
> it wasn't fair; and it really was not. But when at last he caught
> her; when, in spite of all her silken rustlings, and her rapid
> flutterings past him he got her into a corner whence there was no
> escape; then his conduct was most execrable. For his pretending
> not to know her; his pretending that it was necessary to touch
> her head-dress, and further to assure himself of her identity by
> pressing a certain ring on her finger, was vile! Monstrous! No
> doubt she told him her opinion of it when, another blind man
> being in office, they were so very confidential together, behind
> the curtains.

William Tayler, from his below-stairs viewpoint, described in his journal
a less restrained Festive Season. His account suggests that the notion of
Christmas becoming a mere justification for excess is not new:

24th December 1837. This is Sunday, many drunken people about the streets, some getting drunk ready for tomorrow. There are more people go before the Magestrate at Christmas time for getting drunk than there is all the year besides and but very few give it a thought what the time is for. 25th. This is Christmas Day, which is, I am sorry to say, almost forgot in London except by the drunkards. We had here roast beef, plum pudding, turkey, and a bottle of brandy to make punch, which we all enjoyed very much. In many gentlemen's famleys, there is a great deal of egg hot [egg-nog] and toast and ale at these times and great seremoney in putting up the mistletoe bow in the servant hall or the kitchen, but our famly is too small for any thing of the kind.

He explained the significance of that great British institution, Boxing Day. In those days it was the time at which all whose efforts had made the past year more endurable for the respectable classes called to claim their reward, but those in the household's servants' quarters who had put business in the way of local tradesmen might also expect gratitude:

26th. This is what is called about here Boxing Day. It's the day the people goe from house to house gathering their Christmas boxes. We have had numbers here today – sweeps, beadles, lamplighters, watermen, dustmen, scavengers – that is the men who clean the mud out of the streets – newspaper boy, general postmen, twopenny postmen [special deliveries] and waits. These are a set of men that goe about the streets playing musick in the night after people are in bed and a sleep. Some people are very fond of hearing them, but for my own part, I don't admire being roused from a sound sleep by a whole band of musick and perhaps not get to sleep again for an houre or two. All these people expect to have a shilling or half a crown each. Went out this morning, saw plenty of people rowling about the streets in the hight of their glorey. Mrs P [his employer] gave me half a sovereign for a Christmas box, one of the trades people gave me half a crown, another gave me a shilling. I mite get fuddled two or three times a day if I had a mind, as all the trades people that serve this house are very pressing with their glass of something to drink their health this Christmas time.

Gatherings like the one described by Dickens were an important opportunity for the sexes to mix. Marriage might eventually result, but this did not by any means guarantee a happy future for the flirtatious young women whom Tayler observed at a genteel tea-party. His comments are an illuminating insight into the hollowness of 'respectable' society:

> We have a party here today, some to dinner and some to tea. It's amuseing to see the young ladies, how they manover to make the gentlemen take notice of them. They will loose their pocket handkerchiefs or drop their gloves, that the gents mite offer to find them, or they will keep a wine glass or cup and sauser in their hand until after the servant is gone out of the room, so that some of the gents mite take it of them. This gets them to change a fiew words. The girls are up to hundreds of these little manovers at parties, to induce the men to begin talking to them. Their mothers take care to give them good instruction how to manage before they leave home. There is very fiew of them that get husbands after all, except they are very handsome or got large fortunes, as young gentlemen generally place their affections on some poor but pretty girl and takes her into keeping and when tired of her, turns her off and gets another. Those that are turned off mostly go on the toun as comom prostitutes. If a gentleman maries a lady, it's for her money, and in a short time he gets tired of her and takes up with his kept girl again and treats his wife like a dog. Therefore women in high life has not the opertunity of getting married as those in lower stations, as men in lower stations of life cannot afford to keep girls. Therefore they marrey. But men in higher life can afoard to keep these lasses, therefore they do not care about marrying except for money, and then of course there is no happiness. The husband neglects his wife, that gives the wife reason to go with other men, and there is a regular system of whoredom carreyed on by both parties. I mean, that is the case with a great many. Of course, there are some exceptions, some good and some bad.

Weddings were very different to those today. They had to take place in the morning (it was not legal to hold one after noon until the 1880s).

The veil did not become popular until the latter half of the century; prior to that, a bonnet was worn. There was likewise no tradition of brides wearing a white dress; indeed they often wore black. At weddings of the middle and upper classes the bride might wear any colour, and would simply put on her best dress. The departure, together, of a lower middle-class bride and groom for the church from a small terrace was visualized by 'Boz':

> One fine morning, at a quarter before eight o'clock, two glass coaches drove up to Miss Willis' door, at which Mr Robinson had arrived in a cab ten minutes before, dressed in a light-blue coat and double-milled kersey pantaloons, white neckerchief, pumps, and dress gloves, his manner denoting, as appeared from the evidence of the housemaid at No 23, who was sweeping the door-steps at the time, a considerable degree of nervous excitement. It was also hastily reported on the same testimony that the cook who opened the door, wore a large white bow of unusual dimensions.
>
> At last the Miss Willises' door opened; the door of the first glass coach did the same. Two gentlemen, and a pair of ladies to correspond – friends of the family, no doubt; up went the steps, bang went the door, off went the first glass coach, and up came the second.

Among this class, there would perhaps be a party at the couple's home and a 'wedding breakfast'. They might also be able to travel for a day or so to a seaside resort, but there would otherwise be no question of a reception or a honeymoon – a far cry from the extensive 'wedding tours' of their social betters. Many couples simply moved into their married home and began domestic life at once.

For the middle classes, marriage could be for love, but within the professions and the higher reaches of commerce, and within Society, this was a not normally an option. Young men would not risk their future respectability by making an unsuitable marriage. For the aristocracy this was resoundingly true. Many of its members met their future partners during the Season, a series of social events – balls, banquets, parties, sporting events – held every year between Easter and August. This was considered a suitable time for arranging marriages because the whole

of Society was in London at once, because it offered innumerable
opportunities for families and their marriageable offspring to size each
other up, and because young women of good family made their entrance
into the adult world by being presented to the monarch. Though the
old aristocracy was a relatively close-knit group, and the nature of the
Season was that it should be exclusive, social barriers in Britain have
always been permeable for those with enterprise and connections.
Queen, a ladies' periodical, opined in the 1860s that, whereas in the past:

> **Presentations were confined to the true aristocracy of the
> country, the peerage, the superior landed gentry, persons of
> distinction in art, science and letters and the holders of offices of
> dignity under the Crown. It is now no longer so. Presentations
> are so vulgarised that literally ANYBODY who has sufficient
> amount of perseverance or self confidence may be presented. The
> wives of all Members of Parliament are presented and they in turn
> present the wives and daughters of local squires and other small
> magnates. There is no knowing where this is to stop.**

Young women would be outfitted at great expense for the various events
they were to attend. They and their parents would be praying that a
death in the family did not cause them to abandon the Season and have
to dress for the whole of the next year in mourning black. Out-of-town
families paid often extortionate amounts to rent houses in the West End,
and hoped for a return on their investment through an advantageous
alliance. The Season was, in other words, a marriage-market, often
conducted with ruthlessness and cynicism. The poet Alfred Austin
characterized it in a work he wrote about a Society ballroom:

> **This scene, your anti-sensual strictures doom,
> Is not an orgy but an auction-room,
> These painting damsels, dancing for their lives,
> Are only maidens waltzing into wives,
> Those smiling matrons are appraisers shy,
> Who regulate the dance, the squeeze, the sigh,
> And each base cheapening buyer having chid,
> Knock down their daughters to the noblest bid.**

Sala, as usual, left us his own observation. He viewed a wedding at St James's Church in Piccadilly, with an array of bridesmaids and a best man from an Indian Army regiment:

> How eloquent, and, by turn, pathetic and humorous I could be on the bevy of youthful bridesmaids – all in white tulle over pink glace silk, all in bonnets trimmed with white roses, and with bouquets of camellias and lilies of the valley! How I could expatiate on the appearance of the beauteous and high-born bride, her Honiton lace veil, her innumerable flounces; and her noble parents, and the gallant and distinguished bridegroom, and his 'best man', the burly colonel of the Fazimanagghur Irregulars; and the distinguished personages who alight from their carriages at the little wicket in Piccadilly, and pass along the great area amid the cheers of the little boys! They are so noble and distinguished, that one clergyman can't perform the ceremony, and extra parsons are provided. The register becomes an autograph-book of noble and illustrious signatures; the vestry-room has sweet odours of Jockey Club and Frangipani lingering about it for hours afterwards.
>
> See, the bridal procession comes into garish Piccadilly, and amid fresh cheers and the pealing of the joy-bells, steps into its carriages.

Domestic Life

Once married, a couple might have a short period of irresponsible gaiety before the onset of family life. Sala noticed some couples on their way to dinner (one pair on their way to the Trafalgar, a tavern at Greenwich famous for whitebait suppers, and with a balconied bow window that looked over the Thames). He gives a useful insight into the diet, as well as the dress-style, of the Victorians:

> In that snug, circular-fronted brougham, a comfortable couple, trotting out to dinner in the Alpha Road, St John's Wood. Plenty of lobster sauce they will have with their salmon, I wager; twice of boiled chicken and white sauce they will not refuse, and oyster patties will they freely partake of. A jovial couple, rosy, chubby,

childless, I opine, which makes them a little too partial to table enjoyments. They should be well to do in the world, fond of giving merry, corpulent little dinners of their own, with carpet dances afterwards, and living, I will be bound, at Maida Hill, or Pine Apple Gate. There is another couple, stiff, starched, angular, acrimonious-looking. Husband with a stern, Lincoln's Inn conveyancing face, and pilloried in starch, with white kid gloves much too large for him. Wife, with all manner of tags, and odds and ends of finery fluttering about her: one of those women who, if she had all the rich toilettes of all King Solomon's wives on her, would never look well dressed. I shouldn't like to dine where they are going. I know what the dinner will be like. Prim, pretentious, dismal, and eminently uncomfortable. There will be a saddle of mutton not sufficiently hung, the fish will be cold, the wines hot, and the carving-knives will be blunt. After dinner the men will talk dreary politics, redolent of stupid Retrogression, and the women will talk about physic and the hooping-cough.

Yet another couple – A severe swell, with drooping moustaches of immense length, but which are half whiskers. A pretty lady – gauzy bonnet and artificial flowers, muslin jacket, skirts and flounces oozing out at the sides of the carriage; and a Skye terrier with a pink ribbon. I know what this means. Greenwich, seven o'clock dinner (they are rather late, by the way, but they pass us on London Bridge, and the coachman will drive rapidly) water souche [fish soup], whitebait, brown bread and butter, and iced punch; cigar on balcony, and contemplation of the moon. Ride on, and be happy. Rejoice in your youth – and never mind the rest. It will come, O young man, whether you mind it or not.

Soon after marriage, members of all classes would set out to produce children as soon as possible. It was necessary to have several. No matter how well off a child's family, there was a serious risk of death from any of several diseases, and for the mother there was the possibility of dying in childbirth. Victorian children were not pampered (even in wealthy homes they might be subject to harsh discipline and corporal punishment) and they had to be tough to survive the vital years of infancy: one in five died within the first year of life.

The children would be looked after by nurses or nannies and presented to their mother only at bedtimes or other significant moments. She needed to have little to do with actually bringing them up. She would, in fact, have little to do at all. Servants kept the home running smoothly under her nominal supervision; if her husband entertained, she had only to plan the seating for dinner-parties and decide the menu. She had to fill her days with other things: shopping, paying and receiving calls, attending committees for a multitude of good works (Victorian philanthropy owes much to the boredom of middle-class women) and making things – principally embroidery – for sale on behalf of charities.

One task of undoubted importance, performed even by the well-off, might surprise us. In an era when toilet-paper had not been invented, households created their own (the word 'bumf' for sheets of printed paper is short for 'bum-fodder' for this reason; such a term would not, of course, have been used by respectable people). Diana Holman Hunt recalled a visit to her grandmother during which she was put to work at this task. Though this memory belongs to a slightly later era, it nevertheless captures the no-nonsense manner of the Dickensian householder. The old lady issued her with the necessary equipment:

'Here is your knife. You will find the stiletto, the template and string in the Indian box over there.'
I ripped the blade through the stiff paper folded around the template. Some of these bags from Palmer's Stores are very thick and covered with writing. When I had cut a hundred sheets, I pierced their corners and threaded them with a string; I tied this in a loop to hang on a nail by the 'convenience'. I made a mental note of the softer pieces and put them together in the middle, between the back of a calendar and an advertisement for night-lights.

This combination of practical chores and charitable works was the currency of many women's lives in an era in which they had no political rights and few commercial or creative opportunities. Again, Dickens aimed satirical darts with a good deal of accuracy in the guise of 'Boz':

In winter, when wet feet are common, and colds not scarce, we have the ladies' soup distribution society, the ladies' coal distribution society and the ladies' blanket distribution society; in summer, when stone fruits flourish and stomach aches prevail, we have the ladies' dispensary, and the ladies' sick visitation committee; and all the year round we have the ladies' child's examination society, the ladies' bible and prayer-book circulation society, and the ladies' childbed-linen monthly loan society. The two latter are decidedly the most important; they create a greater stir and more bustle than all the others put together.

When the young curate was popular, and all the unmarried ladies in the parish took a serious turn, the charity children all at once became objects of peculiar and especial interest. The three Miss Browns (enthusiastic admirers of the curate) taught, and exercised, and examined, and re-examined the unfortunate children, until the boys grew pale, and the girls consumptive with study and fatigue ...

Mrs Johnson Parker, the mother of seven extremely fine girls, reported to several other mammas of several other unmarried families, that five old men, six old women, and children innumerable, in the free seats near her pew, were in the habit of coming to church every Sunday, without either bible or prayer-book. Was this to be borne in a civilized country? Could such things be tolerated in a Christian land? Never! A ladies' bible and prayer-book distribution society was instantly formed: president, Mrs Johnson Parker; treasures, auditors, and secretary, the Misses Johnson Parker: subscriptions were entered into, books were bought, all the free-seat people provided therewith, and when the first lesson was given out, on the first Sunday succeeding these events, there was such a dropping of books, and rustling of leaves, that it was morally impossible to hear one word of the service for five minutes afterwards.

Going to Church

There were many thousands of women whose talents and energies were fixed on the Church. They could not participate in ministry, but they could perform invaluable work as organizers of charity events, teachers of Sunday Schools, or simply as disciples of particular clergymen.

Though a census carried out in 1851 concluded that less than half of
the British population attended a church (it was based on statistics
gathered on a single Sunday), the established Church held a place in
social life that is all but inconceivable today. Victorian Britain was a
deeply religious place. In 1829, legal restrictions on Catholic worship
were removed for the first time since the Reformation. The Clapham
Sect, a gathering of idealistic intellectuals that included William
Wilberforce, agitated for the abolition of slavery in the 1820s and
fostered a new enthusiasm for nonconformism. In the 1850s this was
built upon by the American evangelists Moody and Sankey, whose visits
to Britain brought a full-blown 'Revival' of faith, and by the sermons of
the popular and influential London preacher C.H. Spurgeon. Within
the Church of England, the Oxford Movement led to a different sort of
revival: a return to ritual and ornament that emulated the styles of the
Middle Ages. Enthusiasm for, and opposition to, this trend divided the
Anglican Church between ritualists ('high') and those who preferred
simpler forms ('low'). Everywhere, as the population expanded, there
was church-building; and many of these edifices, such as those designed
by A.W. Pugin or William Butterfield, have become well-loved features
of the capital. Everywhere, too, Christianity was the subject of debate,
enquiry and celebration. Religion had a degree of vibrancy and social
influence that cannot be overestimated.

The cartoonist Osbert Lancaster, though of a later generation,
expressed something that was also true of Dickens' time. He described
how the importance of ecclesiastical matters was taken for granted
and was reflected in the space devoted to clergymen's portraits in the
illustrated papers. These followed immediately after pictures of monarchs
and military heroes:

More familiar were the pages devoted to the more prominent
contemporary divines. No flourishing moustachios nor jewelled
orders here, but every variety of whisker from the restrained
mutton-chop to the full Newgate fringe, and billowing acres of
Episcopal lawn. At the time these portraits were taken the social
prestige of the [ecclesiastical] Establishment, and even, on a
different level, of Nonconformity, was at its height. In the society
in which my parents moved, the clergy still played a prominent and

honoured role. Their merits as preachers were eagerly discussed
and the exact degree of their 'Highness' or 'Lowness' keenly
debated. Many of the originals of those portraits were, therefore,
quite familiar to me by name as being preachers under whom
members of my family had at one time or another sat, while on
the knees of one of them, a celebrated Evangelical preacher from
whose well-attended Watch Night sermons the more impressionable
members of the congregation were regularly carried out on
stretchers, I myself had once had the honour of being perched.

Today the Church makes no objection to congregations 'dressing down'.
In the 19th century it was taken for granted that churchgoers would
dress as well as they could possibly afford to. Quite apart from the matter
of 'keeping up appearances', the parish church was the centre of a close-
knit local community (of gossip, sociability and charity) and, like any
community, it had a hierarchy. There was unapologetic class distinction,
manifest not only in the dress of parishioners but in where they sat. The
pews, with their doors and high wooden sides, were rented by the year.
Those in prominent positions naturally cost more, or might be, *de facto*,
the permanent possession of one family. There were 'free seats' elsewhere
in the church, but these would be at the back or in the gallery, where
servants would sit among the local poor.

A pew in the front of the church, with the accompanying deference of
the pew-opener and the parish beadle, would have been a status symbol
of which today's equivalent might be having one's own box at the opera.
Dickens captured this sociological aspect of Victorian churchgoing in his
description of a wealthy widow:

Her entrance into church on Sunday is always the signal for a
little bustle in the side aisle, occasioned by a general rise among
the poor people, who bow and curtsey until the pew-opener
has ushered the old lady into her accustomed seat, dropped a
respectful curtsey and shut the door: and the same ceremony is
repeated on her leaving church, when she walks home with the
family next door but one, and talks about the sermon all the way,
invariably opening the conversation by asking the youngest boy
where the text was.

Osbert Lancaster recalled the spectacle of the congregation leaving a fashionable church:

> For the present generation it is almost impossible to imagine how impressive a spectacle was the weekly Church Parade outside any one of a dozen or more London churches at the close of Morning Prayer on any fine Sunday. The street would be deserted save for one or two victorias and broughams at the church gates (never very many, although the congregation contained a high proportion of 'carriage folk'. St John's was rather Low and it was not thought right for any except the frail and aged to work their coachmen on the Sabbath), and the soft strains of Dykes would come floating out among the plane trees of Ladbroke Hill as the verger opened the doors at the final verse of the closing hymn. Then a short pause, a rustling murmur as the congregation rose from its knees gathering up prayer books and adjusting veils and gloves, and the first worshippers would emerge blinking a little in the bright sun pursued by the rolling chords of the voluntary. Soon the whole churchyard and street was a mass of elaborate, pale-shaded millinery, among which the glittering top hats, ceaselessly doffed and replaced, provided the sharper, more definite accents.

A clergyman, by definition the most respectable of beings, would often be a subject of great interest to lady members of his congregation. At a time when stipends in good parishes were generous and their occupants wealthy (the Church was still, as in Jane Austen's time, a suitable profession for the younger sons of good families), a rector or curate was a desirable husband. 'Boz' discussed the fascination exerted by these men:

> Our curate is a very young gentleman of such prepossessing appearance, and fascinating manners, that within one month after his first appearance in the parish, half the young-lady inhabitants were melancholy with religion, and the other half desponding with love. Never were so many young ladies seen in our parish church on Sunday before. He was about five-and-twenty. He parted his hair on the centre of his forehead in the form of a Norman arch, and had a deep sepulchral voice of unusual

solemnity. Innumerable were the calls made by prudent mammas on our new curate, and innumerable the invitations with which he was assailed. Pews in the immediate vicinity of the pulpit or reading-desk rose in value; sittings in the centre aisle were at a premium: an inch of room in the front row of the gallery could not be procured for love or money.

He began to preach extempore sermons, and even grave papas caught the infection. He got out of bed at half-past twelve o'clock one winter's night, to half-baptise a washerwoman's child in a slop-basin, and the gratitude of the parishioners knew no bounds. He sent three pints of gruel and a quarter of a pound of tea to a poor woman who had been brought to bed of four small children, all at once – the parish were charmed. He got up a subscription for her – the woman's fortune was made. He spoke for one hour and twenty-five minutes at an anti-slavery meeting – the enthusiasm was at its height.

The curate began to cough. Here was a discovery – the curate was consumptive. How interestingly melancholy! If the young ladies were energetic before, their sympathy and solicitude now knew no bounds. Anonymous presents of black-currant jam, and lozenges, elastic waistcoats and warm stockings, poured in upon the curate until he was completely fitted out with winter clothing as if he were on the verge of an expedition to the North Pole: verbal bulletins of the state of his health were circulated throughout the parish half-a-dozen times a day; and the curate was in the very zenith of his popularity.

In the event, his popularity evaporated when an even more 'interestingly melancholy' clergyman arrived at a nearby chapel.

However trivial, insincere or superficial this approach to religion may seem, it must be remembered that Dickens was writing satire, not fact. It is not at all surprising, or blameworthy, that the parish church gave to local people a sense of belonging, a source of diversion and a feeling of self-importance. For all the significance that many congregations gave to outward appearance and deference to the wealthy, there were numerous churches beyond the reach of forms and fashion whose members did immeasurable good for the society around them.

GAZETTEER

Dickens' London is not difficult to find. In many corners of the city –
Clerkenwell, Islington, Camden, Southwark – there are not only houses
but streets and whole districts of houses dating from the 1820s, 30s and
40s. Similarly, the stuccoed squares and terraces of **Belgravia, Bayswater**
and **South Kensington** look much as they did in the mid-19th century.

South of the River
In **Borough High Street** many of the buildings and alleys have a
Dickensian feel. It was at the **White Hart** here that Mr Pickwick met
Sam Weller. The inn has gone, though it is commemorated by a plaque.
Part of a coaching inn survives nearby, however. **The George**, originally
built in 1677, has galleries and taprooms that Pickwick would recognize.

Round the corner in **St Thomas Street** are important reminders of
London's medical history. Opened in 1726, **Guy's Hospital** represented a
breakthrough in hospital design. Its wards were roomy, well-lit and well-
ventilated, grouped around two courtyards. This still looks much as it did
when built, and in one of its courtyards is preserved a stone shelter from
Old London Bridge. Bob Sawyer in *Pickwick Papers*, who held a party at
his rooms in nearby **Lant Street**, was a medical student at Guy's.

Opposite the hospital is a grimmer relic. Concealed in the loft of a
church is the former womens' operating theatre of another hospital, St
Thomas'. This was in use from 1821 until the hospital moved in 1865. It
vividly demonstrates why only the toughest could survive surgery.

A few minutes' walk to the south is the site of the **Marshalsea Debtors'
Prison**. Only part of the high brick wall, skirting the nearby churchyard,
remains. The church itself, **St George the Martyr**, is the scene of Little
Dorrit's christening, and of her marriage to Arthur Clennam. It is known
as the 'Little Dorrit Church.'

Other Churches and Cemeteries
There are other churches with Dickens connections. In **the Strand**,
the church of **St Mary** was the setting for his parents' wedding in
1809, while he himself was married to Catherine Hogarth at **St
Luke's** in **Sydney Street, Chelsea**, in 1836. Most significant of
all is **Westminster Abbey**, where Dickens' grave can be seen in
Poets' Corner. His parents are buried in **Highgate Cemetery**.

Map of DICKENS' LONDON, showing places mentioned in the text

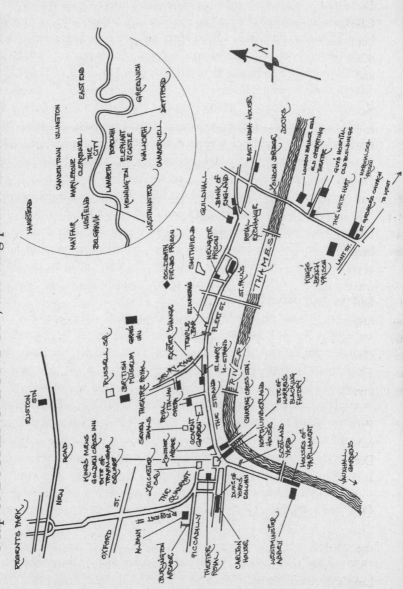

Dickens' Residences

Only one of Dickens' homes still exists. His family's house in **Bayham Street, Camden**, was demolished almost a century ago, and his lodgings from 1834–7 at **Furnival's Inn** in **Holborn** (where he wrote *Pickwick Papers*) have been replaced by the **Prudential Building**, in which he is commemorated by a bronze bust. The house in **Devonshire Terrace, Marylebone**, in which he lived from 1839–51 (and wrote *A Christmas Carol*, *Dombey and Son*, *The Old Curiosity Shop*, *Martin Chuzzlewit* and *David Copperfield*) is marked by a stone relief depicting the mature Dickens, together with some of his characters. His house in **Tavistock Square, Bloomsbury** (1851–60) has also vanished. Here he wrote *Bleak House*, *Little Dorrit*, *A Tale of Two Cities* and *Great Expectations*.

The house at **48 Doughty Street**, off **Theobalds Road** in **Holborn**, in which he lived from 1837–9, and wrote *Oliver Twist* and *Nicholas Nickleby*, has been restored as a museum. It houses a library of Dickens editions as well as over 700 of his letters. It is run by the Dickens Fellowship, and is unique among London's museums in that it is open on Christmas Day.

Other Important Sites

Opposite the end of Doughty Street is **Gray's Inn**, containing the building – **No. 1, Smith Square** – in which the young Dickens worked as a clerk for Ellis and Blackmore from 1827–8. Nearby, **Ely Place** was the scene of a dinner party in *David Copperfield* and **Field Lane**, a now-vanished alley off **Shoe Lane** in **Farringdon**, was the site of **Fagin's 'den'**. Near the south gate of Gray's Inn are **Staple Inn**, which features in *The Mystery of Edwin Drood*, and **Lincoln's Inn Fields**, where Dickens' friend and biographer, John Forster, lived. Round the corner, set back behind the larger buildings of **Kingsway** and **Aldwych**, is a premises purporting to be **The Old Curiosity Shop**. Though there is no truth in this claim, the shop itself – looking incongruously quaint among its functional neighbours – is thought to date from the reign of Elizabeth I.

The City

A wonderful Dickensian survival is the **George and Vulture** – still an 'eating house' – at which Mr Pickwick stayed. In **Fleet Street**, another establishment that has kept its historic atmosphere is the **Cheshire Cheese**, where a table said to have been favoured by the novelist is still pointed out. Nearby are the giants on the clock of **St Dunstan's Church**, while **Temple Bar**, which filled the young Dickens with awe, has been reassembled farther east, in **St Paul's Churchyard**. **Smithfield Market**, north of St Paul's, was rebuilt in Dickens' time and still functions. It is within sound of the bells of **St Sepulchre's**, the church that stands opposite the site of **Newgate Prison**.

The West End

In **Craven Street** near **Charing Cross Station** is a house – **number 40** – whose knocker is said to have inspired the image of Marley's face in *A Christmas Carol*. **Rules**, in **Maiden Lane**, is the capital's oldest restaurant, opened in 1798. Dickens dined there regularly. It was a short distance from the office of the magazine he edited, *All the Year Round*, in **Wellington Street**. **The Theatre Royal, Drury Lane**, retains its Regency interior and its rotunda. **Burlington Arcade**, off **Piccadilly**, also looks as it did in Georgian times. It is described in *The Uncommercial Traveller*. Further afield, **London Zoo** – though naturally greatly expanded – retains its original buildings. It was a favourite haunt of Dickens.

Shops

Lock, the hatters at **No. 6, St James's Street**, preserves its Georgian frontage, and hats from the Dickensian era – stovepipes and shakoes – can still be glimpsed inside. **G. Smith and Sons**, a tobacconist at **74 Charing Cross Road**, still boasts the traditional symbol of a wooden Highlander.

Museums

The Cuming Museum in **Walworth**, thought to be the original of the collection described in *The Old Curiosity Shop*, houses the pump from the **Marshalsea Prison** as well as the shop sign of the dog licking the bowl. Another sign, the 'Little Midshipman,' is in the **Dickens House Museum**. 'Tippoo's Tiger,' the mechanical toy once displayed at **East India House**, is now in the **Victoria and Albert Museum**. Nearby, in the **Science Museum**, is a model of **Gurney's steam coach**, while the **London Transport Museum** contains **Shilibeer's Omnibus** as well as a **'knifeboard'**. The **Museum of London** at the **Barbican**, the **Ragged School Museum** in **Tower Hamlets** and the **Geffrye Museum** in **Hackney** all have exhibits or collections dealing with the Dickensian era.

CHRONOLOGY

1812   7 February. Charles Dickens born at Portsmouth.

1817   His father, John Dickens, posted to Chatham, Kent, as clerk in Naval Pay Office.

1820   *Accession of King George IV.*

1822   John Dickens transferred to London.

1824   John Dickens arrested for debt and incarcerated in King's Bench and the Marshalsea. Charles works in Warren's Blacking Factory. Charles educated at Wellington House Academy.

1827   Becomes solicitor's clerk.

1829   Begins journalistic career as court reporter, Doctors Commons.

1830   *Accession of King William IV.*

1831   Dickens becomes parliamentary reporter.

1833   His first short story, 'A Dinner at Poplar Walk', accepted by *The Monthly Magazine*.

1834   Becomes reporter on *The Morning Chronicle*.

1836   *Sketches by Boz* published.
First parts of *Pickwick Papers* appear.
Marries Catherine Hogarth.

1837   *Accession of Queen Victoria.*
Pickwick Papers continues.
Eldest son Charles born. Moves to 48 Doughty Street.

1838   *Oliver Twist* published.
Visits Yorkshire to research for *Nicholas Nickleby*.

1839   *Nicholas Nickleby* appears.
Moves to Devonshire Terrace.

1840   *Master Humphrey's Clock, Vol. I.*

1841   *Master Humphrey's Clock, Vol. II.*
The Old Curiosity Shop.
Barnaby Rudge.

1842   The Dickenses tour America.
American Notes published.

1843   *A Christmas Carol.*

1844   *The Chimes.*
        Martin Chuzzlewit.

1845   *The Cricket on the Hearth.*
        Dickenses return to England after extended visit to Italy.

1846   *Pictures from Italy.*

1848   *Dombey and Son.*
        The Haunted Man.

1850   *David Copperfield.*
        Household Words, a magazine edited by Dickens, first issued.

1851   **May. Opening of the Great Exhibition.**
        John Dickens dies.

1852   *A Child's History of England, Vol. I.*

1853   **Outbreak of Crimean War.**
        A Child's History of England, Vol. II.
        Bleak House.
        Dickens gives first public reading.

1854   *A Child's History of England, Vol. III.*
        Hard Times.

1856   **Crimean War ends.**
        Dickens buys Gad's Hill Place.

1857   *Little Dorrit.*

1858   Separates from Catherine Hogarth. Begins regular public readings.

1859   *A Tale of Two Cities.*

1861   *Great Expectations.*
        The Uncommercial Traveller.

1865   *Our Mutual Friend.*
        Dickens injured in railway accident at Staplehurst while returning
        from France with his mistress, Ellen Ternan.

1866–8 Extensive reading tours in Britain and USA.

1869   Ill health forces him to curtail reading tour.

1870   Received in audience by Queen Victoria.
        The Mystery of Edwin Drood, his last work, left unfinished.
        9 June. Dies. Buried in Poets' Corner, Westminster Abbey.

BIBLIOGRAPHY

Ackroyd, Peter, *Dickens*, Vintage, 1999

Ackroyd, Peter, *Dickens' London*, Headline, 1987

Allwood, Rosamund, catalogue for exhibition in Jeffrey Museum, 1982

Anon., *1849–1949, A Story of British Achievement*, Harrod's, 1949

Anon., *A Description of London*, W. Darton, 1824

Anon., *Early Victorian England, 1830–65*, Oxford University Press, 1934

Anon., *Hatchard's 1797–1997*

Anon., *London As It Is Today*, H.G. Clarke, 1851

Anon., *London and its Vicinity*, John Weale, London, 1851

Anon., *Notes and Reflections*, Longman, Rees, Orme, Brown and Green, 1826

Anon., 'The Science of Garotting', *Cornhill Magazine*, Vol. 7, 1863

Austin, Alfred, *The Season, A Satire*, 1861

Beaver, Patrick, *The Crystal Palace*, Phillimore, 1986

Birkenhead, Sheila, *Peace in Piccadilly*, Hamish Hamilton, 1958

Butler, E.M. (ed.), *A Regency Visitor*, Collins, 1957

Cameron, David Kerr, *London's Pleasures*, Sutton Publishing, 2001

Charles Dickens and Southwark, Southwark Local History Library, 1974

Corbett, Edward, *An Old Coachman's Chatter*, Richard Bentley, 1890

Desmond, Ray, *The India Museum, 1801–1879*, HMSO, 1982

Dickens, Charles, *A Christmas Carol*, various editions

Dickens, Charles, *Bleak House*, various editions

Dickens, Charles, *David Copperfield*, various editions

Dickens, Charles, *Dombey and Son*, various editions

Dickens, Charles, 'Gone Astray', in R. Vallance (ed.), *Dickens' London*, Folio Society, 1966

Dickens, Charles, *Great Expectations*, various editions

Dickens, Charles, *Little Dorrit*, various editions

Dickens, Charles, *Martin Chuzzlewit*, various editions

Dickens, Charles, *Nicholas Nickleby*, various editions

Dickens, Charles, *Oliver Twist*, various editions

Dickens, Charles, 'On Duty with Inspector Field', *Household Words*, 14 June 1851, in R. Vallance (ed.), *Dickens' London*, Folio Society, 1966

Dickens, Charles, *Our Mutual Friend*, various editions

Dickens, Charles, *Pickwick Papers*, various editions

Dickens, Charles, *Sketches by Boz*, Chapman & Hall, W.D.

Dickens, Charles, *The Old Curiosity Shop*, various editions

Dickens, Charles, 'The Prisoner's Van', *Sketches by Boz*, in R. Vallance (ed.), *Dickens' London*, Folio Society, 1966

Dickens, Charles, 'The Streets, Morning', *The Morning Chronicle*, 21, July 1835, in R. Vallance (ed.), *Dickens' London*, Folio Society, 1966

Dickens, Charles, 'A Visit to Newgate', *Sketches by Boz*, in R. Vallance (ed.), *Dickens' London*, Folio Society, 1966

Disher, Maurice W., *Victorian Song. From Dive to Drawing Room*, Phoenix House, 1955

Egan, Pierce (ed.), *Grose's Classical Dictionary of the Vulgar Tongue*, Sherwood, Neely and Jones, London, 1823

Ford, J., *Prizefighting*, David & Charles, 1971

Godfrey, Alan, reprint of 1873 Ordnance Survey map of St Paul's, Alan Godfrey Maps, 1987

Grant, James, *Sketches in London*, W.S. Orr, 1838

Greenwood, James, *The Seven Curses of London*, Stanley Rivers, 1869

Hayward, Arthur, *The Dickens Encyclopedia*, Routledge, 1924

Holman-Hunt, Diana, *My Grandmothers and I*, 1960, in (Clocktower) paperback, 1999, by Michael Russell, in Judith Flanders, *The Victoria House*, Harper Collins, 2003

Horn, Pamela, *High Society, The English Social Elite, 1880–1914*, Alan Sutton, 1992

Illustrated London News, 1866, in Alison Adburgham, *Shopping in Style: London from the Restoration to Edwardian Elegance*, Thames & Hudson, 1979

Keers, Paul, *A Gentleman's Wardrobe*, Weidenfeld & Nicolson, 1987

Knight, Charles, *London, Volume V*, Charles Knight, 1843

Lancaster, Osbert, *All Done From Memory*, Houghton Mifflin, 1953

London, John o', *London Stories*, T.C. & E.C. Jack, Old House Books, 1911

Mayhew, Henry, 'Labour and the Poor', *Morning Chronicle*, 1862, in R. Allen, *The Moving Pageant*, Routledge, 1998

Newcastle Commission Report, 1861

Prestige, G.L., *St Paul's in its Glory*, SPCK, 1955

Pritchard, R.E., *Dickens' England*, Sutton Publishing, 2002

Punch, Vol. 1

Quennell, Peter (ed.), *Mayhew's Characters*, William Kimber, 1951

Quennell, Peter (ed.), *London's Underworld* (reprinted from *London Labour and the London Poor*), Spring Books, 1969

Quennell, Peter (ed.), *Mayhew's Characters*, Spring Books, 1969

Quennell, Peter (ed.), *Mayhew's London*, The Pilot Press, 1949

Rowell, George, *Queen Victoria Goes to the Theatre*, Paul Elek, 1978

Sala, G.A., *Twice Round the Clock*, Edward Marsh, London, 1862

Schlesinger, M., *Saunterings in and About London*, Nathaniel Cooke, 1853

Seacole, Mary, *Wonderful Adventures of Mrs Seacole in Many Lands*, 1857, reprinted Falling Wall Press, 1984

Sekon, G.A., *Locomotion in Victorian London*, OUP, 1938

Select Committee on the Education of Destitute Children, 1842

Shaw, Captain D., *London in the 'Sixties*, Everett & Co., 1908

The Times, 17 January, 1829

The Times, 2 February, 1852

The Times, 26 March, 1833

The Times, Monday 26 May, 1851

Ward, A.C., *Everybody's Lamb*, G. Bell & Sons, London, 1933

Warrell, W., *Scribes Ancient and Modern (Otherwise Law Writers and Scriveners)*, Lindsey & Co., London, 1889: Guildhall Library pamphlet 4482

Warwick, Alan, *The Phoenix Suburb*, The Norwood Society, 1972

Wey, Francis, *A Frenchman Sees London in the 'Fifties*, adapted by Valerie Pirie, Sidgwick & Jackson, 1935, in Alison Adburgham, *Shopping in Style: London from the Restoration to Edwardian Elegance*, Thames & Hudson, 1979

Willis, Frederick, *101 Jubilee Road*, Phoenix House, 1948

Wise, Dorothy (ed.), *Diary of William Tayler, Footman, 1837*, Westminster City Archives, 1998

Young, G.M (ed.)., *Early Victorian England 1830–1865 Vol II*, OUP, 1989

SOURCES

The publisher has endeavoured to contact the owner of all quoted material still in copyright for permission to reproduce. Acknowledgement is due to the following sources. (Page numbers in square brackets are those of the original source.)

(quoted in) Ackroyd, Peter, *Dickens*, Sinclair-Stevenson/Vintage, 1999 241 [71], 250 [86]. Reproduced by kind permission of The Random House Group Ltd.

(quoted in) Ackroyd, Peter, *Dickens' London*, Headline, 1987 78 [49]

(quoted in) Adburgham, Alison, *Shopping in Style: London from the Restoration to Edwardian Elegance*, Thames & Hudson, 1979 61 [110], 124 [112]. Reproduced by kind permission of Thames & Hudson.

(quoted in) Allen, R., *The Moving Pageant*, Routledge, 1998 193 [127]

Allwood, Rosamund, catalogue for exhibition in Jeffrey Museum, 1982 104 [26]

Anon., *1849–1949, A Story of British Achievement*, Harrod's, 1949 63 [9–10]

Anon., *Early Victorian England, 1830–65*, Oxford University Press, 1934 119 [290]

Anon., *Hatchard's 1797–1997* 68 [6]

(quoted in) Beaver, Patrick, *The Crystal Palace*, Phillimore, 1986 145 [41–2]

(quoted in) Birkenhead, Sheila, *Peace in Piccadilly*, Hamish Hamilton, 1958 283 [151–2]

Butler, E.M. (ed.), *A Regency Visitor*, Collins, 1959 41 [213–4], 44 [37], 152 [53], 173–4 [83], 250 [226–7], 257 [227], 259 [227]

(quoted in) Cameron, David Kerr, *London's Pleasures*, Sutton Publishing Ltd, 2001 159 [180]

(quoted in) *Charles Dickens and Southwark*, Southwark Local History Library, 1974 177 [20]

(quoted in) Desmond, Ray, *The India Museum, 1801–1879*, HMSO, 1982 155 [23–4]

Disher, Maurice W., *Victorian Song: From Dive to Drawing Room*, Phoenix House (Orion Publishing Group Ltd), London 1955 57 [131]

(quoted in) Flanders, Judith, *The Victorian House*, Harper Collins, 2003 292 [296]

(quoted in) Godfrey, Alan, notes to reprint of 1873 Ordnance Survey map of St Paul's, Alan Godfrey Maps, 1987 26

(quoted in) Horn, Pamela, *High Society, The English Social Elite, 1880–1914*, Sutton Publishing Ltd, 1992 289 [76]

Keers, Paul, *A Gentleman's Wardrobe*, Weidenfeld & Nicolson, 1987 44 [42]

Lancaster, Osbert, *All Done From Memory*, Houghton Mifflin, 1953 294–5 [39–40], 296 [72–3]

London, John o', *London Stories*, T.C. & E.C. Jack, Old House Books, 1911 117 [134–5], 120 [136]

(quoted in) Prestige, G.L., *St Paul's in its Glory*, SPCK, 1955 26 [43]

(quoted in) Pritchard, R.E., *Dickens' England*, Sutton Publishing Ltd, 2002 32 [185]

Quennell, Peter (ed.), *London's Underworld* (reprinted from *London Labour and the London Poor*), Spring Books, 1969 40 [40], 40 [42–3], 238 [141–2]

Quennell, Peter (ed.), *Mayhew's Characters*, Spring Books, 1969 84–5 [98–9]

(quoted in) Quennell, Peter (ed.), *Mayhew's Characters*, William Kimber, 1951 135–6 [183–4], 137–8 [280], 182–3 [221–2], 191 [223], 205 [101 & 105], 205–6 [65 & 67], 231 [145]

(quoted in) Quennell, Peter (ed.), *Mayhew's London* The Pilot Press, 1949 16 [337–8}

(quoted in) Rowell, George, *Queen Victoria Goes to the Theatre*, Paul Elek, 1978 172 [24]

Seacole, Mary, *Wonderful Adventures of Mrs Seacole in Many Lands*, reprinted Falling Wall Press, 1984 51 [58]

Shaw, Capt D., *London in the Sixties*, Everett and Co., 1908 41 [9], 241–2 [76], 261–2 [154–5], 263 [158–9]

(quoted in) Vallance, Rosalind (ed.), *Dickens' London*, Folio Society, 1966 24 [24–5], 25 [21], 27 [21], 28–9 [19–20], 50 [19], 87–8 [35–6], 243 [136–7], 245–6 [85–6], 255–6 [111–12], 256 [115], 258 [118–9], 259 [121–2]

Ward, A.C. (ed.), *Everybody's Lamb*, G. Bell & Sons, London, 1933 106–7 [161–2]

Warrell, W., *Scribes Ancient and Modern (Otherwise Law Writers and Scriveners)*, Lindsey & Co., London, 1889: Guildhall Library pamphlet 4482 98–9

(quoted in) Warwick, Alan, *The Phoenix Suburb*, The Norwood Society, 1972 145 [108], 160 [60], 161–2 [69–70]. Reproduced by kind permission of The Warwick Family and The Norwood Society.

Wey, Francis, *A Frenchman Sees the English in the Fifties*, adapted by Valerie Pirie from *Les Anglais chez Eux*, Sidgwick & Jackson, 1935, quoted in *Shopping and Style: London from the Restoration to Edwardian Elegance* by Alison Adburgham, Thames & Hudson, 1979 124 [112]. Reproduced by kind permission of Thames & Hudson.

Willis, Frederick, *101 Jubilee Road*, Phoenix House (Orion Publishing Group Ltd), London, 1948 67 [38–9], 198–9 [90], 199 [88]

Wise, Dorothy (ed.), *Diary of William Tayler, Footman, 1837*, Westminster City Archives, 1998 119 [75], 200 [62], 201 [75], 201 [17–18], 201 [44], 202 [79], 202–3 [34–5], 286 [78–9], 286 [78–9], 287 [72–3]

INDEX

accents 6–7, 10, 57–8
actors
  'fleeting...celebrity' 191
  life and status 179–80
  'mumming' at fairs 182
  notable performers 177–9
  Penny Theatre performers 186–7
  'private business' 182–3
Admiralty 22
advertising
  public advertising 41, 80–1, 138–40
  on shops 77–9
agricultural depression 212–13
Albany 282–3
Albert, Prince Consort 148, 285
alcohol
  drinking by children 36, 222
  wide consumption of 222
Amburgh, Isaac van 172
Anglican Church 293–4
animals
  baiting of 162–3
  menageries/zoos 28, 146–8
  street performances with 137–8
  see also livestock
apprentices 64, 98–9, 196–9
  end-of-term rituals 198–9
Apsley House 30
  'bullet-proof shutters' 276–7
  'situation...finest in metropolis' 276
Artful Dodger 54, 235
Artillery Ground 158
artisans' hats 45
Astley, Philip 148
Astley's Royal Equestrian Amphitheatre 148–50
Athenaeum, The: 'Tippoo's Tiger' 155
Austin, Alfred: 'auction-room' of the Season 289

babies
  'baby farmers' 204
  corpses of 20
  gin as soother 222
bachelor apartments 282–3
badger-baiting 162, 163
balloon ascents 158–9, 161
Bank of England 19, 24
  'eleven hundred clerks' 92
  'impressive new building' 19
  'omnibuses...disgorge the clerks' 89–90
  'quite detached' building 92
bankruptcy 246–51
Banqueting House 22
Barker, John 73
Barker's 69
Bartholomew Fair 167
Bayswater 159, 272
bazaars 69–73
Bazalgette, Joseph 32
bear-baiting 162, 163
beauty, notions of 46
beer 213, 222
beggars
  children as 36
  'Negro beggars' 54–5
behaviour
  coarseness of 8, 36
  general rudeness 37–8
  'rudest licence' at the theatre 174
  treatment of minorities 51–2
Belgravia 268, 272
Belzoni, Giovanni 151
Bermondsey 18, 22, 209
Berry Brothers and Rudd 68
Beulah Spa 159–62
  demise of 161–2
  'fashionable...elegant' 160
Billingsgate 211
Bishopsgate 19
Blackheath 16
black people 51, 54–6
Bleak House
  Captain Hawdon's scribe work 97–8
  'flakes of soot' 20
  Mr Tulkinghorn's memory 91
  reference to Astley's 149
Blimber, Doctor 280
'Bloomer Costume' 150
Bloomsbury 151, 268, 299
Bond Street 63
Borough 22
Borough High Street 114, 298
Boswell, James 162
Botany Bay 259
Bow Street Police Office 245–6
'Bow Street Runners' 239
boxers 164–7
boxing
  bare-knuckle fighting 11, 164–7
  regulations 163, 164
  'renders him...a cripple' 166
  Spring vs. Langan contest 164–6
Boxing Day 286–7
brandy 222
Bricklayer's Arms 17
Bridge House Hotel 117–18
Brighton 111
British and Foreign Schools Society 231
British Museum 33, 151–3
Brixton 279
Broad Street (later Broadwick) 213
Brompton 22
Brompton Road 63
Brummell, 'Beau' 95
Brummell, William 95
Buckingham House (later Palace) 30
building construction
  demolition and evict 33

speculative building 23
'bulk and file' 236
bull-baiting 11, 162, 163
Bull and Mouth 113
'bunters' 221
Burford, Thomas 143
Burlington Arcade 30,
    68, 301
Burlington House 30
Burton, Decimus 142, 160
Butterfield, William 294
Byron, Lord 164, 166, 282

cab-drivers 128–9
cabriolets 128
Calcraft (hangman) 262–3
Camberwell 22, 231
Camden Town 22, 280
Cannon Street Station 31
caps 45
Carlton House 21, 30, 49
Carlyle, Thomas 134
Carpenter, Mary: 'barely
    above starvation' 233
carriages
    carriage-makers 198
    high cost of 266
    shopping trips 67
casual workers 208–11
Catholics 294
cats 20
cemeteries 33
Chancery Lane 87
Chaplin, William 113
Charing Cross 275
Charing Cross Station 28,
    31, 301
Charles I, King 29
Charles II, King 169
Chartism 10
Cheapside 19
Chelsea 63
children
    and alcohol 36
    as beggars 36
    as crime victims 237
    harsh discipline 291
    infant mortality 213,
        215–16, 291
    'street arabs' 211–12
    as thieves 238–9

as workers 35, 36, 208,
    209, 216–17, 231
    see also babies
chimney-sweeps 36
Chiswick 268
cholera 10, 213
Christianity 294
Christmas 285–6
Christmas Carol, A
    Topper's courtship ruse
        285
    'Walk-ER!' 58–9
    see also Scrooge, Ebenezer
churches
    the 'Church Parade' 296
    rented pews 295
Chuzzlewit, Martin 207–8
City of London 24–5
    'farming out' of paupers
        226–7
    office workers 87–91
    as residential area 24
    small size of firms 91
Clapham Sect 294
Classical Dictionary of the
    Vulgar Tongue 13
    see also Grose, Francis
clay pipes 36
Clennam, Arthur
    'little counting-house'
        of 96–7
    meets 'Barnacle junior'
        95
    'Sunday evening...
        gloomy...and stale' 21
    'too depressed' to mix in
        prison 249–50
    visits the Barnacles
        274–5
clergymen 296–7
Clerkenwell 246
clerks
    life as 94–7, 100–2
    travelling to work 87–90
    see also Scribes Ancient and
        Modern
clothes
    attending church 295
    cleaning 43
    dressing for the Season
        289

men's 43–4, 47–9, 50–1,
    88–9, 277, 282, 291
    and social position 47–8,
        277
    theatre dress code 172
    wedding clothes 288
    women's 46–7, 278, 289,
        291
'clouting' 235
coaches
    accommodation 112–13
    cost of travelling 110,
        111
    'fast mail' coaches 64,
        109–11, 113
    steam powered coaches
        116–17
    types of passenger 113
    'very perilous' 109
coaching inns 114
cock-fighting 162
Cockney dialect 7
Cockney songs 57
    Tony Weller is 'werry
        sorry' 57
Codlin and Short 134–5
cohabitation 217
Coldbath Prison 246
Coleridge, Samuel Taylor
    177
Commercial Road 22
commuting
    City workers 87–90
    and the omnibus 122
    and the railways 33,
        120–2
    by steamboat 129–31
    and suburbanisation 122,
        268
confidence-tricksters 237
Cook, Thomas 266
Copperfield, David
    on 'amazing' London
        15–16
    aunt's pickpocket fears
        235
    Covent Garden 'delight'
        173
    'forlorn and desolate'
        schoolroom 280
    'giants of St Dunstan's' 27

'I loved Dora Spenlow'
  284–5
on London Bridge 17
meets Daniel Peggotty 29
'supreme comfort of
  prisoners' 254–5
well-known cap of 45
see also David Copperfield
Corbett, Edward
  '8 miles an hour' 110–11
  coach maintenance 110
Cornhill Magazine: the
  garroter's technique 244
Corn Laws 10
corpses
  as common London sight
    20, 219–20
  shallow burial of 33
  Thames scavengers of
    209–11
corsets 47
courtship 284–5, 287,
  288–9
Covent Garden 193,
  241–2
Covent Garden, Theatre
  Royal 169, 170–1, 177
  David Copperfield at 173
  Edmund Kean's collapse
    178–9
Cranfield, Thomas 231
Cratchit, Bob 96, 107
crime
  arrest and charge 244–6
  infamous districts 241–3
  juvenile thieves 238–9
  'no...property was safe'
    241
  'out of control' 10
  street crime 235–9
  violent crime 243–4
Crimean War 10
crinolines ('hoop skirts')
  47, 124
crossing-sweepers 36–7
Crummles, Mr and Mrs
  180–1
Crystal Palace 33
  destroyed by fire 146
  'elevation of... working
    classes' 145

and Great Exhibition 47,
  144–5
move to Sydenham Hill
  145–6
self-cleaning system 47
superior attractions of
  160
cudgels 162
'curtails' 236

David Copperfield 160
  on Golden Cross Inn 29
  Micawber's arrest 247–8
  Micawber's shabby
    elegance 47–8
  Salem House school
    280–1
  see also Copperfield,
    David
Davis, Eliza 52
debtors' prisons 246–51
Defoe, Daniel 162
department stores 73
Deptford 16
Description of London
  Covent Garden profits
    170–1
  East India House
    'curiosities' 154
  on rebuilt Drury Lane
    170
Dickens, Charles
  acting aspirations 176
  boyhood journey to
    London 15
  Camden Town home 22
  City impressions 24
  class distinctions in
    church 295
  Cockney dialect 57
  coins 'sandwich board'
    term 40
  on conveyance of
    prisoners 245–6
  on 'early clerk population'
    87–8
  father's incarceration 247
  'Fog everywhere' 9
  'for relief...there is the
    parish' 222–3
  goatee beard 46

'golden dog' shop sign 78
'The Last Cab-Driver'
  128
literary inspiration 113
on Northumberland
  House 28–9
portrayal of Jews 52–3
Seven Dials 'wickedness'
  242
on shop opening ritual
  64
on Temple Bar 27–8
Vauxhall disappointment
  155–6
visits Seven Dials with
  Insp. Field 243
Warren's blacking factory
  247, 251
as 'writing-clerk' 45
see also Household Words:
  'Gone Astray'; Sketches
  by Boz; individual works
Dickens, Charles, Jnr 278
Dickens, John 247
Dickins & Smith (later
  Jones) 62
diptheria 213
dirtiness 20, 36
disease 8, 10
  overcrowding 213
  visible signs of 36
Disraeli, Benjamin 52
dogs
  animal-baiting 163–4
  feral dogs 20
  selling of turds 209
  stealing 236
Dombey and Son
  Doctor Blimber's
    establishment 280
  Florence meets 'Good
    Mrs Brown' 35
  the 'little Midshipman'
    78
  railway building chaos
    31–2
  'We lost one babby' 215
Dr Barnardo's Homes 11
dresses 47, 288
drinking water 19, 20
Drury Lane, Theatre Royal

169, 170, 177, 179, 301
Ducrow, Andrew 148
'dundrearies' 46
dung: sale of 209
'dust-heaps' 16, 208–9

Early Closing Association
    73
East End 22
East India Company 24, 91
    disbanding of 155
    Lamb's 'pension for life'
        106–7
    Museum of 153–5
education
    girls 278–9
    and the poor 11, 231–3
    university for middle-
        classes 266, 281
    see also schools
Egyptian Hall 62, 151
Egyptian Panorama 140
Elgin Marbles 152
Elias, Sam ('Dutch Sam')
    167
Ellis, Thomas Flower 283
employment
    children 35, 36, 208,
        209, 216–17, 231
    clerks 87–91, 94–7
    coaching employees
        113–14
    labourers 204
    shop assistants 64–6, 67,
        73, 75
    trades 38–9, 41, 204–6
    women 36–7, 39–40,
        193, 195–6, 204, 279
    see also hours of working;
        street vendors
entertainment
    menageries 28, 146–8
    museums 151–5
    outing venues 150–1
    panoramas 140–6
    pleasure gardens 155–62,
        159–62
    street performers 41–2,
        56, 133–8
    tea gardens 156–8
Eton College 278

Euston Station 31, 121–2
    guidebook description
        118–19
Evelyn, John 162
executions
    condemned cells 255,
        259–60
    Magwitch's penalty 253
    'New Drop' gallows 255
    public hangings 11,
        260–3
Exeter 'Change' 28, 69,
    146

Fagin 52, 259–60
Fagin, Robert 251
fairs 167–9
'fan lay' 236
'Fantoccini' 135
fares
    coaches 111, 122
    omnibuses 123
    railways 120, 122
'farming' paupers 215,
    226–7
Farringdon 120
Fascination Fledgeby 53,
    283
Fenchurch Street Station
    31
Field, Inspector 243
firework displays 161
Fleet Prison ('Navy Office')
    247
Fleet River 33
Fleet Street 27, 300
Flint & Clark (later
    Debenham's) 68
Flora Tea Gardens:
    parachute descent at 159
Florence 35
food
    diet of poor 35, 217,
        221–2
    dining out 284, 290–1
    'fast food' sellers 221–2
    a servant's diet 201
    workhouse consumption
        226
football 11
footmen 67

foreign journeys
    departure points 114, 118
    steamboats 130
Foreign Office 33
Forster, John: on 'agonised'
    Dickens 176–7
Fortnum & Mason 68
French Revolution 276
Fry, Elizabeth 253
funerals, 'helping' at 208

gardening 267–8
Gargery, Joe 197
'garotting' 244
gas lighting 26, 79–80
General Post Office, One
    Minute to Six, The 104
gentlemen's clubs 30,
    283–4
George IV, King 10, 30,
    152
German bands 134
gin 222
giraffes 147
Gladstone, William 206,
    282–3
Gloucester Coffee House
    113
Gloucester Terrace 273
gloves 43
gold 93–4
Golden Cross Inn 29–30,
    114–16
Grant, James
    actors' 'miserable
        pittance' 186
    'dancing booths' at
        Greenwich' 169
    debtors feel 'degraded'
        251
    on debtors' prisons 247
    Greenwich Fair 'marvels'
        167–8
    'horror' of the workhouse
        227–8
    Marylebone workhouse
        224–5
    'miserable' police cells
        245
    outdoor relief and 'starved
        looks' 229

on Peel's recruits 240
Penny 'Gaff' audiences
   183–4, 187
on Penny Theatre actors
   186–7
on 'miserable-looking'
   Penny Theatres 183–8
'perfect equality' of
   workhouses 224
police 'defective and
   inefficient' 239–40
poor relief 'idleness and
   fraud' 225–6
on 'romance' of
   workhouse lives 228
workhouse organization
   226–7
workhouses 'conducive to
   health' 230
Great Exhibition 10
middle-class attendance
   266
public lavatories at 74
serious pleasures of 138
Great Expectations
'All otherth ith Cag-
   Maggerth' 59
Magwitch and 'wittles'
   57
Magwitch's
   'punishment...being
   Death' 253
Wemmick's commuting
   23
see also Pip
Great Fire 25
Great Reform Bill 10, 276
Great Russell Street 138
'Great Stink' 32
Great Western Railway
   120
Green Park 30
Greenwich 117, 118
Greenwich Fair 167–9
Greenwood, James
cohabitation amongst
   poor 217
Covent Garden
   scavengers 211–12
joy at first 'parcel of food'
   217

matrimony amongst the
   poor 217–18
worker at 'age of ten'
   216–17
Greville, Colonel 152
Grose, Francis 13
the 'barrow man' 252
a 'bulk and file' 236
the 'fan lay' 236
'pretending to be
   postmen' 237
prison 'chummage' 249
to 'stall a person up'
   236–7
Grosvenor Estate 268
Guildhall 25
Gurney, Sir Goldsworthy
   116

'hackney carriages' 128–9
hairstyles 46
Hamilton, Sir William 152
Hampstead 22, 268
Hampton, Mr 159
Hancock, Walter 116
hansom cabs 131
Harmon, John: 'made...
   living by Dust' 209
Harrod, H.C. 63
Harrod's 63–4
Harrow school 278
Harvey Nichols 68
Hatchard's bookshop 68,
   276
hats
   men 45
   women 46
Haymarket 30, 169
   hay sellers 23
   prostitutes in 39–40
Haymarket, Theatre Royal
   169, 171–2
Hazlitt, William: Kean's
   'electrical shocks' 177
Heal's 63
health
   Londoners' 'unhealthy
   appearance' 35
   see also disease
Hertford, Marquess of 27
Hertford House 275

Hetherington, John 45
Hexham, Gaffer 210–11
Hexham, Lizzie 210–11
Hicks, George Elgar 104
Highgate 22, 268
Highgate cemetery 33, 298
highwaymen 239
Hogg, Quentin 232
Holborn 62, 273, 300
Holborn Viaduct 33
holidays
   annual children's holidays
   233
   and the middle-classes
   265, 266
   package tourism 11
   paid holidays 100
   shop closure 77
Holland, Henry 30
Holland, Robert 159
Holman Hunt, Diana:
   creating toilet paper 292
homes
   of middle classes 266–72,
   291–3
   poor people's lack of
   kitchens 221
   of upper classes 272–7
hop-picking 100
Horner, Mr 143
Horsemonger Lane Prison
   247
horses
   aroma of 18
   gradual displacement of
   116–17, 131
   'had 1,800 horses' 113
   and omnibuses 123
   sale of dung 209
hours of working 101
   City clerks 95
   scribes 98, 101
   seamstresses 195–6
   shop assistants 66, 76
household utensils:
   supplying and mending
   85
Household Words: 'Gone
   Astray'
   City impressions 24
   Guildhall Giants 25

St Dunstan's clock 27
'striking' rural costume
50–1
see also Dickens, Charles
Houses of Parliament 21,
33
housing
lodging-houses 220–1
the 'lodging slum' 237
men's bachelor
apartments 282–3
new building 23
renting for the Season
289
slums 54, 212, 218–21
Howell and James 67
Hudson's Bay Company 91
hulks 251–3
Hyde Park 23, 277–8
Hyde Park Corner 22, 30

illegitimacy 213
Illustrated London News:
'dizzying' Regent Street
61
immigrants
black people 6, 51, 54–6
European workers 6, 56,
213
foreign prostitutes 39–40
Irish 6, 31, 53–4
Italian entertainers 56
Jews 52–3
indentures 198
Indian Mutiny 155
Industrial Schools 232
inns 17
Interment Act,
Metropolitan 33
Ireland: potato famine 213
Irish
as 'Irish cockneys 54
as labourers 31, 53
as policemen 240
poverty of 54, 121
Isle of Dogs 22
Islington 6, 194
Italians 6, 7, 56, 133

Jackson, 'Gentleman' John
166

James Lock (hatters) 68,
112
James Smith 69
Jews
Dickens' portrayal 52–3
as landlords 220, 221
population 52
trades 52
John Lewis 69
Jonson, Ben 167

Kean, Charles 178–9
Kean, Edmund
'completely broke down'
178
spontaneity of 177
Kemble, Fanny: the
'magical machine' 119
Kennington 22, 194
Kensal Green cemetery 33
Kensington 272
Kensington Palace Gardens
273
Kew 268
King's Bench Prison 247,
250
King's Cross Station 31
King William Street 33
knee-breeches 43
knife attacks 243–4
'knife-board' seats 87, 124
Knight, Charles
on 'Italian boys' as
entertainers 56
a street telescope show
138
Knightsbridge 63

labouring 204
Lafitte, Jacques 123
Lamb, Charles
gets 'a pension for life'
106–7
visits old colleagues
107
Lambeth 22, 148, 220
Lancaster, Osbert
on prominence of clergy
294–5
'weekly Church Parade'
296

Langan, John 164–6
Leadenhall Street 153
legal profession
seasonal working 100
see also scribes
Leicester Square 143
Lenin, Vladimir Ilyich 56
Lethaby, Dr: 'filthy or
overcrowded' rooms
219–20
Liberty, Arthur Lasenby 73
licensing hours 222
life expectancy 8, 213
lighting
gas 26, 79–80
perils of theatre 170
whale-oil 18
Little Dorrit
'Highlander' shop sign 78
'melancholy' Sundays 21
nepotism and 'Barnacle
junior' 95
shop window 'tickets of
prices' 78–9
'squeezed house' of the
Barnacles 274–5
see also Clennam, Arthur
livestock 16, 23, 194
sale and slaughter of 26
Locke, William: on 'Ragged
School' pupils 232
lodging-houses 220–1
Lombard Street 19, 113
London Bridge 17, 18
London General Omnibus
Company 131
London as it is Today
British Museum treasures
152
Coldbath Fields as
'healthiest' prison 246
the 'Colosseum'
142–3
on Madame Tussaud's
151
the 'Moving Panorama'
141–2
Mr Wylde's Model of the
Globe 144
obtaining theatre tickets
172

the Polyrama 144
Soho Bazaar 69
Theatre Royal,
   Haymarket capacity
   171
Thomas Burford's
   panorama 143
'Tippoo's Tiger' 154
London, John o': railway
   opening 117
London Labour and the
   London Poor 12
   see also Mayhew, Henry
London Missionary
   Museum: 'ingenuity of…
   savages' 153
London Season 62, 196,
   266, 288–9
London Underground 11,
   32, 120
London Zoo see Zoological
   Gardens
Long Acre 198
Lowther Arcade: 'most
   noted toy-mart' 70
Ludgate Circus 88
Ludgate Hill 15, 62, 83

Macadam, John 110
Macaulay, Thomas
   Babington: 'chambers in
   Albany' 283
Mace, Jem 167
Macready, William
   as Dickens' friend 176
   saw audience as 'brutes'
   179
Madame Tussaud's 150–1
Magwitch, Abel 57, 253
Mansion House 19, 21
manufacturing 28
Maple's 63
market gardens 16
markets
   early-morning workers
   193
   scavengers of 211–12
marriage 287–90
   'much pride…taken' by
   poor 217–18
Marshalsea Prison 247, 298

Martin Chuzzlewit:
   pawnshop visits 207–8
Marx, Karl 56
Marylebone 151, 224–7
Mayfair 22, 62, 272
Mayhew, Henry
   black beggars 54–5
   blind street musician 134
   'dust' like 'volcanic
   mountain' 16
   early-morning poor 193
   female crossing-sweeper
   36–7
   'Gun-Exercise Exhibitor'
   136
   'Happy Families' show
   137–8
   'helping at funerals' 208
   lodging-house 'bunters'
   220–1
   lodging-houses 220–1
   'Negro mendicants' 54–5
   parish aid 'hurted him
   sorely' 229
   polluted water 218
   prostitutes 39–40
   'small ware' seller 205
   stationery peddler 205–6
   street boys' knowledge
   54, 231
   a street performer's life
   135–6
   a street-trader's progress
   84–5
   strolling actors 182–3
   'unchaste' servants 203
   'young pickpockets' 40
   'young thieves are ragged
   boys' 238–9
   'young women…who
   steal' 238–9
Melbourne House 22
menageries 28, 146–8
Mendoza, Daniel: on
   boxing injuries 166
Metropolitan Police 239
Metropolitan Railway 32,
   120, 204
'mews' 273
Micawber, Mr
   'arrested early one

morning' 247–8
   'shabby' elegance of 47–8
middle classes
   homes of 266–72
   marriage 288
   schools 279–81
migration 213
Mile End Road 22, 225
milkmaids 17, 39
Millbank 254
milliner's apprentices
   196
Monmouth Street 83
Montague House 151
Moorfields 153
Moorgate 33
Morning Chronicle, The:
   'early clerk population'
   87–8
motor-buses 131
motor-taxis 131
'mudlarks' 209
museums 151–5

Nash, John 22, 30
National Gallery 33
National Schools Society
   231
Nelson, Lord 26
nepotism 94–5
Newgate Market 26
Newgate Prison 26, 255–9,
   301
Newington 22
New Oxford Street 33
New Poor Law Act 229
New Poor Law
   Commissioners 224–5
New South Wales 253
newspapers 69, 103–4, 112
Nicholas Nickleby
   crowd 'scarcely…notice'
   shops 80
   Dickens 'agonised' at
   stage version 176–7
   'dumbed down'
   Shakespeare 172
   female theatricals 181
   'hungry eyes' regard
   'profusion' 65–6
   Lord Verisopht's

apartments 62
male actors 180–1
'night tables' 283
noises 7–8, 17, 21
'noisy dog racket' 236
nonconformism 294
Northumberland House
    28–9, 275–6
Norwood 268
Notting Hill 194
Nubbles, Kit 149
Nunhead 268

Old Curiosity Shop, The
    'gorgeous mysteries' of
        Astley's 149–50
    Punch and Judy show
        134–5
Old Kent Road 17
Oliver Twist
    Bill Sykes's costume 48
    Fagin awaits death by
        hanging 260
    'farmed' by 'elderly
        female' 215
    'lowest orders of Irish' 54
    sleeping 'under the
        counter' 75
    'villainous-looking' Fagin
        52
    see also Twist, Oliver
omnibuses 11, 122–31
    commuting for 'well-off'
        87, 124, 125, 130, 242
    the crews 126–7
    'disgorge...clerks by
        hundreds' 89–90
'onion hunters' 236
Our Mutual Friend
    Fledgeby and the Albany
        283
    'made...living by Dust'
        209
    portrayal of Riah 53
    scavengers of the
        drowned 210–11
'outdoor relief' 223
    abuse of 225–6
    amounts of 226
    numbers of recipients
        225

'of a grotesque nature'
    229–30
overcrowding 10, 218–20
Oxford Movement 294
Oxford Street 62
oysters 222

Paddington Station 31
    'really wonderful' 119
Pall Mall 30
panoramas 140–6
Pantheon Bazaar 62
    'fancy articles' displayed
        71–3
    female clients of 281–2
parachutes 159
parasites 219
Paris 123, 158
Paris, E.T. 143
parish system 223
Parker, Jacobus 206
parlours 269
Parsons, Gabriel 160
patronage 95
pattens 44
pawnshops 207–8
Paxton, Joseph 47
Peel, Sir Robert 239
Peggotty, Daniel 29
penal reform 253–4
'penny gaffs' 183–8
pensions 106–7
Pepys, Samuel 162
'Peterloo Massacre' 50
'pfifferari' 7
Phelps, Samuel 179
Phigalian Marbles 152
philanthropic societies 11,
    231
photography 11
Piccadilly 22, 23, 30, 62,
    67–8, 151, 193
Piccadilly Circus 30
pickpockets 40, 50, 167,
    235–6
Pickwick Club 29
Pickwick Papers
    coaching inn
        accommodation 114
    the 'Pugnacious Cabman'
        128–9

Weller senior's dialect
    57–8
the Wellers as coachmen
    109, 114
Pickwick, Samuel
    at Golden Cross Inn
        29–30
    'sitting for your portrait'
        248–9
piemen 221
Pip
    at 'evening school' 197–8
    convict coach
        companions 111–12
    and Magwitch's escape
        130, 253
    'please what's Hulks?'
        252–3
    on Smithfield and
        Newgate 26–7
    'straw-yard' hackney 129
    on Thames shipping 130
    'to be apprenticed' 197
    and 'ugly' London 15
    visits Mr Pocket 96
    see also Great Expectations
plate glass 61
pleasure gardens 155–62,
    159–62
police
    bribery 240
    dismissals for misconduct
        241
    Metropolitan force
        established 239, 241
    Thames patrols 239
    uniforms 45, 241
Pool of London 18
poor
    diet 35, 217, 221–2
    education 231–3
    housing 54, 212, 218–21
poor laws 226
poor-rates 226
population 10, 212
postage stamps 11
post-boxes 11
Post Offices 103–5
potatoes
    baked potato sellers 221
    Irish famine 213

presentations to monarch
289
Primrose Hill 22
prisons
  debtors' prisons 246–51
  the hulks 251–3
  modern 'penitentiaries'
    254
  traditional prisons 255–9
privies 218
prostitution 39–40, 68, 204
public lavatories 11, 74–5
public schools 278, 281
Pückler-Muskau, Prince
  Hermann
  on 'ambulant' advertising
    41
  boys 'under sentence of
    death' 259
  British Museum
    'Mischmasch' 152
  'coarseness' at theatre
    173–4
  living 'agreeably' in
    prison 250
  prisoners 'smoke and
    play' 257
  on women's pattens 44
Pugin, A.W. 294
Punch
  Beulah's demise 161–2
  exhausted seamstresses
    196
  omnibus rivalry 123
  the performing sailor 137
Punch and Judy shows 135
Putney 268

Queen: 'Presentations are
  so vulgarised' 289
Queen's Theatre 180
Queen Victoria Street 33
quills 95, 98
Quilp, Mr: coach
  'journeys...very perilous'
    109

race 51
Raffles, Sir Stamford 146
Ragged School Union
  (RSU) 11, 231–3

'Railway Mania' 101–2
railways 10
  arrival in London
    117–22
  building of 31–2, 204
  carriage 'classes' 119–20
  London stations 31,
    118–20
  railway companies 120
  second class for middle
    classes 266
rat-catching 163–4
Ratcliff Highway 220
rats 20
'reader merchants' 235
Regent Circus 30, 62, 113
Regent's Park 22, 30
Regent Street 30, 61–2,
  64
religion 11, 293–7
Riah 53
Richmond 268
Richmond, Bill 166
rickets 36
road-building 110, 111
'Rollers' 239
rookeries 54, 212, 241
Rothschild's 91
Rotten Row 277, 278
Roubilliac, Louis François
  152
Royal Adelaide 118
Royal Exchange 24, 33,
  91–2
Royal Humane Society
  210
Royal Italian Opera House
  30
Royal Mews 29
Royal Society of Arts 74
Royal William 118
rubbish tips 16
rural London 23

Sadler's Wells 160, 179
Sainsbury, John 69
St Bartholomew's church
  167
St Clement Dane's 28
St Dunstan-in-the-West
  27

St George's-in-the-East
  220
St Giles 83
St Giles-in-the-Fields 242
St James's 22
St James's Hall 62
St James's Park 23
St James's Street 30
St Martin's-le-Grand 104,
  113
St Mary le Bow 19
St Pancras 226
St Pancras Station 31
St Paul's Cathedral 15, 19,
  21, 25–6
St Paul's Churchyard 62
St Sepulchre's church 255,
  262, 301
Sala, George Augustus
  'bowed out' of Pantheon
    72–3
  buying children 'ugly
    toys' 70–1
  'Can any scene...equal
    Rotten Row?' 278
  'children of the poor' 76
  dining-out styles 290–1
  on girls of good family
    281–2
  'grimy little steamboats'
    131
  on 'hideous' fumes 19
  'lazar-house of painting'
    71–2
  a middle-class family
    270–2
  'never ride inside'
    omnibuses 124–5
  on 'newspaper boys' 104
  on Pantheon
    conservatory 72
  popular theatre offerings
    174
  'sempstresses' walking to
    work 195
  on shop opening
    'ceremony' 64–5
  'spruce clerks' with
    'crimson braces' 88–9
  on street performers 41–2
  on third-class travel

121–2
three o'clock at Royal
Exchange 92
'train of omnibuses'
89–90
'transported...from Vanity
Fair' 68
wedding in 'garish
Piccadilly' 290
'Salmon, Mrs' 27
Salvation Army 11
Sanderson 69
'sandwich boards' 40
sanitation
polluted water 19, 20,
213, 218
private dwellings 218–20
Saunterings in and About
London 12
see also Schlesinger, Max
saveloys 222
Savile Row 62–3
Sayers, Tom 167
scavengers 210–11, 221
Scharf, George 41, 137
Schlesinger, Max
on advertising 'energy'
80–1
'advertising monsters'
139–40
Bank of England 'saloon'
93
'brutal conduct' on streets
37–8
'dress' and 'social
position' 48
early-morning scene
194–5
gas-lit shops 79–80
on gentlemen's clubs 284
Government dividend
payout 93–4
'hauteur' of omnibus
drivers 126
'horses, grooms' behind
'iron gates' 273–4
'London omnibus...
prepossessing' 125–6
on a middle-class house
268–9
omnibus 'brakes' 127

omnibuses as 'necessities'
125
passengers 'caught' 126
on penny theatre actors
191
a Penny Theatre
performance 189–91
'pushing' in public places
38
rushing for Post Office
104–5
skill of drivers 127
street vendors 83
'the English kitchen in
its...glory' 270
'These fashionable
quarters are...quiet' 273
upper-class 'simplicity
...of...appearance' 277
where 'pawnbrokers...
hang out' 59
schools
Industrial Schools 232
middle-class 'academies'
279–81
Mr Wopsle's great-aunt's
197–8
penny-a-week schools
216
'Ragged Schools' 11,
231–3
Scotch House 69
Scotland Yard: gain in
prosperity 76
Scribes Ancient and Modern
apprenticeships 98–9
essential materials 98–9
excuses for failure 102–3
legal scribes' work
100–1
Vacation 'misery' 100
Scrooge, Ebenezer
buys 'prize Turkey' 58–9,
77
tiny 'clerk's fire' 90
'treadmill and the Poor
Law' 228
under-the-counter bed
75
see also Christmas
Carol, A

scurvy 213
Seacole, Mary: boys 'poke
fun' at 51
seamstresses 195–6
Season see London Season
servants 67, 199–203, 265,
269, 272, 282, 292
Sessions House 26, 255
Seven Dials 242–3
sewerage system
building of 32–3, 204
source of 'moderate
wealth' 209
Sewers, Metropolitan
Commission of 32
Shakespeare, William
'dumbed down' 172
Kean's 'flashes' 177
Macready's 'rediscovery'
of 179
Penny Theatre 'mangling'
of 187
private theatre
performance 175–6
Roubilliac's statue 152
Shaw, Captain D.
Covent Garden hazards
241–2
the dangers of 'the Dials'
242
execution preparations
261–2
'fatal noose...around
every neck' 262–3
'lowest scum' at 'public
execution' 261
on 'swearing' 38
shawls 47
Sheppard, Jack 256
Shillibeer, George 122–3
ships
cross-Channel steamers
118
steamboats 129–31
Thames shipping 15, 18,
129–31
Shipton, Mother 27
shirts 43–4
shoe blacks 206
shoes
lack of 44

men's 44
women's 46
Shoolbred, James 63
shop assistants 64–6, 67, 73, 75
shops
advertising 77–81
bazaars 69–73
'carriage-trade' 66–7
closing scene 77
department stores 73
'dressing the window' 65–6
first shopping centre 28
opening hours 66, 73, 76, 77
opening ritual 64–5
quality stores 66–9
shopping streets 61–4
small shops 75–7
side-whiskers 46
'silk-snatchers' 236
Sketches by Boz 13
arranging a coach journey 114–15
balloon attempt 158–9
'changed' Scotland Yard 76
'childhood' and Astley's 149
'City man...and...his garden' 267–8
the coach journey begins 115–16
'dingy little back office' 97
entrance to Newgate 255–6
fascination of curates 296–7
Greenwich Fair 'fever' 167
'horror-stricken' by 'condemned pew' 258
on ladies' occupations 292–3
lower middle-class wedding 288
a middle-class couple 266–7
Newgate women's wards

256–7
Newgate's condemned cells 259
on 'private theatres' 175–7
shop closing scene 77
shops' downward progress 81–2
tea garden clientele 156–8
'the would-be aristocrats' 265
see also Dickens, Charles
Sketches in London 239
slang 58–9
slavery 294
slums ('rookeries') 54, 212, 241
smallpox 36, 213
smells 18–19
'Great Stink' 32
Smith, Sydney: 'frozen' in St Paul's 26
Smith, William Henry 69
Smithfield 23, 26, 167, 301
Snow, Dr John 213
snuff 36
Soane, Sir John 19
Soho 62, 213
soldiers
British dislike of 50
'simple lounging gait' ploy 50
'slouching' Guards 49–50
Somerset House 21
South Kensington 152
Southwark 6, 226, 247
Soviet Union 9
Sowerberry (undertaker) 75
Spa Road Station 117
Spencer House 275
Spenlow, Dora 284–5
Spring, Thomas Winter 164–6
Spurgeon, C.H. 294
stables 17
status 23
steam
steam-driven coaches 116–17

steamboats 129–31
see also railways
Steerforth 281
stockings 46
Stockton and Darlington Railway 119
Strand 28, 62, 123
'street arabs' 211–12
street lighting 18
street performers 7, 41–2, 56, 133–8
street vendors 83–5, 204–6, 221–2
suburbs
middle class exodus 268
and the omnibus 122
and the railways 33, 121
suicide 206
Sundays
'Everything...bolted and barred' 21
and shop assistants 73
Sunday Schools 231
Surrey Zoological Gardens: 'collection...is large' 147–8
Swan With Two Necks 113
swearing 8, 38
swindlers 237
Sikes, Bill 48
Syon Park 276
syphilis 36

Tabard inn 114
tanneries 18, 209
Tayler, William 13
Boxing Day 'glass of something' 286–7
'Christmas Day... drunkards' 286
a gentleman's servant 202
on Paddington station 119
'regular system of whoredom' 287
a servant's life 200–3
a servant's 'offence' 203
tea gardens 156–8, 159

teeth 35, 36
Telford, Thomas 110, 111
Temple Bar 27–8, 301
Thackeray, William: on
  Great Exhibition 144–5
Thames
  buildings on banks 18
  drownings 209–10
  human scavengers
    209–11
  police patrols 239
  'putrid fermentation' 32
  shipping in 15, 18,
    129–31
  stink of 19, 32
  as water supply 19, 218
theatres 8
  grand theatre 169–80
  'penny gaffs' 183–8
  travelling companies
    180–3
'tights' 43
Times, The
  advertisements for
    'academies' 279
  'Fleas of all nations' 150
  Great Exhibition 145
  Kean's last performance
    178
  'Mme Tussaud & Son'
    150
  'model water-closets and
    public lavatories 74–5
  Zoological Gardens
    notice 147
Tiny the Wonder 164
Tite, William 91
tobacco 36
toilet paper 292
Tom Thumb, General 151
Tootle, Mr 215
top hats 45
Tottenham Court Road 63
Tower of London 21, 146
Townley Marbles 152
Traddles 281
trades 38–9, 41
Trafalgar Square 21, 29,
  33, 275
Trafalgar (tavern) 290
traffic 16, 17, 20–1

transport see coaches;
  omnibuses; railways;
  ships; walking
transportation 253, 259
Tree, Miss F. 178
Trevithick, Richard 116
Trotwood, Betsey 235
trousers ('pantaloons') 43
Tulkinghorn, Mr 91
Turpin, Dick 256
Twice Round the Clock 12
  see also Sala, George
    Augustus
Twist, Oliver
  Fagin's headquarters 54,
    242
  'farmed' by parish 215
  'sleeping among the
    coffins' 75
  workhouse beginnings
    214–15
  see also Oliver Twist
typhus 213

unemployment
  and legal 'vacations' 100
  and the workhouse 225
uniforms 48–9, 50, 56,
  123, 152
United Services Club 276
University of London 266,
  271
upper classes
  appearance and
    behaviour 277–8
  arranged marriages 288–9
  houses 272–7
  schools of 278

Vauxhall Gardens 155–6,
  158
Verisopht, Lord 62
vermin 219
Victoria and Albert
  Museum 155, 301
Victoria, Queen 10
  at Drury Lane pantomime
    172
  death of 131
  hair 'in a bun' 46
  and morality 155

opens Great Exhibition
  145
opens Royal Exchange
  91
presentations to 289
and Surrey Zoological
  Gardens 148
Victoria Station 31
Victoria Street 33
voting 276

wages
  apprentices 98
  scribes 102
  servants 201
walking 16, 23, 87
Walworth 23, 147, 279
Wapping 220
Warde, Mr (actor) 178
Warrell, W. 98–103
water: pollution of 19, 20,
  213, 218
Waterloo Road 220
waxworks 27, 150–1
weddings 287–90
Weller, Samuel 7, 109, 114
Weller, Tony 7, 57–8, 109
Wellington, Duke of 30
  railway objection 120
  and Reform Bill riots
    276–7
  steam coach passenger
    116
  swearing habit of 38
Wellington House
  Academy 280
Wemmick, Mr 23
West End 22, 39–40, 195
Westbourne Terrace 273
Westminster Abbey 21,
  298
Westminster, City of 27
Westminster, Palace of 22
  and 'Great Stink' 32
Westminster school 278
Wey, Francis: 'rickety'
  London omnibuses
    124
whale-oil 18
whisky 222
Whitechapel 220

White Cross-Street Prison
  247
Whitehall 22, 87, 94–5
White Hart 114, 298
White Horse cellar 113
Whiteley's 69, 73
Wilberforce, William 294
Wilkins, Dick 75
William IV, King 10, 152
Willis, Frederick
  'aristocracy of labour'
    199
  'Ringing Him Out'
    198–9
  shops 'radiated quality'
    66–7
windmills 17
window-dressing 65–6
women
  clothes 46–7, 48

hairstyles 46
hats 46
loads on heads 36
middle classes 281–2,
  290–3
occupations 36–7, 39–40,
  193, 195–6, 204–5, 279
in prison 256–7
as thieves 238–9
upper classes 278–9
Wood Street 19
Wopsle, Mr 197
workhouses 204, 206,
  222–30
inhabitants' work 223
inmate numbers 224–5
Oliver Twist's experiences
  214–15
outdoor relief
  administration 229–30

training for children 197
Wren, Christopher 27
Wylde, Mr 144

Yorkshire Stingo 123

Zoological Gardens,
  Regent's Park
  'picturesque...as possible'
    146
  'rare...specimens' 147

PICTURE CREDITS

Cover: City of London image from the author's collection; portrait of Charles Dickens, Bridgeman Art Library/Getty Images.

Plates: 1 Author's collection, 2, 4, 11, 14, 18, 26 & 29 Museum of London; 3 The Art Archive/Alfred Dunhill Collection/Eileen Tweedy; 5 & 20 V&A Images; 6 & 7 The Stapleton Collection/Bridgeman Art Library; 8 & 12 Mary Evans Picture Library; 9 & 21 Topfoto; 10, 27 & 28 Topfoto/HIP; 13 & 22 Dickens House Museum, London/Bridgeman Art Library; 15 Mary Evans/Hans Schwarz Collection; 16 The Art Archive/London Transport Museum/Eileen Tweedy; 17 NRM – Pictorial Collection/Science and Society Photo Library; 19 The Stapleton Collection/Bridgeman Art Library; 23 Barnardo's Picture Library; 24 Musée d'Orsay, Paris/ Bridgeman Art Library; 25 Birmingham Museums and Art Gallery/Bridgeman Art Library; 30 Topfoto/HIP/Museum of London; 31 Fine Art Photographic Library/Corbis; 32 The Art Archive/National Railway Museum York/Eileen Tweedy; 33 Bettmann/Corbis.

Chapter openers: all images taken from *London, A Pilgrimage* by Gustave Doré reproduced courtesy of Dover Publications, Inc. 31 East 2nd Street, Mineola, NY 11501, USA. 1 'Ludgate Hill – A Block in the Street'; 2 'The Great Tree – Kensington Gardens'; 3 'Bishopsgate Street'; 4 'St Paul's from the Brewery Bridge'; 5 'A City Thoroughfare'; 6 'At Evans's'; 7 'Wentworth Street, Whitechapel'; 8 'Newgate Exercise Yard'; 9 'Holland House – A Garden Party'.

backing on the visitor with disorder, the visitor was shut up, pending his announcement, in a close back-parlour.

The wealthiest aristocracy lived not even in these rarefied districts but in their own town mansions. Most of these have since been demolished and virtually none are still owned by the original family, but two survivors – Spencer House in St James's and Hertford House, which now houses the Wallace Collection – give some notion of their size and grandeur. Many had their frontages hidden from the street by a high wall, so that the public could see only the rooftops.Northumberland House, where the young Dickens had admired the lion atop the façade, was among the most ostentatious. Many of the homes of the nobility were Georgian or Regency buildings, but Northumberland House was considerably older: it had been completed in 1610 before the West End existed, so it was situated not in a fashionable district but amid the bustle of the Strand, with shops and taverns jammed against it on both sides. It was, however, huge. When it opened to the public for a short time during the Great Exhibition, a guidebook offered this description:

The front is 160 feet in length, and the court is 81 feet square. The garden between the house and the river consists of a fine lawn, surrounded by a gravel walk. This house came into the family of the Percies [sic] by the marriage of a nephew of the Earl of Northumberland with a daughter of the Earl of Suffolk. The lion on the central parapet is a copy of the celebrated one by Michael Angelo, and is the crest of the Percies.

The Jacobean exterior concealed splendid interiors of more recent design. Arranged around a courtyard, they included a drawing-room entirely walled with mirrors and coloured glass, a picture gallery more than 30m/100ft in length, and a huge marble staircase that was considered 'without exception the most splendid feature of the building.' As the area around Charing Cross began to change its character, it became increasingly extraordinary that what was effectively a country house, with a large formal garden running down to the Thames, should survive within a few feet of Trafalgar Square. Cut off by new development and openly coveted by railway builders, the house only just

survived Dickens' lifetime, despite valiant attempts to save it. Its site
was covered by other buildings but the famous lion was rescued and can
be seen today on the roof of Syon Park, a country house to the west of
London that is still owned by the Dukes of Northumberland.

A mansion that fared better, but was much newer, was Apsley House,
the home of the Duke of Wellington. The same guidebook described the
house but was equally interested in its owner:

> The situation is one of the finest in the metropolis, standing
> at the very beginning of the town. The principal front, next
> Piccadilly, consists of a centre with two wings, having a portico
> of the Corinthian order, raised upon a rusticated arcade of three
> apertures, leading to the entrance hall. The front is enclosed by a
> rich bronzed palisade, corresponding with the gates to the grand
> entrance to the Park. The ball room, extending the whole length of
> the mansion, and the picture gallery, are superb. The banqueting
> room is splendidly decorated, being of dead white, richly gilt.

The 'Iron Duke' himself was often to be seen on horseback, travelling
down Piccadilly to visit Hatchard's bookshop, the United Services
Club or the House of Lords. His military exploits had made him a hero
(indeed a monstrous statue of him was to be placed on an arch opposite
his house in 1846, several years before his death), but his subsequent
political career had made him unpopular with radicals and his home had
been attacked.

The French Revolution had demonstrated the danger of an angry mob
whose energies were directed against the aristocracy. There had been
no equivalent upheaval in Britain, but the passing of the Great Reform
Bill in 1832, which had widened the franchise and effectively ended
aristocratic dominance of Parliament, had seemed almost as bad. The
Duke and his peers no longer had things all their own way. Schlesinger
noticed the effect of this state of affairs on Wellington's home:

> It has rarely been the lot of a man so frequently to witness his
> own apotheosis as the Duke of Wellington; and yet how gloomy
> looks Apsley House on the fresh green borders of the park. The
> windows, shut up from year's end to year's end, and protected by

bullet-proof shutters of massive iron – the very railings in front of
the house boarded up, to exclude the curiosity of the passers-by
– all owing to the riots which preceded the passing of the Reform
bill – riots in which the castles of the Tories were burnt down in
the provinces, while in the metropolis the populace threatened the
life of the greatest Englishman of the age.

The Park

Only a few yards from Apsley House, the aristocracy, and indeed the
whole of London's *beau monde*, was on display in the afternoons. Rotten
Row, the track for riders and carriages that runs from east to west
through Hyde Park, was an essential place of resort for those who wished
to be seen. To drive or ride there in the late afternoon, or at the least
to lean on the wooden rails and watch those passing, was an essential
social ritual for anyone who aspired to beauty and fashion. While
the dandies who lined the rails might be extravagant in their dress,
Schlesinger realized that the comparative drabness of the aristocrats was
symptomatic both of their confidence and their fear of arousing envy.
His observation was a useful summing-up of the attitude of Society
toward the display of wealth:

Those who have seen the Prater [a pleasure garden] of Vienna
will be rather disappointed with the aspect of the drive in Hyde
Park, where the upper classes of London congregate in the
evening between five and seven o'clock, partly to take the air, and
partly because it is considered fashionable. Extravagant turn-outs
and liveries, such as the Viennese produce with great ostentation,
are not to be found in London. The English aristocracy like
to make an impression by the simplicity and solidity of their
appearance; and the metropolis is the last of all places where
they would wish to excite attention by a dashing and extravagant
exterior. They have not the least desire either to dazzle or to awe
the trades-people or to make them envious. They are too sure of
their position to be tempted to advertise it; whoever wants this
assurance cannot pretend to belong to the aristocracy.

The aristocracy, however, did like to display their skill in horsemanship, and its young female members, especially, found in 'the Row' an opportunity for energy and high spirits that had no other outlet apart from the ballroom. It was these young women, trotting, cantering and galloping to and fro, whom the sauntering, overdressed men principally came to admire. Sala witnessed the daily procession:

> I am glad to say that I am by no means alone as I lean over the rails. Whether it is that they can't or won't ride, I know not; but I find myself surrounded by groups of exquisites, who, to judge by their outward appearance, must be the greatest dandies in London. Such peg-top trousers! Such astounding waistcoat patterns! Such lofty heels to the varnished boots! Such Brobdignagian moustaches and whiskers! Such ponderous watch-chains! Such breezy neckties and alarming scarves! Ladies, too – real ladies – promenade in an amplitude of crinoline difficult to imagine and impossible to describe; some of them with stalwart footmen following. Little foot-pages; swells walking three, sometimes four, abreast; gambolling children; severe duennas; wicked old bucks, splendidly attired, leering furtively under the bonnets – what a scene of more than 'Arabian Nights' delight and gaiety!
>
> The Danaes! The Amazons! The lady cavaliers! The horsewomen! Can any scene in the world equal Rotten Row at four in the afternoon, and in the full tide of the season? Rotten Row is a very Peri's Garden for beautiful women on horseback. I count the male riders absolutely for nothing, though there may be marquises among them.

Schools and Schooling

The sons of the aristocracy were sent to school at Westminster, Harrow or Eton (to which Dickens sent his own son, Charles junior – proof that social barriers were not absolute) while their daughters were largely educated at home. Although careers were not open to girls, there were numerous accomplishments that they had to possess. Apart from the duties of running a household, it was desirable that they be able to